Ethics of Media

D1649402

Ethics of Media

Edited by

Nick Couldry
Goldsmiths College, London, UK

Mirca Madianou
University of Leicester, UK

and

Amit Pinchevski
The Hebrew University of Jerusalem, Israel

palgrave
macmillan

First published 2013 by
PALGRAVE MACMILLAN

Palgrave Macmillan in the UK is an imprint of Macmillan Publishers Limited, registered in England, company number 785998, of Houndmills, Basingstoke, Hampshire RG21 6XS.

Palgrave Macmillan in the US is a division of St Martin's Press LLC, 175 Fifth Avenue, New York, NY 10010.

Palgrave Macmillan is the global academic imprint of the above companies and has companies and representatives throughout the world.

Palgrave® and Macmillan® are registered trademarks in the United States, the United Kingdom, Europe and other countries.

ISBN 978–0–230–34763–2 hardback
ISBN 978–0–230–34783–0 paperback

This book is printed on paper suitable for recycling and made from fully managed and sustained forest sources. Logging, pulping and manufacturing processes are expected to conform to the environmental regulations of the country of origin.

A catalogue record for this book is available from the British Library.

A catalog record for this book is available from the Library of Congress.

Contents

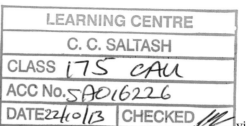

Part III Mediations

Part IV Practices

Figures

Contributors

Ronald C. Arnett (PhD, Ohio University, 1978) is Chair and Professor of the Department of Communication and Rhetorical Studies and the Henry Koren, C.S.Sp., Endowed Chair for Scholarly Excellence at Duquesne University, Pennsylvania, US. He is the author/co-author of eight books and three edited books. His most recent books are *An Overture to Philosophy of Communication: The Carrier of Meaning* and *Communication Ethics in Dark Times: Hannah Arendt's Rhetoric of Warning and Hope*.

Roy Brand is Lecturer of Philosophy at the Graduate School of Bezalel Academy of Art and Design, and the Director and Chief Curator of Yaffo 23, Jerusalem, Center for Contemporary Art and Culture. He is the editor and translator of *Philosophy in a Time of Terror: Dialogues with Habermas and Derrida,* and editor and consultant curator of *Bare Life: Contemporary Art Reflecting on the State of Emergency*. His book *LoveKnowledge: The Life of Philosophy from Socrates to Derrida* was published in 2012.

Lilie Chouliaraki is Professor of Media and Communications at the London School of Economics, UK. She is the author of, among others, *Discourse in Late Modernity* (2000 with N. Fairclough), *The Spectatorship of Suffering* (2006/2011) and *The Ironic Spectator* (2012).

Clifford G. Christians is Research Professor of Communications at the University of Illinois, US, where he has joint appointments as Professor of Journalism and Professor of Media Studies Emeritus. He is author/co-author of *Media Ethics: Cases and Moral Reasoning* (9th edn), *Ethics for Public Communications, Good News: Social Ethics of the Press, Normative Theories of the Media, Moral Engagement in Public Life: Theorists of Contemporary Ethics* and *Handbook for Mass Media Ethics*.

Nick Couldry is Professor of Media and Communications and Joint Chair of the Department of Media and Communications, Goldsmiths, University of London, UK, where he is also Director of the Centre for the Study of Global Media and Democracy. He is the author/editor of ten books, including most recently *Media, Society, World: Social Theory and Digital Media Practice* (2012) and *Why Voice Matters: Culture and Politics after Neoliberalism* (2010).

Daniel Dayan is Professor of Media Theory at Institut d'Etudes Politiques, Paris, France. He is a fellow of the Marcel Mauss Institute, l'Ecole des Hautes Etudes en Sciences Sociales, and of the Levinas Institute, University of Paris-VII, Denis Diderot. He has been a lecturer, visiting professor and professor at numerous US and European universities, including Stanford, US; the Annenberg School of Communications, University of Southern California, US; the University of Oslo, Norway; the University of Geneva, Switzerland; the University of Pennsylvania, US; the Centre National de la Recherche Scientifique, France; and the New School for Social Research, New York, US. He received the ICA Fellows Award in 2010 for the book *Media Events: The Live Broadcasting of History*, co-authored with Elihu Katz.

Joseph Livingstone is studying for a postgraduate degree in philosophy at King's College London, UK.

Sabina Lovibond is an Emeritus Fellow of Worcester College, Oxford, UK, where she taught philosophy from 1982 to 2011. Her publications include *Realism and Imagination in Ethics* (1983), *Ethical Formation* (2002), *Iris Murdoch, Gender and Philosophy* (2011) and a variety of other work, mainly in ethics and feminist theory.

Peter Lunt is Professor of Media and Communication and Head of the Media and Communication Department at the University of Leicester, UK. He is the author of several books, including *Media Regulation: Governance in the Interests of Citizens and Consumers* (2012 with Sonia Livingstone), *Stanley Milgram* (2009) and *Talk on Television* (1994 with Sonia Livingstone).

Mirca Madianou is Senior Lecturer in Media and Communication at the University of Leicester, UK. She has published extensively on news audiences and the social consequences of new media, especially in relation to processes of nationalism/transnationalism and emotions. She is the author of *Mediating the Nation: News, Audiences and the Politics of Identity* (2005) and *Migration and New Media: Transnational Families and Polymedia* (2012 with Daniel Miller).

Onora O'Neill combines writing in political philosophy and ethics with a range of public interests and activities. She comes from Northern Ireland and has worked mainly in Britain and the US. She was Principal of Newnham College, Cambridge, UK, from 1992 to 2006; President of

the British Academy from 2005 to 2009; chaired the Nuffield Foundation from 1998 to 2010; has been a cross-bench member of the House of
Lords since 2000 (Baroness O'Neill of Bengarve); and chairs the Equality and Human Rights Commission. She currently lectures and writes
on accountability and trust, on justice and borders and on the future of
universities, the quality of legislation and the ethics of communication,
including media ethics.

Angela Phillips is Reader in Journalism at Goldsmiths, University of
London. She worked for many years as a Journalist and established the
MA in Journalism at Goldsmiths. She gave evidence to the Leveson
Inquiry into the Press, on behalf of the Media Reform Coalition and
is co-author of *Changing Journalism*, Sage.

Amit Pinchevski is Senior Lecturer in the Department of Communication and Journalism at the Hebrew University of Jerusalem. He is the
author of *By Way of Interruption: Levinas and the Ethics of Communication*
(2005) and co-editor of *Media Witnessing: Testimony in the Age of Mass
Communication* (2009 with Paul Frosh).

Piotr M. Szpunar is a doctoral candidate at the Annenberg School
for Communication, and the Department of Political Science at the
University of Pennsylvania, US. His research interests include war and
terrorism, collective memory, political philosophy and the philosophy
of communication. His previous work has been published in *Cultural
Studies, Media, Culture & Society, International Journal of Communication, Memory Studies, Journalism: Theory, Practice, and Criticism* and *Social
Semiotics*.

Damian Tambini is Senior Lecturer at the London School of Economics,
UK. He serves on the Advisory Board of the Center for International
Media Ethics and is a trustee of Reporters Sans Frontieres UK. From
June 2002 to August 2006 he was Head of the Programme in Com-
parative Media Law and Policy at Oxford University, UK. He was
Director of the Media Policy Project at the Institute for Public Policy
Research, UK (1999–2002); a postdoctoral fellow at Nuffield College,
Oxford, UK (1998); Humboldt University, Berlin, Germany (lecturer,
1997); and the European University Institute, Florence, Italy (PhD,
1996). He is the author of numerous books and articles on media and
telecommunications governance.

Stephen J. A. Ward is Professor and Director of the George S. Turnbull Center for Journalism, which is part of the School of Journalism and Communication of the University of Oregon, US. Previously, he was the Burgess Professor and Director of the Center for Journalism Ethics at the University of Wisconsin-Madison, US, and Director of the Graduate School of Journalism at the University of British Columbia in Vancouver, Canada. A former war reporter and newsroom manager, he is an award-winning author of numerous books and articles on journalism and media ethics, including his recent *Global Media Ethics: Problems and Perspectives* (2013) and *Ethics and the Media: An Introduction* (2011).

Barbie Zelizer is the Raymond Williams Professor of Communication and Director of the Scholars Program in Culture and Communication at the University of Pennsylvania's Annenberg School for Communication, US. A former journalist, she is known for her work in the area of journalism, culture, memory and images, particularly in times of crisis. She is author/editor of 13 books, including the award-winning volumes *About to Die: How News Images Move the Public* (2010) and *Remembering to Forget: Holocaust Memory through the Camera's Eye* (1998), and more than 100 articles, book chapters and essays. Recipient of a Guggenheim Fellowship, a Freedom Forum Center Research Fellowship, a fellowship from Harvard University's Joan Shorenstein Center on the Press, Politics and Public Policy and a fellowship from Stanford University's Center for Advanced Study in the Behavioral Sciences, she is also a media critic, whose work has appeared in *The Nation*, PBS News Hour, *The Huffington Post, Newsday* and other media organs. Co-editor of *Journalism: Theory, Practice and Criticism*, she is also a recent president of the International Communication Association.

Joanna Zylinska is Professor of New Media and Communications at Goldsmiths, University of London, UK. The author of four books – most recently *Life after New Media: Mediation as a Vital Process* (2012 with Sarah Kember) and *Bioethics in the Age of New Media* (2009) – she is also a translator of Stanislaw Lem's major philosophical treatise *Summa Technologiae* (2013). Together with Clare Birchall, Gary Hall and Open Humanities Press, she runs the JISC-funded project Living Books about Life, which publishes open-access books that are at the crossroads of the humanities and the sciences. She combines her theoretical writing with photographic art practice.

1
Ethics of Media: An Introduction

Nick Couldry, Mirca Madianou and Amit Pinchevski

In September 2012 a series of violent protests erupted in the Middle East, North Africa and Asia in response to a *YouTube* film that caricatured Islam's Prophet Muhammad. The protests, which were directed primarily towards the US where the short film was made, echoed the similar violent reactions to the publications of the Prophet Muhammad cartoons in the Danish daily *Jyllands-Posten* in 2005. Were the protesters right to express their anger at what were evidently provocative and offensive media representations of their faith? Were the filmmakers and cartoonists entitled to freedom of speech and is this freedom limitless? Or was this a clear case of media harm? And what, if any, is the responsibility of the audiences who not only watch and read but also produce, circulate and 'like', potentially harmful content?

The film protests were one incident in a series of recent events that sparked intense debate on the ethics of media. In the UK the phone-hacking scandal, implicating not only the *News of the World* and the tabloid press more widely but also the police and the government, has generated an ongoing discussion on media ethics and regulation, which culminated with the reporting of the Leveson Inquiry. Before the hacking scandal and Leveson, *WikiLeaks* raised questions of accountability and trust on a global scale (Brevini, Hintz and McCurdy 2013). But, crucially, the backdrop to these developments and the concern with an ethics of media is the sheer pervasiveness of the media not only as centralized institutions but also as technologies and means through which we sustain relationships with each other. We live *with* and *in* media, and this book is the attempt of its editors and contributors to identify the normative contours of this new life. *What are the 'ethics' of media? What forms would we expect them to take? What understanding of 'media' is needed to bring such ethics, if such exist, into focus?*

1

We pose these questions and publish this book at a time when media institutions' ethical standards (or lack of them) have dominated recent public debate to an unusual degree (in the UK at least), yet the characteristics, even the identity, of 'media' have become ever more difficult to define. How is it possible that public figures frequently argue about the morality of journalists, yet the conceivability of an ethics of media remains, for some, problematic? In this book, no single answer is offered to this question; this is not a field where single or univocal answers are possible. Instead, our point of departure is to treat ethics as a category to be theoretically and even empirically explored rather than defined in abstraction from the details of our practices with media. The chapters aim to display the *diversity* of competing answers to the question 'What are the ethics of media?' whether from specialist researchers of media or from philosophers. We hope thereby to establish beyond doubt that *debate* about the 'ethics of media', whatever forms they take, is integral to a world and of lives increasingly suffused with media content and media devices. We cannot live so intensively with media without generating questions about the ethical dimensions of that life, questions that, as with other aspects of our lives, hold no promise of consensual answers.

The centrality of ethics to any public discourse about media has not always been so clear. Ethics has, for many decades, been a formal part of journalistic training in most countries, within the context of voluntary or legally binding codes of conduct for journalists of varying degrees of strictness (Bertrand 2000; Keeble 2001). But, important though such codes are, journalists' working rules and norms are only one part of the domain of ethical questions raised by media. Janet Malcolm caused a sensation when in two articles published in *New Yorker* magazine in the 1980s she questioned the morality of a particular journalist's treatment of a convicted murderer whose story that journalist had told (Malcolm 1990), but the sensation only underlined how rare such questioning is. Over the longer term, the public world of countries such as the US and the UK has been surprisingly devoid of discussion about the wider morality of what media institutions do, not least because it is rarely in the interests of those same institutions to promote such discussion. Speculation about the role that chasing paparazzi played in the death by car crash of Princess Diana in a Paris tunnel in August 1997 was an exception, but it did little to halt the longer-term growth in newspapers' reliance on an industry of image capture and circulation (Howe 2004). Philosopher Onora O'Neill's BBC *Reith Lectures* in 2002 provoked debate about growing mistrust in media and a number of other institutions, and the causes of such mistrust (O'Neill 2002), but no consequences followed for media institutions. Only the emergence of sustained evidence of malpractice across *three* core institutions (media, police and government) forced the *News of the World* 'phone-hacking' scandal onto the front pages and prime-time news bulletins, and onto the agendas of government. At the end of this Introduction we return to the aftermath of that scandal which has attracted global attention and major financial consequences for News Corporation at the end of this Introduction. It may be that we will look back on the past decade as one that finally installed the ethics of media at the heart of public debate in mature democracies.

While hardly a new preoccupation, it was only recently that ethics achieved centrality in the humanities and social sciences, culminating with what has been dubbed 'the turn to ethics' (Garber, Hanssen and Walkowitz 2000). Ethics is foregrounded in many recent works in cultural theory (Bauman 1993; Bhabha 2004; Butler 2006; Gilroy 2004) and the mainstream of communication and media studies is now following suit. An important precursor is the work of Clifford Christians (Christians, Ferré and Fackler 1993; Christians, Rotzoll and Fackler 1991). Drawing on wider debates about humanitarianism and community in Christian discourse and beyond, his work has combined philosophical analysis and contextualization with rigorous discussion of examples from media practice. Strikingly, however, in spite of the richness of this work, its influence has been largely confined to the US where the tradition of 'public journalism' has provided an important context (Glasser 1999), and even there its implications have been, at least until recently, neglected by the wider field of media and communications research. A paradoxical consequence of that neglect was that, for scholars like us, interested in connecting media research to wider ethical debates in the mid-2000s, the field seemed almost undiscovered territory; however misleading that sense of 'newness', it proved to be an impetus to the recent revival in the field of media and communication ethics (Couldry 2006; Madianou 2005; Pinchevski 2005). A further impetus to thinking normatively about media was the emergence of a globalized media space, enacted most vividly in the terrible events of 9/11. Roger Silverstone's book *The Media and Morality* (2007) was a notable response to that challenge, and was joined by a number of writings that reflected on the centrality of normative questions to media research, often in the context of globalization (Couldry 2008; Eide, Kunelius and Phillips 2008), but sometimes also in a national context (Morrison et al. 2007). Another impetus was political theory and media analysis on the normative implications of media's presentations of distant suffering, as demonstrated most dramatically by the global audience for the Asian tsunami of 2004 (Boltanski 1999; Chouliaraki 2006). Since then, a number of summative works have begun to consolidate this mainstreaming of normative discussion within media research (Christians, Glasser, McQuail, Nordenstreng and White 2010; Ward 2011; Ward and Wasserman 2010).

It was in the middle of this emerging validation of ethical debate within the mainstream of media research that we, the editors of this volume, organized a series of small colloquia bringing together philosophers and social scientists to highlight ethics of media as a topic: in Cambridge, UK, in April 2008; in Paris, France, in June 2008; and in Chicago, US, at the annual conference of the International Communication Association in May 2009. Several of the chapters here started life as participations in one or more of those events, but this book is far from being a set of conference proceedings, since we have also drawn in new participants (Angela Phillips, Damian Tambini), and a number of chapters move a long way from the conference contributions of their authors.

The result of these efforts, we hope, is a volume that offers some useful signposts, even if not always convergent ones, onto an expanding domain of reflection about whether the media we now have are consistent with lives we want to lead.

Overlapping uncertainties

The territory of media ethics is difficult: marked by branching paths, ambiguous directions and potholes into which the traveller can easily fall. We can illustrate the sheer difficulty of 'ethics of media' through some quotations.

'Journalism is a profession *in search of* norms', wrote Clifford Christians and his co-authors (1991: 417, added emphasis), a diagnosis that echoes loudly in the UK of the *News of the World* scandal: a problem, then, of *framing* an ethics of journalism and, perhaps, more widely of media. 'The liberal values that underlie any democratic society...are kept outside the realm of journalism', wrote Israeli legal philosopher Rafael Cohen-Almagor (2001: 79); 'as long as this is the case', he continued, 'the term "media ethics" will remain a cynical combination'. Here, then, is a problem of *will* on the part of journalists and of *focus* on the part of the rest of us. How indeed can we bring everyday values to bear on the paradoxical specialism of journalism (paradoxical because it remains a particular craft whose specialism is the description of everything outside itself)? Underlying the problem of bringing the moral questions raised by media into proper focus is a deep institutional issue: if, as in the conventional model of liberal democracy, the press's role is to monitor all the institutions of government, what institutions are left to monitor whether appropriate normative standards apply within the press itself? This was a problem already for the great French historian and proto-sociologist Alexis de Tocqueville, who worried in his diagnosis of emerging American democracy:

> If any one could point out an intermediate, and yet a tenable position, between the complete independence [of the press] and the entire subjection of the public expression of opinion, I should perhaps be inclined to adopt it; but the difficulty is to discover this position. de Tocqueville.
>
> (1964: 204–205)

de Tocqueville's worries about institutional frameworks remain unresolved today: indeed, they are at the heart of the Leveson Inquiry which reported in the UK in November 2012. (For a discussion of various aspects of the inquiry, see contributions by O'Neill (Chapter 2); Madianou (Chapter 11); Phillips (Chapter 15); and Zelizer (Chapter 16).)[1] The first and last parts of this volume cover questions that relate to these various problems: Part I, 'Framings', and Part IV, 'Practices', which also begins to turn to questions of policy and regulation.

A different area of difficulty – but also a huge stimulus to the field of 'ethics of media' – is the changing nature of 'media' themselves. In 2006 *The Economist* asked: 'what *is* a media company?' (20 April 2006, added emphasis). Whether you are a media professional or a media researcher, media ontology – what media 'are' – has been transformed over the past decade. All of us have to consider forms of production with very different features and dynamics from the traditional media of press, radio, television and film. Meanwhile, those who lack that specialist interest use media interfaces for an increasing range of activities, both as background infrastructure and as their principle focus of attention. As new media technologies have blurred the line between production and consumption, media texts and everyday interactions, ethical concerns have become relevant not only to institutional practitioners but to all media users. Media, in some form, are everywhere, making it all the more pressing to consider the boundaries of an ethics of media. Moreover, digital media may be understood to create new types of ethical problems.[2] For instance, new media practices, such as citizen journalism, and transnational developments, such as *WikiLeaks* (Tambini, Chapter 14), compel us to reassess notions of accountability and trust. Technological convergence blurs the boundaries between public and private interactions and between mediated interpersonal and institutional communication. Can private views expressed in social media still be considered private? Can they be governed by freedom of expression – an individual right – or do we need new principles to assess their new status (Madianou, Chapter 11)? The middle two parts of this volume are designed to focus first on the growing proliferation of media interfaces (Part II, 'Interfaces') and second on the proliferating ways in which everyday life is represented by media institutions and media-related practices (Part III, 'Mediations').[3]

We can schematically – as an introduction to the summary of the volume's chapters that follows – list a series of overlapping questions which are inherent to the domain of 'ethics of media' and which various authors address in one way or another. These are the intersecting themes and questions that chapters from across the volume seek to address.

The *first* question is the institutional quandary raised early on by de Tocqueville: How does one identify or build institutions appropriate to overseeing or intervening in the normative standards that democracy's own watchdogs (the media) adopt? Clearly, government cannot take on this role without undermining media's role as watchdog over the state; any regulatory body set up by legislation and with powers of intervention granted by the state must, at the very least, be able to demonstrate an independence from the state and from government. The path to institutional innovation here may be blocked by constitutions that give primacy to the freedom of the press, as O'Neill notes (2002, and Chapter 2), requiring a re-examination of what we really mean when we talk of the press, not just individuals (journalists, citizens), having 'freedom' of speech. Where institutional innovation is not blocked, there may be scope for rethinking how a regulatory process might work, involving a range of citizens in an open deliberative process that, whatever its legislative origins, is designed to exceed the control of the state (Couldry 2006: 137–139). The issue of accountability of media institutions was at the heart of the phone-hacking scandal and its aftermath, which resulted in the Leveson Inquiry in the UK. It is clear that discussion about how to build new institutions for regulating the media has only just begun.

A *second* problem is how to define the focus of 'ethics of media'. Are media in general, or is journalism in particular, the subject of a *particular* type of ethics such as medical or legal ethics (Zelizer, Chapter 16)? If so, on what basis can this demarcation from general ethics be justified – media's distinctive role in democracy; media's role as a truth-teller that represents our common life; or the consequences of circulating media contents on social stability and trust? And, once made, from where can ethical principles be developed to serve this distinctive area of life? If, on the other hand, media and/or journalism are *not* the subject of a distinctive area of ethics, what are the general ethical frameworks that apply to them? Alternatively, do specific *and* general (professional and universal) ethical norms *intersect* in media practice?

A *third* question is whether there is any stable starting-point for ethics of media at all? What if particular media practices (e.g. the circulation of media images on scales up to and including the global) raise normative uncertainties that we have as yet no language for resolving (Oswell 2012)? Does this create a new 'limit situation', as Paul Ricoeur (2007: 35–36) puts it, that requires a sustained exercise in collective ethical invention before any starting-points for ethics of media can be established? Alternatively, are the uncertainties currently felt about the ethics of certain media practices (e.g. the free circulation of images of individuals on social media, such as *Facebook*) precisely *characteristic* of the problems we tend to call 'ethical', as distinct from problems where a rule-based solution is available? If so, how do we conceive of the way beyond such uncertainty? Perhaps through a notion of 'uncodifiability' that neo-Aristotelian ethics resolves through its account of the stable dispositions called 'virtues' which, when acquired and refined in practice, tend to generate solutions that are not graspable in advance or in the abstract (Couldry, Chapter 3); or perhaps through an insistence that ethics confronts an unresolvable space of contradiction (e.g. a conflict between knowledge and care) for whose resolution there are no recipes beyond an openness to interruption (Brandt and Pinchevski, Chapter 7; Zylinska, Chapter 6).

At this point we move into a *fourth* and broader area of questioning: What are the choices between frameworks of philosophical thinking about ethics and morality that are more, or less, helpful for thinking about media in general and journalism in particular? Is the choice of such a framework purely a matter of personal philosophical taste, or are there substantive reasons why one framework or another is better suited to an ethical grasp of media, or the practical conditions under which media get made and circulate? The choice between normative frameworks (what we might call 'meta-ethics' (Miller 2003)) may be difficult or some eclecticism may be permitted; alternatively, media may be a site of multiple contestations, making viewers' own meta-ethical reflections an important contribution to any eventual ethics of media (Lunt and Livingstone, Chapter 12) – an approach that reflects parallel developments in the anthropology of 'lay moralities' (Howell 1997).

Fifth, are media involved in generating complex forms of harm that require detailed empirical enquiry before their ethical analysis can be advanced further (Madianou, Chapter 11)? If so, there may be arguments for developing an ethics of media as an area of exploratory *empirical* work that draws on sociology and anthropology, and the study of everyday formulations of ethics and meta-ethics (cf. Morrison et al. 2007; see also Lunt and Livingstone, Chapter 12). This point relates to the recognition that media as processes of mediation constitute a very different mode of communication compared with interactions as co-presence on which most liberal ethics principles (e.g. freedom of expression) are premised. If mediation introduces structural transformations to communication then we need to understand these transformations before we can address the ethical implications for producers as well as audiences (as is evident in questions of witnessing, see Frosh and Pinchevski 2009).

Sixth, can we override – and so perhaps resolve, or at least simplify – some of the above open questions by appealing to a macroframework which already specifics these functions of media for particular agreed purposes and so requires certain norms of performance? Is democracy one such framework (O'Neill, Chapter 2)? If so, what are the implications for debates about media ethics in countries that are not democracies – are they still possible, or premature? Or perhaps it is the performance conferred by the media, the ways in which the media do things with image, sound and text, that should be at the centre of any ethical inquiry (Dayan, Chapter 10)?

Finally, what is the scale on which an ethics of media aspires, and perhaps needs, to apply? The potentially *global* circulation of media contents in a world banally linked up by the internet, and more exceptionally linked up by traditional media, argues for a media ethics conceived on a global scale (Couldry, Chapter 3; Christians and Ward, Chapter 5). Despite the initial optimism regarding the potential of new communication technologies to foster a global public sphere and cultivate cosmopolitan sensibilities, recent evidence suggests that the dominant genre of humanitarian communication resembles what Chouliaraki

(2010) terms 'post-humanitarian', where proposals for action are simplified and equated with the clicking of one's mouse rather than grounded on moral imperatives or dialogical reflexivity (Beck 2006). If social media orientate humanitarian action at a communitarian rather than a cosmopolitan level (Madianou 2013), what is the moral value of this engagement and how should it be assessed? The upshot is that it remains a question for debate *how best* to formulate ethical principles for such a global mediated space where no consensus exists across religions and cultures on questions of value (Tambini, Chapter 14).

These are not questions that allow easy resolution. Different questions have greater salience, depending on your starting-point as an author and a user of media. As a result, there is not, even in principle, a point on the ethical horizon where answers to these questions converge. It is better instead to conceive of 'ethics of media' as a highly contested field of first-order and second-order reflection about how far what we do with media is, or can be, consistent with our normative principles and how far these normative principles may be transformed because of what we do with the media. It is indeed the richness of dispute around such issues that confirms 'media' as an inescapable problematic of contemporary life.

Outline of the book

The chapters in Part I, *Framings*, address the conceptual fault-lines in the field of ethics and media and make original contributions to current debates. Onora O'Neill (Chapter 2) opens the book's discussions by questioning the current orthodoxy on media freedom, which is popularly considered beyond challenge. O'Neill disentangles often conflated concepts, such as individual rights of self-expression and generic rights to freedom of expression, and argues that the former cannot apply to powerful institutions such as media organizations. Appeals to the protection of individuality and self-expression cannot provide a useful account of press freedom which operates at a larger scale and with far-reaching consequences. For O'Neill, media freedom cannot be an unconditional right of self-expression 'but a freedom to publish in an intelligible and assessable way'. These are the standards that need to balance media freedom together with independent regulation that forbids censorship of content but regulates media process.

In his contribution, Nick Couldry (Chapter 3) frames media ethics as 'an effective tool for asking appropriate normative questions about everyday media practice', broadly defined. Drawing on neo-Aristotelian virtue ethics, Couldry sets out to overcome the conceptual fault-line in contemporary moral philosophy between notions of the good and right, and asks: 'How should we live well together through the media?' and 'Which are the virtuous dispositions that can contribute to our living well *with* and *through* media?' Couldry focuses on accuracy, sincerity and care as the key virtues that allow us to live together in the common fabric of a mediated world. Just as the shared institution of language requires us to show care when we use it, so do our media, which increasingly sustain 'our commonly experienced connectedness'.

Ron Arnett (Chapter 4) examines the question of media ethics in relation to the question of tradition. Invoking Hannah Arendt's critique of modernity, Arnett proposes the notion of tradition as what mediates between past and present, and hence as what can inform media ethics insofar as the mediating of an event and its implications in the public domain. According to Arendt, modernity is a project bent against tradition, and it is for this reason that her critique deems tradition as redeeming. Arnett follows Arendt on this route, considering how tradition might be responsive to change in the interplay between past and future. The question of tradition becomes ever so crucial in the mediated public domain, where multiple traditions are brought into play.

Clifford Christians and Stephen J. A. Ward (Chapter 5) propose a perspective from moral realism that leads to a global ethics for media. From this perspective, ethical propositions are not a matter of individual belief but express an independent ethical truth about a given situation. This makes for an anthropological basis for moral realism, giving priority to 'the necessary and sufficient conditions of being member of the human species'. Christians and Ward proceed to develop the groundwork necessary for a flexible framework of media ethics that allows for pluralism without relativism, and for universal principles that are compatible with change and difference as well as with the particularities of cultures. Anthropological moral realism offers a challenge for scholars of global media ethics to evaluate some of their fundamental assumptions.

Part II, *Interfaces*, features chapters that engage with specific ethical situations arising in media interfaces, with the latter three focusing on the image as the interface. Joanna Zylinska (Chapter 6) ventures an ethical reading of online blogging. Working against common assumptions regarding the narcissistic and self-indulgent impulses of online communication, Zylinska argues that blogging and social networking actually enable novel and alternative forms of ethical relations. The suggestive question organizing her discussion, 'What if Foucault had a blog?', occasions the revision of Michel Foucault's techniques of the self as sites for engagement with others rather than insistence on the self-same. What informs the 'blogger's delirium' is an attraction to the outside, a form of narcissism that is Other oriented. In this respect, Zylinska suggests an unlikely rapprochement between the seemingly opposing ethics of Foucault and Emmanuel Levinas, revealing the two as compatible forms of shifting the self's ontological boundaries, at least insofar as online social interaction is concerned.

Roy Brandt and Amit Pinchevski (Chapter 7) present an ethical phenomenology of photography, one that is importantly informed by the philosophy of Levinas. Taking up his notion of the face, Brandt and Pinchevski ask whether we can regard a photograph as facing and addressing, having the potential of looking back at us when we look. Engaging critically with recent accounts by Judith Butler and Giorgio Agamben, Brand and Pinchevski read Levinas's notion of the face as constituting a link between image and address, making this double feature the premise for ethics of seeing. Photography invites a special kind of facing, one that, along the lines of Roland Barthes's notion of the punctum, invokes absence within presence and hence the face as a trace. Ultimately, this approach seeks to retain the tension between image and address, and the ambiguity this tension produces as a necessary condition for facing the photographed face.

Piotr Szpunar (Chapter 8) also attempts to mobilize Levinas's ethics for a media context. However, his argument, by contrast, involves reasserting the primacy of responsibility not only for the Other but also for the Other's Other – that is, the Third. To the extent that the ethical relation entails the interruption of alterity (Pinchevski 2005), and with it the potential of unsettling established order, moral or otherwise, Szpunar seeks to take the interruptive potential of ethics into the triangular relation, where multiple alterities make their claim. He does so by pursuing an analysis of journalism, specifically of the 'about to die' image of photojournalism (Zelizer 2010), which according to him brings the question of ethics as described by Levinas closer to the question of politics, a question that was only hinted at by the philosopher.

Lilie Chouliaraki (Chapter 9) is concerned with the paradox of in/communicability about war. Drawing on iconic photojournalism from the two world wars and the so-called War on Terror of the last decade, Chouliaraki argues that despite its lack of 'a code of words', the mediation of war reveals the changing moral order of modernity. Chouliaraki traces a shift in the aesthetic representation of the battlefield from the sublime to the traumatic, which she attributes to institutional and technological changes in the media themselves as well as a wider shift from a deontological to a utilitarian morality. The current genre of war as a 'humanitarian endeavour', a fusion of classical liberal ethics and 'late modernity's biopolitical predicament for subtler but more effective forms of violence', conjures up a human imaginary which speaks not only about war but also about our societies and our moral responsibilities as witnesses.

The chapters in Part III continue in detailed ways to unravel particular processes of 'Mediation'. They all bring together social theory and ethics in order to understand the ethical implications of living together in a mediated world. A decade ago the late Roger Silverstone had already set the stage for this inquiry by explaining (Silverstone 2002) why and how the media are fundamentally involved in morality. Everyday processes of social life, Silverstone argued, are inseparable from their mediation – that is, the way by which they are rendered meaningful by social agents, institutions and technologies. The media implicate us morally: audiences are not merely spectators but witnesses who find themselves having to negotiate between, and respond to, the moral issues that arise from the seemingly innocent act of everyday involvement with the media. Too often we find ourselves either collusive or complicit, sometimes both, in the plights of mediated others. Silverstone urged us to take responsibility for the ways in which the media make us irresponsible: 'The mediated symbolic is not imposed upon us as a space of no escape. It is one, historically, we have chosen, one that we choose on a daily basis, and one whose choice we have chosen to deny. Choice involves agency. Agency involves the possibility of challenge and refusal' (Silverstone 2002: 777).

In his contribution, Daniel Dayan (Chapter 10) focuses on the journalist as a mediator, as one who shows, as 'monstrator'. Engaging critically with Silverstone's notion of media hospitality, Dayan offers an alternative in the paradigm of monstration – the performativity of media. Referring to three models of the journalist (as witness, translator and monstrator), he argues that the ethical stakes of journalism lie not in the production of objective knowledge, in what Austin called the constative, but in the way mediated knowledge is so performed, in the performative – in monstration. Following Hannah Arendt's conception of politics as the act of appearing in public, Dayan develops the idea of monstration as a critique to the media hospitality, calling for a renewed sense of factuality – one that bridges between care and truth.

Mirca Madianou (Chapter 11) argues that understanding the workings of mediation – a structurally different condition from face-to-face communication – is a prerequisite for any discussion of ethics of media.

Madianou returns to O'Neill's earlier critique of rights-based models of media ethics (Chapter 2) and argues that a sociological analysis of the symbolic power of mediation highlights an additional reason why freedom of expression – an individual right – cannot be applied to mediated communication which involves a different temporal and spatial scale including potentially infinite audiences. Drawing on the witness statements at the Leveson Inquiry into the culture, practice and ethics of the UK press among other narratives of individuals who found themselves inadvertently exposed in the media, Madianou illustrates the asymmetries of mediation and observes that technological convergence can heighten the symbolic power of mediation. Despite the potential of digital media for bypassing original gatekeepers (disintermediation), cases of mediated harm can contribute to the problem of materialization (Butler 2005) and annihilation of voice.

A more optimistic scenario is proposed by Peter Lunt and Joe Livingstone's 'meta-ethical' analysis of moral discourse on *The Jeremy Kyle Show*, a popular British daytime talk show known for its sensationalism. For them, the programme is part of a politics of recognition (Honneth 1996 where otherwise marginalized voices may be granted visibility. Exposing the diversity of moral judgements and ethical disputes, it mediates the wider narrative of 'contradictions, tensions and indignities of living in late modernity' (Boltanski and Thévenot 2006). Rather than assessing the show against normative standards, Lunt and Livingstone shift their attention to the ethical disputes as they arise among the programme participants as a means to understand their *meta*-ethical assumptions when asserting their arguments. In other words, rather than asking what is right or wrong, the concern here is on what we mean by saying something is right or wrong.

Part IV, *Practices*, picks up the thread of practices of mediation developed in the previous chapters and gives them a sharper focus. The emphasis here is largely on *journalistic* practices, from the rise of the 'ethical living' journalism genre to *WikiLeaks* and the pressures of tabloid newswork. Sabina Lovibond's contribution (Chapter 13) continues the analysis of discourses of ethics which circulate within media (Lunt and Livingstone) and draws on ethical theory to reflect on newspaper journalists' framings of ethical living in relation to broader economic and environmental effects of the individual's consumption choices. In an unusual move for a philosopher, she departs from well-rehearsed discussions of ethical codes of conduct for media professionals and focuses on ethics as a subject matter of journalism. Lovibond recognizes that ubiquitous media provide a channel for first-order ethical debate even though the present analysis of 'ethical living' journalism appeals to a limited nature of ethics.

Damian Tambini (Chapter 14) deals with the tension between national security and cosmopolitan ethics focusing on *WikiLeaks*. The global, stateless nature of *WikiLeaks* and its lack of formal accountability reveal the limits of current state-based models of legal and self-regulatory frameworks. This 'limit situation' (Couldry 2012; cf. Ricoeur 2007) necessitates a new ethics of media, and Tambini contributes to this debate through his analysis of the US cables scandal. Drawing on a 'practical' approach to ethics (O'Neill 2000), Tambini asks what ethical rules might organizations such as *WikiLeaks* seek to voluntarily adhere to and how these norms would differ from those within national legal and ethical systems. Tambini puts forward a proposal for cosmopolitan ethics, which, although not yet achieved, would be the only way to give equal weight to all voices in the global space of appearance.

Angela Phillips (Chapter 15) examines the tension between individual journalists' ethical practices and institutional power, and argues that fierce market competition and institutional cultures undermine individual ethical practices. This is precisely what happened at the *News of the World* tabloid and the hackgate scandal which launched the Leveson Inquiry in the UK. The British system is particularly vulnerable to extreme pressures of competition as they combine with weak voluntary self-regulation. Phillips's comparative review identifies parallels, but also examples of best practice among European countries where ethical practices are encouraged and journalism is protected from cutthroat competition. For Phillips such protection is vital if we agree that ethical journalism is vital for democracy.

Not all would agree with this last statement. Barbie Zelizer's interpretation (Chapter 16) of the consequences of the *News of the World* scandal is markedly different. She argues that journalistic practices not only defy the establishment of meaningful ethical standards but also cut short the potential for ethical practice in the ground. Part of the problem, for Zelizer, of applying universal codes is that journalistic practice itself increasingly defies standardization, while the temporal, geographic, institutional and technological parameters of newswork further complicate matters. A set of collective ethical standards would narrow down the remit of journalism and attempt to reify its practices at a time when newswork is taking multiple and even unexpected forms. In so doing, Zelizer argues, ethics codes may undo what is most ethical about journalism.

With this final chapter, this book's debate reaches an appropriately unsettled ending. Zelizer's argument, distinctively, can draw on a rich tradition of journalistic and more broadly rhetoric education within the US, extended by recent debates within and beyond the US academy on 'public journalism' (Glasser 1999). But there are also connections back to chapters and philosophical perspectives earlier in the book. Zelizer's suspicion of ethics codes has something in common with Couldry's insistence on John McDowell's neo-Aristotelian principle of the 'non-codifiability' of the ethical (Couldry 2012: 189, discussing McDowell 1998), and with Levinas's refusal to reduce ethics to 'a fully conceptualized framework' (Pinchevski 2005: 96). So issues about how, whether and when to ask ethical questions about communication, and specifically the communications of media institutions, remain unresolved.

And yet, in at least one democracy (the UK), public demand for a stronger underpinning of ethical practice in the mainstream press is intense. The shocking immorality revealed by the UK phone-hacking scandal gave Lord Leveson little choice but to return to de Tocqueville's unanswerable question and call in his report for a non-governmental mechanism of some sort that could restore the irrevocably damaged legitimacy of existing self-regulatory mechanisms for monitoring press standards (the UK Press Complaints Commission). But as yet no new institutional framework has been agreed, and the wider question of how ethics of media can appropriately enter civic debate and representative public deliberation is also, not surprisingly, unresolved. This controversy is, perhaps, best seen as part of a peculiarly British legitimation crisis (involving not just the press but also the BBC, parliament, banks and police) that is, perhaps, of ultimately parochial interest, but it can also stand as proxy for the urgent issue of media accountability and, crucially, the open question that resonates throughout international media and communication research in the early 21st century: How can (perhaps should) we think about the ethics of our lives with media?

The ethics of media cannot be other than a contested domain, a space where even the very desirability of such an ethics remains up for interrogation, even as all of us, professional journalists or general audiences, circulators or actual subjects of media materials, confront the complexity of the normative challenges in which today's globally extended supersaturated media environment implicates us. Whatever your views on what is at stake in the 'ethics of media', this book, we hope, will prove to be a useful stimulus to such reflection.

Acknowledgements

The authors are grateful to the organizers and supporters of the various symposia which formed the background to much of this book: the Centre for Research in the Arts, Social Sciences and Humanities at Cambridge University (particularly its then director, Mary Jacobus, Catherine Hurley and Michelle Maciejewska), which funded The Ethics of Media: Philosophical Foundations and Practical Imperatives conference in April 2008; Dr Waddick Doyle at the American University of Paris, who hosted a symposium on media ethics in June 2008; the Philosophy, Theory and Critique Division of the International Communication Association, which hosted a preconference on media ethics in Chicago in May 2009; and Goldsmiths, University of London's Department of Media and Communications (particularly Dr Gareth Stanton), which contributed to the funding of each of these events. We also thank the other participants in those events who could not be represented in this volume.

Notes

1. Available from http://www.official-documents.gov.uk/document/hc1213/hc 07/0780/0780.asp.
2. The increasing importance of new media and the new ethical problems that they generate were largely neglected by the Leveson Inquiry report.
3. In choosing the part title 'Mediations', we do not thereby intend to take a position in the recent debate about which English term best captures such processes of representation and their cumulative consequences: 'mediation' or 'mediatization' (Krotz 2009; Lundby 2009; Hjarvard 2008; cf. Couldry 2012, Chapter 6).

References

Bauman, Z. (1993) *Postmodern Ethics*. Oxford: Blackwell.
Beck, U. (2006) *The Cosmopolitan Vision*. Cambridge: Polity.
Bertrand, C.-J. (2000) *Media Ethics and Accountability Systems*. New Brunswick: Transaction.
Bhabha, H. K. (2004) *The Location of Culture*. London: Routledge.
Boltanski, L. (1999) *Distant Suffering*. Cambridge: Cambridge University Press.
Boltanski, L. and Thévenot, L. (2006) *On Justification: Economies of Worth*. Princeton: Princeton University Press.
Brevini, B., Hintz, A. and McCurdy, P. (eds.) (2013) *Beyond WikiLeaks*. Guildford: Ashgate.
Butler, J. (2005) *Giving an Account of Oneself*. New York: Fordham University Press.
Butler, J. (2006) *Precarious Life: The Powers of Mourning and Violence*. London: Verso Books.

Chouliaraki, L. (2006) *The Spectatorship of Suffering*. London: Sage.

Chouliaraki, L. (2010) 'Post-humanitarianism: Humanitarian Communication Beyond a Politics of Pity', *International Journal of Cultural Studies* 13(2): 107–126.

Christians, C., Ferré, J. and Fackler, M. (1993) *Good News: Social Ethics and the Press*. New York: Longman.

Christians, C., Glasser, T., McQuail, D., Nordenstreng, K and White, R. (2010) *Normative Theories of the Media*. Chicago: University of Illinois Press.

Christians, C., Rotzoll, K. and Fackler, M. (1991) *Media Ethics: Cases and Moral Reasoning*. 3rd edition. New York: Longman.

Cohen-Almagor, R. (2001) *Speech, Media and Ethics: The Limits of Free Expression*. Basingstoke: Palgrave.

Couldry, N. (2006) *Listening Beyond the Echoes*. Boulder, CO: Paradigm Books.

Couldry, N. (2008) 'Media Ethics: Towards a Framework for Media Producers and Media Consumers', in S. Ward and H. Wasserman (eds) *Media Ethics Beyond Borders*. Johannesburg: Heinemann.

Couldry, N. (2012) *Media Society World*. Cambridge: Polity.

de Tocqueville, A. (1964) [o.p. 1835–1840] *Democracy in America*. London: David Campbell.

Eide, E., Kunelius, R. and Phillips, A. (eds) (2008) *Transnational Media Events: The Mohammed Cartons and the Imagined Clash of Civilizations*. Nordicom: Götebor.

Frosh, P. and Pinchevski, A. (eds) (2009) *Media Witnessing: Testimony in the Age of Mass Communication*. London: Palgrave Macmillan.

Garber, M. B., Hanssen, B. and Walkowitz, R. L. (2000) *The Turn to Ethics*. New York: Routledge.

Gilroy, P. (2004) *Between Camps: Nations, Cultures and the Allure of Race*. London: Allan Lane.

Glasser, T. (ed.) (1999) *The Idea of Public Journalism*. New York: Guilford Press.

Hjarvard, S. (2008) 'The Mediatization of Society: A Theory of the Media as Agents of Social and Cultural Change', *Nordicom Review* 29(2): 105–134.

Honneth, A. (1996) *The Struggle for Recognition*. Cambridge: Polity.

Howe, P. (2004) *Paparazzi*. New York: Artisan Books.

Howell, S. (ed.) (1997) *The Ethnography of Moralities*. London: Routledge.

Keeble, R. (2001) *Ethics for Journalists*. London: Routledge.

Krotz, F. (2009) 'Mediatization: A Concept with Which to Grasp Media and Societal Change', in K. Lundby (ed.) *Mediatization*. New York: Peter Lang, 19–38.

Lundby, K. (ed.) (2009) *Mediatization*. New York: Peter Lang.

Madianou, M. (2005) *Mediating the Nation: News, Audiences and the Politics of Identity*. London: UCL Press/Routledge.

Madianou, M. (2013) 'Humanitarian Campaigns in Social Media: Network Architectures and Polymedia Events', *Journalism Studies* 14(2): 249–266.

Malcolm, J. (1990) *The Journalist and the Murderer*. Basingstoke: Macmillan.

McDowell, J. (1998) *Mind, Value and Reality*. Cambridge, MA: Harvard University Press.

Miller, A. (2003) *An Introduction to Contemporary Metaethics*. Cambridge: Polity.

Morrison, D., Kiernan, M. and Svennevig, M. (2009) *Media and Values: Intimate Transgressions in a Changing Moral and Cultural Landscape*. Bristol: Intellect Press.

O' Neill, O. (2000) *Bounds of Justice*. Cambridge: Cambridge University Press.

O'Neill, O. (2002) *A Question of Trust*. Cambridge: Cambridge University Press.
Oswell, D. (2012) *The Agency of Children*. Cambridge: Cambridge University Press.
Pinchevski, A. (2005) *By Way of Interruption: Levinas and the Ethics of Communication*. Pittsburgh, PA: Duquesne University Press.
Ricoeur, P. (2007) *Reflections on the Just*. Chicago: Chicago University Press.
Silverstone, R. (2002) 'Complicity and Collusion in the Mediation of Everyday Life', *New Literary History* 33(5): 745–764.
Silverstone, R. (2007) *Media and Morality*. Cambridge: Polity.
Ward, S.J.A. (2011) *Ethics and the Media*. Cambridge: Cambridge University Press.
Ward, S.J.A. and Wasserman, H. (eds) (2010) *Media Ethics Beyond Borders*. New York: Routledge.
Zelizer, B. (2010) *About to Die: How News Images Move the Public*. New York: Oxford University Press.

Part I
Framings

2
Media Freedoms and Media Standards

Onora O'Neill

Introduction

In Tom Stoppard's 1978 play *Night and* Day,[1] Ruth Carlson, the wife of an expatriate copper mine manager, says to a young journalist: 'I'm with you on the free press. It's the newspapers I can't stand.' This ambivalence is still common. We stand by media freedom but are appalled by the results – and in the UK even more appalled today than we used to be before revelations about media phone hacking into private lives.

In Stoppard's play the idealistic young reporter replies that he shares the older woman's ambivalence:

You don't have to tell me, I know it better than you – the cele-bration of inanity, and the way real tragedy is paraphrased into an inflationary spiral of hackneyed melodramas – Beauty Queen In Tug-of-Love Baby Storm... Tug-of-Love Baby Mum In Pools Win... Pools

An ancestor of this paper was presented under the title 'Does Freedom Trump All Other Media Norms?' at a conference entitled The Ethics of Media: Philo-sophical Foundations and Practical Imperatives, organized by the Centre for Research in the Arts, Social Sciences and Humanities at Cambridge Univer-sity in 2008. A lot has changed in discussions of media ethics in the UK since then, not least with the partial emergence of facts about phone hack-ing by the British press. The present chapter takes some account both of these changes and of a range of arguments that I subsequently developed for a Woodbridge Lecture given at Columbia University in the spring of 2010 under the title 'Ethics for Communication'; in the *News of the World* in the *World Financial Times*, 18 November 2011; and in a Reuters Lec-ture entitled 'The Rights of Journalism and the Needs of Audiences', 22 November 2011, http://reutersinstitute.politics.ox.ac.uk/fileadmin/documents/ presentations/The_Rights_of_Journalism_and_Needs_of_Audiences.pdf.

Man In Beauty Queen Drug Quiz. I *know*. It's the price you pay for the part that matters...

But later he backtracks and says more seriously:

> It's not easy to defend, but it's mainly attacked for the wrong reasons. People think that rubbish journalism is produced by men of discrimination who are vaguely ashamed of truckling to the lowest taste. But it's not. It's produced by people doing their best work. Proud of their expertise with a limited number of cheap devices to put a shine on the shit. Sorry. I know what I'm talking about because I started off like that, admiring it, trying to be that good, looking up to Fleet Street stringers, London men sometimes, on big local stories. I thought it was great. Some of the best times in my life have been spent sitting in a clapped-out Ford Consul outside a suburban house with a packet of Polos and twenty Players waiting to grab a crooked landlord or a footballer's runaway wife who might be good for one front page between oblivion and oblivion. I felt part of a privileged group, inside society and yet outside it, with a licence to scourge it and a duty to defend it, night and day, the street of adventure, the fourth estate. And the thing is – I was dead right. That's what it was, and I was part of it because it's indivisible. Junk journalism is the evidence of a society that has got at least one thing right, that there should be nobody with the power to dictate where responsible journalism begins.

This is an eloquent, if not wholly coherent, defence of what we still have. Apart from the obsolete references to the 'clapped-out Ford Consul', 'packet of Polos and twenty Players', the position is wholly recognizable.

Yet are junk journalism and trailer-trash television, not to mention Fox News and blatant intrusion by parts of the print media into private lives, inevitable costs of media freedom? Do we face a stark choice between a 'world with nobody with the power to dictate where responsible journalism begins' and one of media excess and intrusion? Are currently favoured arguments for media freedom beyond challenge? What exactly do the better of them show? Do any of them show that media freedom should be (close to) unconditional, and incompatible with requiring media standards? If they don't, what conditions may be set on media freedom?

We are so distant in time, culture and technologies from the early versions of classical arguments for free speech, and for press or media freedom, that it takes effort to imagine their original context and point. To me it seems unlikely that any of them now carries quite the sense or weight that it was originally taken to have. Yet the old arguments are still the ones we rely on. Four types of argument for media freedom are, I think, in common use, each with many variations. I shall refer to classical versions of these constantly reused arguments, taking them in rough chronological sequence, and prefacing the discussion with brief general comments on arguments from authority (section 'Arguments from authority: Preliminary remarks'). (More extensive comments on arguments from authority are given in a discussion of its contemporary use in appeals to freedom of expression in section 'Generic freedom of expression').

Arguments from authority: Preliminary remarks

The first and probably the most common type of argument for media freedom simply appeals to constitutional or other authorities that proclaim or enact variously specified rights to free speech or to media freedom. Such arguments may, for example, appeal to the relevant part of the First Amendment to the US Constitution ('Congress shall make no law abridging the freedom of the press') or to Article 10 of the European Convention on Human Rights (ECHR) (to which I shall return), or to other enactments or declarations taken to have authority.

Unfortunately, arguments from authority don't provide deep justifications. The impression that they are convincing often trades on the underlying ambiguity of (human) rights claims, which can be interpreted either as claims about convention(al) or positive rights – convincing only to those who accept the authority of the favoured convention or constitution – or as claims about underlying moral or natural rights, which purportedly justify convention(al) rights.[2] The second understanding of (human) rights aspires to deeper justification, and goes beyond an appeal to the mere fact that a specific conception of some right has been promulgated or endorsed by an accepted – or disputed – authority.

Justifications that do not appeal to authority will fail if they take shortcuts or make unsustainable assumptions, but they at least aim deeper than appeals to authority. The best-known examples of deeper arguments for media freedom have variously claimed that it is necessary for discovering truth; that it is a corollary of individual rights to self-expression; that it is a generic form of freedom of expression (itself, however, often 'justified' only by appeals to the authority of international human rights documents); and that it is necessary for social, cultural and, above all, democratic life.None of these lines of thought justifies unconditional media freedom.

Truth and truth-seeking

Appeals to the needs of truth-seeking are the oldest of these deeper arguments. Milton famously offered a resonant version:

> And though all the winds of doctrine were let loose to play upon the earth, so Truth be in the field, we do injuriously, by licensing and prohibiting, misdoubting her strength. Let her and Falsehood grapple; who ever knew Truth put to the worse, in a free and open encounter?[3]

The argument is too ambitious. Some forms of freedom are indeed necessary for the discovery of truth, but they are not sufficient, and unrestricted freedom damages the search for truth.

Any serious search for truth has to observe structures and disciplines, and is undermined by casual (let alone systematic) disregard of norms of aiming for accuracy, norms for using evidence and other everyday epistemic norms. Where truth is the central concern, disregard of the disciplines of truth-seeking is self-defeating: hence the elaborate disciplines of academic research, writing and publication, and the complex processes of criminal trials. As Bernard Williams points out, 'in institutions dedicated to finding out the truth, such as universities, research institutes, and courts of law, speech is not at all unregulated'.[4]

Media freedoms are not best justified solely by appeals to the needs of truth-seeking for two reasons. First, a great deal of media content does not make truth claims (e.g. horoscopes, short stories, crosswords, drama, music). Second, when media content makes truth claims (e.g. in reporting news, sport or markets) it may have further aims or constraints that mean that it has to use rough and ready versions of the disciplines of truth-seeking, which would be unacceptable where truth-seeking is the overriding aim.

Rights of self-expression

John Stuart Mill shared Milton's view of the importance of freedom for truth-seeking, claiming that

> the peculiar evil of silencing the expression of an opinion is, that it is robbing the human race; posterity as well as the existing generation;

those who dissent from the opinion, still more than those who hold it. If the opinion is right, they are deprived of the opportunity of exchanging error for truth: if wrong, they lose, what is almost as great a benefit, the clearer perception and livelier impression of truth, produced by its collision with error.[5]

However, this argument too cannot support an unconditional conception of media freedoms: like 'free and open encounters', 'collisions with error' are not sufficient for truth-seeking (nor are the metaphorical 'marketplaces of ideas' that are more popular with later liberal writers). Since the disciplines of truth-seeking are constraining, appeals to truth-seeking can at most support conceptions of media freedom that incorporate the relevant constraints.

Mill, however, argues for a more radical view of free speech for individuals than his appeal to the needs of truth-seeking at the start of Chapter 2 of *On Liberty* can support. In Chapter 1 he defends a distinctive view of rights of self-expression for individuals that he does not derive from the needs or benefits of truth or truth-seeking. There he argues that strong individual rights of self-expression are needed if we are to recognize 'the permanent interests of man as a progressive being', and respect individuals' 'sovereignty over their own minds and bodies'. Respect for this 'sovereignty' means that harmless self-expression should not be restricted, even if it is, for example, unintelligible, untrue or cavalier about evidence. Rather, 'the sole end for which mankind are warranted, individually or collectively, in interfering with the liberty of any of their number, is self-protection'.[6]

Where there is no harm to others, Mill concludes, each individual should enjoy 'absolute freedom of opinion and sentiment on all subjects, practical or speculative, scientific, moral, or theological' whether or not they respect the disciplines of truth-seeking.[7]

Appeals to the protection of individuality and individual self-expression don't, however, provide a useful basis for an account of press or media freedom. Self-expression covers speech that is not aimed at and does not reach any audience, so does not communicate. Mill's further arguments in Chapter 2 of *On Liberty* focus specifically on communication. Although they too call speech acts 'expressions of opinion', they actually discuss speech that is directed at audiences and used in discussion, and say no more about individual self-expression. The chapter is fundamentally an argument for the importance of free discussion, in which each adopts 'the steady habit of correcting and completing his own opinion by collating it with those of others'.

The arguments of this chapter provide a far more hospitable basis for a justification of media freedoms than the discussion of rights of self-expression that Chapter 1 can provide. The media are evidently in the business of communication, not of self-expression. Their speech, like that of other powerful organizations, including governments, other public bodies and corporations, is directed at audiences; it fails in its purposes if it is, for example, unintelligible or inaccessible to those audiences. So media speech, like all intended communication, has to meet at least the standards that enable audiences to grasp what is meant; self-expression does not have to attend to those standards.

Because the media include powerful organizations, there may be reasons to think that they should meet further conditions. It is easy for the powerful to mislead the less powerful, and in other cases we set stringent conditions on the communication of powerful organizations. We don't think it acceptable for companies to invent their balance sheets or to distort or hide material considerations in company reports; we don't think it acceptable for public bodies to invent, distort or conceal their performance. Companies and public bodies that act in these and similar ways are likely to face sanctions, prosecution and heavy reputational damage. But media speech is often seen as an exception because of the fear – of which Mill was acutely aware – that setting constraints or conditions on media speech risks censorship, or may chill or stifle debate.

Yet the very concerns and fear that we have about the speech of other powerful organizations are also relevant to powerful media organizations. While we have reason to think that nobody should have the power to dictate where responsible journalism begins, we also have reason to remember Rudyard Kipling's sharp comment that unrestrained media freedom is 'Power without responsibility – the prerogative of the harlot throughout the ages'.[8]

This dilemma is all too topical. The revelations about media intrusions into private lives that became a matter of public knowledge in the UK in 2011 are reasons for thinking that, even if Mill's arguments for individual freedom of self-expression are convincing, they cannot justify press and media freedoms. Nor is intrusive journalism the only reason for doubting the adequacy of assimilating press and media freedom to individual rights to self-expression. The media seek to communicate, so have reasons to be intelligible and to make what they communicate assessable by their readers, listeners and viewers, and to offer reasons and evidence for their assertions. If individuals are unintelligible, or cavalier about accuracy or evidence, they often (not invariably) do little harm, or harm only themselves. When powerful organizations, including the media, take a cavalier approach to intelligibility, or to accuracy or to evidence, the effects can run wider.

Generic freedom of expression

In the last 50 years it has become standard to speak of the media as having not rights of self-expression but generic rights to freedom of expression. Differences between these similar-sounding ideas are often blurred. Freedom of expression is a creature of the great declarations of human rights of the mid-20th century; it is not the same as a right to self-expression.

The Universal Declaration of Human Rights of 1948, Article 19, asserts a generic right to freedom of expression, in the first instance for individuals but then extended to the media; it does not refer to rights of self-expression:

> Everyone has the right to freedom of opinion and expression; this right includes freedom to hold opinions without interference and to seek, receive and impart information and ideas through any media and regardless of frontiers.[9]

Similarly, the ECHR of 1950, Article 10.1, asserts a generic right to freedom of expression, in the first instance for individuals, but then extended to the media; it too does not refer to rights of self-expression:

> Everyone has the right to freedom of expression. This right shall include freedom to hold opinions and to receive and impart information and ideas without interference by public authority and regardless of frontiers.[10]

It is plain that the Declarations and Conventions use the phrase 'freedom of expression' generically to cover both individual and media speech rights, although they give priority to the former, but that here self-expression is not given priority over communication. This broad usage has advantages. It avoids the awkwardness of requiring separate consideration of individuals' freedom of speech and of press or media freedoms – an awkwardness that may, however, reflect real differences. The new term also fits well in a world in which communication, whether by individuals or by the media (or by other organizations), uses a range of symbolic systems (speech, writing, images) and numerous communicative technologies (print, broadcasting, film, internet, multimedia). Any speech act, whether or not it communicates, can be seen as expressive simply because it expresses content – but many cannot plausibly be seen as acts of self-expression, or covered by Mill's arguments for rights of self-expression for individuals.

The rights proclaimed in the great Conventions and Declarations are also highly indeterminate, and are not intended as absolute or unconditional rights. This is made wholly explicit in the *ECHR*, where Article 10, ii (so much less cited than Article 10, i) sets out a range of legitimate restrictions on freedom of expression:

> the exercise of these freedoms, since it carries with it duties and responsibilities, may be subject to such formalities, conditions, restrictions or penalties as are prescribed by law and are necessary in a democratic society, in the interests of national security, territorial integrity or public safety, for the prevention of disorder or crime, for the protection of health or morals, for the protection of the reputation or rights of others, for preventing the disclosure of information received in confidence, or for maintaining the authority and impartiality of the judiciary'.[11]

So while ECHR assigns 'freedom of expression' both to individuals and to institutions, it promptly 'balances', and limits, that freedom with rights for the state to set conditions on its use. It proclaims not unrestricted freedom of self-expression but a defeasible right to media freedom.

So the relevant articles of the two documents assert speech rights for individuals and for the media, but neither refers to rights of self-expression, let alone to the arguments that Mill used to argue specifically for rights of self-expression for individuals. This is entirely reasonable. First, unlike individuals, organizations cannot, strictly speaking, express themselves, having no self to express. Second, Conventions and Declarations do not do justifications: their task is to proclaim or assert, and any justification must be dealt with elsewhere, whether by the arguments of political philosophy or by political processes of agreement and ratification.

Since Conventions and Declarations rely on arguments from authority, and do not offer deeper justification for the rights they proclaim, we must look elsewhere for justification. It is clear enough that the generic freedom of expression proclaimed in ECHR cannot be justified by Mill's arguments for individuals' rights of self-expression. However, even if Mill's arguments for rights of self-expression cannot justify media freedoms, his harm principle might help to resolve their indeterminacy, and indeed versions of the harm principle are often put to such use. I shall consider briefly whether the principle can serve this purpose, and then return to justifications of media freedom that appeal to the discursive needs of social and cultural life, and of democracy.

Generic freedom of expression and the harm principle

Appeals to generic freedom of expression – if justified – could at least provide a broad framework for acceptable configurations of media freedom. However, they are highly indeterminate, and Article 10 ii of ECHR also does not justify the restrictions on media freedom that it asserts. But can appeals to the harm principle resolve the indeterminacy of conceptions of freedom of expression, just as they (supposedly) determine the proper limit of rights to self-expression?

Unfortunately the harm principle provides a hopelessly inadequate way of determining what sorts of media and other public speech may be prohibited or restricted. This can be illustrated by the case of the publication of cartoons of the Prophet Mohammed in Denmark. In September 2005 when Flemming Rose, cultural editor of the provincial paper *Jyllands-Posten* commissioned and published some now notorious cartoons depicting the Prophet, he intended to make a point about free speech and media freedom. As he saw it, these freedoms were at risk in Denmark not because of censorship but because of self-censorship. Some writers and artists, he claimed, were reluctant to comment openly on Islam or on Muslim immigration into Denmark. Publishing cartoons of the Prophet would supposedly exemplify and reaffirm rights of freedom of expression. As Rose saw the matter, publishing the cartoons might offend some people but that would not be a legitimate reason not to publish.

The consequences of his decision to publish emerged slowly, as a vast number of uncoordinated and, in many cases, misinformed responses to the initial publication ensued in many different countries.[12] The months after the cartoons were first published saw millions of words of commentary; a range of unsuccessful diplomatic initiatives; numerous protests and denunciations; and energetic exacerbation of the dispute both by zealous would-be defenders of Islam and by zealous would-be defenders of conceptions of free speech. By the time the protests declined in the late spring of 2006, this war of words had escalated into demonstrations and threats (including numerous death threats); burnings of Danish embassies, Christian churches and other buildings; an extensive boycott of Danish goods in several Middle Eastern countries; and some 240 deaths and 800 injuries. Four months after first publication, Rose expressed limited regret for the dreadful outcome. However, he maintained that 'We do not apologise for printing the cartoons. It was our right to do so.'[13]

This is a clear case in which publication and circulation of various claims and counterclaims – not only by *Jyllands-Posten* – triggered cascades of events, many of them speech acts, that ended in undoubted and enormous harm to many people. If Mill's harm principle offers a way of determining the acceptable limits on media speech, this case should be revealing. However, as soon as one examines the complex interaction of claims and counterclaims that ensued after the initial publication of the cartoons, it becomes clear that the harm principle offers little help.

Rose's position was fairly typical of those who construe press and media freedom maximally, in that he maintains that free speech includes rights to publish content that others find 'offensive'.[14] Although some who hold this view will add that it would be better if rights to free speech were used 'responsibly', many will agree with Stoppard's character that 'there should be nobody with the power to dictate where responsible journalism begins'. On the other hand, many moderate Muslims, and others, claimed that this particular exercise of free speech was unacceptable not because it was offensive (although they thought that it was) but because they thought that it was discriminatory, blasphemous and dangerous (it did not help that *Jyllands-Posten* had a reputation for hostile coverage of immigrants).

However, it is hard to disentangle who carries which responsibility for what actually ensued. Did harms already arise during the war of words, or did they arise only when events escalated into widespread violence and loss of life? Did Danish and Middle Eastern diplomats and politicians contribute to harm when they made too little (in some cases perhaps disingenuous) efforts to address the issues, or treated the concerns of those who disagreed with them too lightly? Did harm escalate because some right-wing politicians and some fundamentalist Christian groups in and beyond Denmark tried to sharpen the confrontation? Was the harm largely caused by Muslims in various countries who republished and recirculated the very material that they claimed should not have been published at all? Was the main cause of harm the action of a narrower group of Muslims who added further, more offensive, material that had not been published by *Jyllands-Posten* to a dossier documenting the supposed wrongs, then circulated that dossier widely in the

Islamic world?[15] Or was the harm caused by those Muslims who used the very rights to free speech they enjoyed in Western countries to urge that those who had published the cartoons should be persecuted, even executed (leading to arrests of some for incitement of hatred)? In this tangled tale it seems impossible to draw clear lines between offence and incitement.

To those who see media freedom as more or less unconditional, advocates of 'responsible' free speech simply fail to understand what rights to press and media freedoms are for. Rose's subsequent comments are typical: 'I think some of the Muslims who have reacted very strongly to these cartoons are being driven by totalitarian and authoritarian impulses, and the nature of these impulses is that if you give in once they will just put forward new requirements.'[16] Yet even the most committed liberals don't seriously think that rights to free speech are unconditional: the problem is that there is uncertainty about which conditions or restrictions are acceptable, and in particular about the point at which acceptable speech that offends gives way to unacceptable speech that incites or defames. In this case, those who published the cartoons, with substantial help from others who then publicized them, including from some who claimed to oppose their publication, magnified a provincial provocation into global insult and led to many deaths. So even if the harm principle has some purchase in determining which restrictions on individual self-expression are convincing (I am not certain, and I have not argued that it does), it clearly lacks sufficient bite to resolve difficult cases that test the limits of media freedoms.

These liberal dilemmas perhaps reflect an underlying ambivalence in liberal thought about free speech. Liberals are often torn between aspirations to justify free speech as minimal, harmless and uncontroversial (that makes justification easier), and an incompatible belief that free speech matters because it is not minimal at all: the pen is mightier than the sword. This double vision is old and respectable. Immanuel Kant called free speech 'the most innocuous freedom', but then insisted that it was hugely important that enlightened despots should respect it.[17] Mill's arguments for 'rights of self-expression' construe speech minimally as 'merely self-regarding action' (today we would probably speak of it as 'merely self-affecting action'), but then he insists that freedom of speech is of the greatest importance. But once we move beyond simple examples, such as shouting 'fire!' in a crowded theatre (perhaps leading to panic, and deaths) or inciting a riot in front of the house of a grain merchant, where speech act and harm are colocated, and causation of harm is relatively easy to ascertain, uncertainties grow.

Rights to free speech have always been seen as limited by other serious considerations, and must be so restricted if we are to respect other rights. Nobody thinks that a right to free speech includes a licence to intimidate, to incite hatred, to defraud, to deceive or the like, and nobody thinks that the law should protect speech acts that injure or put others' lives at risk. But it is unlikely that there is any simple way of identifying a clear boundary between harmless and harmful speech that provides a generic criterion for identifying misuses of freedom of expression before the future unrolls. While it is often said that free speech must include a right to say things that are offensive or provocative, but not the right to defame or insult, let alone intimidate, these supposed distinctions are inevitably unclear because interpretations of speech acts vary with audiences. Some Danes and others read the cartoons as no more than mildly provocative and offensive to a few; some Muslims and others read them as insulting, defamatory, blasphemous and dangerous. If speech were mere self-expression, we might see what happened as in no way the responsibility of *Jyllands-Posten* or of Rose, and the undoubted harms as entirely due to irresponsible action by others; but since speech usually seeks to communicate, this view is too simple.

However, if we think of free speech as communicating with audiences that vary in the ways they can and will engage with what is said and written, we may find reasons to be more circumspect. *Jyllands-Posten* could have communicated its entirely legitimate worries about self-censorship in ways that would have found resonance and respect, and been effective. Those who claimed that the cartoons were distressing to them and others could have used their energies to make sure that they were not more widely circulated: they did not need to pour petrol on the flames. Those who dealt with the political and diplomatic issues could have taken earlier and more effective action. There is no case for censoring the content that Jyllands-Posten sought to convey; there is a case to be made against the action by which both *Jyllands-Posten* and others chose to spread this message.

Media freedom, discussion and democracy

Mill's approach to free speech, including freedom of press, in Chapter 2 of *On Liberty* points to a different, and in my view more plausible, justification for media freedoms. In that chapter he continues to use the generic term 'expression of opinion' to cover both self-expression and speech that aims to communicate, but he focuses on speech directed at intended audiences that aims at communication and discussion. Mill here has in mind a range of discussion, and in particular discussion in which truth claims are made and disputed in 'morals, religion, politics, social relations, and the business of life'. Taken as a whole the chapter does not place much faith in the 'collisions' of truth with error referred to in its first paragraph, but rather stresses hearing and contesting others' reasons and opinions, presenting and considering 'facts and arguments', and correcting and completing one's views. These activities are indispensable for daily and for public life, and they provide a plausible justification not only for freedom of speech but also for media freedoms.

Media freedom is of special importance in contemporary society because media communication bears on all social and cultural life, and above all on democracy. Free media enable citizens to learn and to judge what is going on in the world they inhabit, to discover what is being done in their names, and to assess social, cultural and public affairs. Without free media they are disempowered, social and cultural life may be damaged, and democracy will falter or fail.[18] However, citizens in democracies need media that are not merely free to publish but communicate intelligibly to intended audiences and enable them to judge or assess the content. So media freedom is not a matter of (more or less) unconditional rights of self-expression but of freedom to publish in any way that is intelligible to and assessable by readers, listeners and viewers.

A demand for media intelligibility may seem trivial: intelligibility is necessary for all communication, and communication is the business that the media are in. However, I mention this apparently obvious demand because it is further evidence that media freedom is conditional on communication meeting certain standards, and cannot parallel rights of self-expression for individuals. Media communication fails if it is unfit to reach intended audiences; self-expression need not be audience-directed at all, let alone intelligible to any actual audiences.

A demand for media accuracy, on the other hand, may seem a demand too far. Certainly such a demand cannot be tightly drawn, for two reasons. First, a lot of media speech does not make truth claims: we cannot demand that crosswords or horoscopes are accurate, or evidence based, although we may have other criteria for assessing them. Second, even when media speech makes truth claims, an excessive demand for accuracy could be intimidating or chilling, or too burdensome in the time available, and so on. Nobody can be sure of getting everything right – even with zealous 'fact-checking' (though fact-checking helps and its neglect may support misleading communication). Media that serve rather than damage social and cultural life and democracy need to aim for accuracy but they cannot be required to achieve it: truthfulness can be required but truth cannot.

However, if the media aim for accuracy, the best approximation that they can provide for their audiences is to make their communication assessable by intended readers, listeners and viewers. Making communication assessable by intended audiences may variously require the inclusion of caveats and qualifications, indications of evidence and sources, prompt corrections of error, as well as indicating whether content is reporting or commentary, making it obvious that rumour and gossip are just that, and the like. These and other forms of everyday epistemic responsibility are the types of normative constraint that media communication has to meet if readers, listeners and viewers are to judge what they encounter. It is unclear to me whether any justification could be offered for media communication that fails these standards. The needs of democracy, and more broadly of social and cultural life, therefore justify a determinate conception of media freedom of expression that differs from individuals' rights of self-expression, and is shaped by requirements to meet the necessary conditions for feasible and assessable communication with intended audiences. All of these requirements on media communication are content neutral, and none of them permits or condones censorship. They constrain media process rather than prescribing or proscribing content.

Securing compliance

If we consider the contemporary British media in the light of these standards, we are likely to form disparate views of different parts of the media, some of them highly critical. As the ruminations of Stoppard's character reveal, media failures are not new. The media scandal that emerged in the UK in 2011 illustrates failings that had been around for a long time. But these failings are not ubiquitous.

At one end of the spectrum, the BBC is required by its Charter and by statute to aim to inform (as well as to educate and to entertain), and by and large takes demands for intelligibility, accuracy and assessability, as well as further demands for impartiality, seriously. On the other hand, parts of the British print media seemingly lack either will or means to take a systematic grip on aiming for accuracy when they make truth claims, and they are often cavalier about handling and communicating evidence, and other measures, that would make media content assessable by intended audiences.

Yet ostensibly the British print media are committed to accuracy, which is the first demand of the Press Complaints Commission (PCC) Code of Practice. The former PCC annually reported that it had 'resolved' a rather limited number of complaints, mainly about inaccuracies and invasions of privacy. However, good reporting is a public good, not a consumer product, and complaints procedures are unlikely to secure public goods. The PCC acted only where individuals made a complaint, and understandably individuals often preferred to remain silent rather than risk drawing attention to themselves, even if they could have shown that media claims about them were false or misleading. And where false or misleading reporting is generic (rather than about named individuals or organizations), complaints procedures provide no remedy.

The dismaying inadequacy of the PCC's performance was highlighted early in the investigation of the phone-hacking scandal, but this did not show that media self-regulation must inevitably fail. Debates about the rival merits of supposedly stronger versions of self-regulation, and of forms of regulation that require a statutory basis (so they can call witnesses and impose sanctions), will only be resolved when action is taken to implement Leveson Inquiry (in greater or lesser measure), and when other public and police inquiries into aspects of the phone-hacking scandal, have reported. So I shall bracket the topic here, while noting that it has long been uncontroversial that the PCC form of self-regulation was failing in many ways.

Justifying a determinate conception of press freedom and its limits is one thing; imposing it is another. Stoppard's character insists that any constraint on media freedom risks establishing a 'power to dictate where responsible journalism begins', and may open the door to the very control of content that has been the traditional aim of censors. This fear has inhibited many discussions of media standards. If the media are regulated by any but themselves, it is often said, this will restrict acceptable exercises of press freedom and even limit the self-expression of individuals. This line of thought is both too quick and too comfortable for those with an interest in securing very extensive rights to freedom of expression for the media (though interestingly not for other powerful organizations – the danger of allowing state and corporate power too wide a freedom of expression is well recognized, especially by the media).

Yet why should we assume that the choice is between state censorship of content and nothing? Even the feeble constraints of the PCC are not nothing, and other forms of self-regulation could offer more. For example, the BBC and Reuters have codes for their reporters and editors which deal with a range of important matters. A stronger form of self-regulation might, for example, require disclosure of the financial interests of those writing on market-sensitive topics. It might require the media to let readers know how much 'informants' (or, should I say, 'mis-informants', there being no neutral term) have been paid for particular 'stories'. It might require the media to tell readers, listeners and viewers when content that is not flagged as advertising has been (partly or wholly) funded by third parties. Self-regulation could secure a range of standards that matter for readers, listeners and viewers: however, large parts of the profit-oriented media are likely to reject self-regulation that requires better media process.

And self-regulation is not the only possibility. It may be necessary to secure media standards through forms of state-backed but independent regulation that forbid censorship of content but regulate media process. Most evidently, and least controversially, the UK could enact stronger legislation to limit concentration of ownership (anti-monopoly provisions were weakened in the Communications Act 2003). More controversially, but I think plausibly, it would be possible to require the media to live up to some of the standards for process and conduct that they are so often keen that others observe. What, for example, would be wrong about *requiring* those working for media organizations to sign up to standards of conduct, such as are commonly required of those with power and influence in other public and corporate organizations? What would be wrong with requiring owners, editors and journalists to register their interests, and in particular their financial interests and political affiliations, and to declare in which jurisdiction they pay taxes? What would be wrong about requiring the disclosure of amounts paid or received in order to publish stories? What would be wrong about rating proprietors, editors and journalists, with the aim of identifying those who communicate well, of naming and shaming those who consistently ignore the needs of their audiences, and requiring the publication of these ratings?

Stoppard's character denies that 'rubbish journalism is produced by men of discrimination who are vaguely ashamed of truckling to the lowest taste', and asserts that it is 'produced by people doing their best work' who are 'proud of their expertise'. People who are proud of their expertise are not immune to shame when they produce poor work. If media processes were regulated, many forms of poor and shoddy communication could be deterred or made public. It is entirely possible to regulate media processes in specific and justifiable ways. Prohibitions of censorship of content are compatible with requiring standards for media process, and publishing evidence about the standards actually achieved.

Notes

1. Tom Stoppard (1978) *Night and Day* (London: Faber and Faber).
2. For an assessment of the task of replacing assertion with argument, see Onora O'Neill (2005) 'The Dark Side of Human Rights', *International Affairs*, 81(2) 427–439.
3. John Milton (16xx), 'Areopagitica A Speech for the Liberty of Unlicensed Printing to the Parliament of England', in *Areopagitica and Tractate on Education*, ed. Charles W. Eliot, published at one time by P.F. Collier, now in multiple versions and in the public domain, Vol. 3, p. 45/para 31.
4. Bernard Williams (2002) *Truth and Truthfulness* (Princeton N.J: Princeton University Press) 217. It is interesting, and rather surprising, that Mill makes this point in an aside in *On Liberty:* 'The dictum that truth always triumphs over persecution is one of those pleasant falsehoods'. John Stuart Mill (1859) 'On Liberty', in *On Liberty and Other Writings*, ed. Stefan Collini (Cambridge: Cambridge University Press) 30.
5. *Ibid.* 20.
6. *Ibid.* 13.
7. *Ibid.* 15.
8. Made famous when quoted in an electoral address by Stanley Baldwin on 17 March 1931.
9. Universal Declaration of Human Rights (1948), http://www.ohchr.org/EN/UDHR/Pages/Language.aspx?LangID=eng.
10. European Convention on Human Rights (1950), http://www.hri.org/docs/ECHR50.html.
11. *Ibid.*
12. For a detailed account of the context and aftermath of the publication of the cartoons, see Jytte Klausen (2009) *The Cartoons that Shook the World* (New Haven, CT: Yale University Press). Statistics on deaths and injuries attributable to the publication of the cartoons are given on p. 107.
13. *The Times*, 1 February 2006.
14. I put the term 'offensive' in scare quotes here because it has become a totem of liberal thought, as if offensiveness were the crucial case for freedom of expression. Yet a focus on offence often overlooks the range and variety of the harms that speech may cause, most of them nothing to do with offence. For a contrary view of the importance of protecting speech that others may find offensive, see Stefan Collini (2011) *That's Offensive! Criticism, Identity, Respect* (Kolkata, London and New York: Seagull Press).
15. See Jytte Clausen (2009) *op. cit.*
16. *The Times*, 1 February 2006.
17. Immanuel Kant (1784) *What is Enlightenment?*, tr. Mary J. Gregor (1996) in Immanuel Kant, *Practical Philosophy* (Cambridge University Press, Cambridge) 8, 35–42 (page references to the standard pagination of the

Prussian Academy edition of Kant's works). Kant argued against unrestricted speech rights for office holders (i.e. those with power (military officers, clergy and civil servants are his examples)), but for free speech for those without institutional commitments who speak 'to the world at large'.

18. Alexander Meikeljohn, Free Speech and its Relation to Self Government, 1948, available at http://uwdc.library.wisc.edu/collections/UW/MeikFreeSp.

3
Living Well with and through Media

Nick Couldry

Introduction

Media raise normative questions of various sorts. Some start out from evaluating the organizational structures through which media get made; others start out from our evaluations of the things media institutions and individual media agents do and the implications for our wider media environment in an environment that in the past 15 years has expanded massively with the growth of the internet and countless new digital platforms. It is the second action-related question with which I am concerned in this chapter, and for which I use the term 'media ethics'. I mean media ethics to be distinct from, for example, Habermas's reflections on the adequacy of the mediated public sphere for democratic functioning.

Journalistic codes of ethics exist in almost every country but comprise only a small part of what I mean by media ethics.[1] Media ethics must address the broader questions – of concern to all citizens – which Durkheim termed 'civic morals' that lie beyond the detailed internal debates for which he reserved the term 'professional ethics' (Durkheim 1992). Media ethics asks what the standards are by which we should judge the satisfactoriness of media institutions' own codes of ethics. It is this broader perspective that has for a long time been missing in discussions about journalistic ethics. But as Israeli legal philosopher Raphael Cohen-Almagor notes, there is a wider problem if 'the liberal values that underlie any democratic society, those of not harming and respecting others, are kept outside the realm of journalism' (Cohen-Almagor 2001: 79). Moral philosopher Onora O'Neill analogously argues that 'we need to rethink the proper limits of press freedom. The press has no licence to deceive and we have no reasons to think that a free press needs such licence' (O'Neill 2002: 102). Both writers appeal to the wider moral or ethical standards within the framework of which we might judge the particular codes adopted under the banner of ethics by actual journalists. It is those wider standards with which media ethics as I understand it is concerned.

There is a particular emphasis in my discussion on media *ethics*. I signal here an allegiance to the tradition of neo-Aristotelian virtue ethics. I believe this is the philosophical tradition best suited to building a conversation about media standards from minimal premises. I aim for an argument based on minimal premises for two reasons. First, media contribute to the shaping of actions and world-views on a variety of scales, up to and including the global (the global distribution of a media message is a possibility that can never be excluded). So any conversation about media ethics involves a global scale. But how do we start such a conversation without also taking into account the huge differences of world-view (religious, political, cultural and moral) among those potentially affected by media who we would want to take part in such a conversation? Second, debate today about media standards must intervene in the daily workings of media industries that are under intense financial and competitive pressure and in conditions of production that have changed radically in the digital age (Fenton et al. 2009). Two quotations from recent debate in the UK illustrate the difficulties. On the one hand, newspaper owner Richard Desmond told the Leveson Inquiry into the standards of the UK press: 'I don't quite know what the word [ethics] means...everybody's ethics are different' (quoted, *Guardian* 13 January 2012). On the other hand, one respected journalist argues that the working conditions of today's UK press 'positively prevent [journalists from] discovering the truth' (Davies 2007: 28). If we want therefore to challenge the insouciance of a Richard Desmond or alter the conditions that Nick Davies diagnoses, it is best to build an argument from minimal premises whose plausibility can command wide assent.

The task of interrupting what media do every day is difficult, but as the 2011–2012 scandal over the *News of the World*'s phone-hacking practices illustrates dramatically, it is essential, not just for the quality of democracy but for the quality of public and social life, whether aspiring to democracy or not. I hope that media ethics, as understood in this chapter, can be a modest but effective tool for asking appropriate normative questions about everyday media practice, whether conducted by professionals or by anyone who acts with and through media, including digital media platforms.

Some preliminaries

Why Aristotle as a starting-point for media ethics? Clearly there are philosophical choices. What of Kant and the whole post-Kantian tradition? What of Nietzsche, Heidegger, Derrida? Rather than review philosophical history in detail, let me note some signposts within philosophical debate that help to make sense of the path taken by this chapter.

Where to start?

First, there is Alisdair Macintyre's historical rereading of the Enlightenment view of rationality and knowledge – and the Nietzschean and other critiques that responded to that view – as based upon an unhelpful rejection of the Aristotelian tradition of virtue ethics. MacIntyre asked: 'was it right in the first place to reject Aristotle?' (1981: 111). And his own approach to the choices for a late 20th-century moral philosophy reopens the path back to Aristotle.

Our contemporary sense of the renewed relevance of Aristotelian ethics is linked also to Ludwig Wittgenstein. The return to Aristotle, and specifically Aristotelian ethics, in Anglo-American philosophy from the late 1950s, and especially from the 1980s, is incomprehensible without the huge influence of Wittgenstein, particularly his philosophy of language and mind, and his highly original approach to philosophical method. But Wittgenstein is also a pivotal figure in the long split between Anglo-American and Continental philosophical traditions because, as Henry Staten (1986) argues, Wittgenstein's philosophical method can in many ways be seen as an anticipation of Derridean deconstruction. Wittgenstein's dismantling of Enlightenment models of 'self-knowledge' removed some important obstacles to looking back beyond the Enlightenment to the Aristotelian model of virtue ethics which had been discarded.

Against the spirit of the Enlightenment's grander rationalist ambitions, both Aristotle and Wittgenstein draw readily on everyday language or judgement, and are impatient with scepticism abstracted from everyday practice. Stanley Cavell's gloss on Wittgenstein's discussion of 'following a rule' is vivid here:

> We learn and teach words in certain contexts, and then we are expected, and expect others, to be able to project them into further contexts. Nothing insures this projection will take place (in

particular, not the grasping of universals nor the grasping of books of rules), just as nothing insures that we will make, and understand, the same projects. That on the whole we do is a matter of our sharing routes of interest and feeling, modes of response... all the whirl of organism Wittgenstein calls 'forms of life'. Human speech and activity, sanity and community, rest upon nothing more, but nothing less, than this. It is a vision as simple as it is difficult, and as difficult as it is (and because it is) terrifying.

> (Cavell 1972: 52, quoted in McDowell 1998: 60)

Cavell's discussion has particular relevance to my argument since it is quoted by John McDowell in his essay 'Virtue and Reason' when discussing resistance to the characteristically Aristotelian 'identification of virtue with knowledge' (McDowell 1998: 53). In McDowell's version of virtue ethics, Wittgenstein's method is treated as having implications not just for philosophy of language but for ethics too. A modest view of the role of philosophy makes possible a modest, but distinctive, view of the cognitive dimension of ethics. Here is McDowell:

> a coherent conception of excellence locates its possessor in what is, for him at least, a world of particular facts, which are often difficult to make out. Faced with a prima facie [ethical] conflict, one has to determine how things really are.
>
> (1998: 21–22, added emphasis)

It might seem odd to characterize as modest a claim to determine 'how things really are', especially when the 'form of life' we are discussing is a set of practices as large and wide-ranging as contemporary media. My sense, nonetheless, is that by building, as McDowell suggests, from our appreciation of 'particular facts' about how media operate in the contemporary world, we have a more useful starting-point for the tangled problems of media ethics than by relying on supposedly consensual norms, rights or obligations.

Consider briefly a different starting-point: the work of Emmanuel Levinas on communication. Choosing Levinas as our starting-point for a global media ethics would involve a conception of what philosophy can do quite different from the modest conception just mentioned. For the areas of questioning about language and communication that Wittgenstein seeks to close down – because he sees the problems they raise as illusory – are exactly the areas which Levinas' approach to communication, so clearly expounded and developed by Amit Pinchevski

(2005), insists on opening up. Paradoxically, both Wittgenstein and Levinas want to move beyond the Enlightenment's misconceived problem of solipsism, but they do so in mutually exclusive ways, relying on very different conceptions of philosophy. Wittgenstein's famous private language argument (Wittgenstein 1958) seeks to establish the irreducibly social nature of language – a topic no less important to Levinas – by arguing that our imagined sense of a solipsistic self existing in isolation from the socially sustained fabric of language derives from earlier philosophy's doomed attempt to solve the illusory problems that arise when everyday language is used outside the language games in which alone it makes sense. As Wittgenstein put it, properly conducted, 'philosophy is a battle against the bewitchment of our intelligence by means of language ... since everything lies open to view, there is nothing to explain. For what is hidden ... is of no interest to us' (1958, paras 109, 126). For Levinas, by contrast, the self/other dichotomy remains the key philosophical problem. It must be thought beyond but never forgotten, requiring for its transcendence a radical and continually repeated move: the invocation of a 'preontological' obligation that lies beyond, and prior to, both self and Other, prior to the self's detachment from or attachment to the Other (Pinchevski 2005: 8). The drastic nature of Levinas' notion of the preontological (criticized by Paul Ricoeur 1992: 337–338) derives from Levinas' sense of the urgent need to go on overcoming a philosophical problem – of the disjuncture of self from Other – which Wittgenstein had argued philosophy must simply forget.[2]

Ethics versus deontology?

Why in particular choose the neo-Aristotelian tradition of virtue ethics? One incidental reason is that it is rich in writers who have sought to bridge the gap between Anglo-American and Continental philosophy.[3] But there is another larger reason. I said earlier that I want to build a framework of media ethics based on minimal premises, because of the complexity of the normative context in which we now act: the world is riven by major differences of belief and value, and media as a specialized technical and professional practice now intervenes in, and represents, the actual lives we lead. Bernard Williams saw the complexity of modern moral debate as the basis for defending ethics over deontology (Williams 1985). He insists that the openness of the Socratic question (How should I live?) is helpful because it implies a second question (How should any of us live? or How should we live together?) (Williams 1985: 20). Answering these questions does not require us to construct an abstract system of media obligations that any rational person as such is compelled to accept. Our aim can be more modest: to find starting-points for discussion, perhaps factual starting-points, around which consensus has a chance of emerging. In a world of fierce conflicts of value, it may be more effective to adopt a media ethics closer[4] in spirit to Aristotle's 'naturalism' than to Kant's 'transcendental idealism' (cf. Lovibond 2002: 25).[5]

Here we face the apparent fault-line in contemporary moral philosophy between approaches based on notions of 'the good' (ethics, which specifies virtue)[6] and approaches based on a notion of the 'right' (deontology, which specifies duty).[7] I say 'apparent' because this fault-line's usefulness has been questioned (O'Neill 1996: 9–23) and, indeed, I will later argue for an eclecticism that in part ignores it. However, in clarifying the basic orientation that led me to choose Aristotle, not Kant, as a starting-point for my work on media ethics, a brief discussion of this supposed fault-line is helpful.

The fault-line can be summed up historically in the difference between Aristotle's question (What is the good life for human beings?)[8] and Kant's question (broadly: What actions are the duty of any rational being?).[9] There are, of course, immediate complications. It is possible to follow in the tradition of ethics without believing in Aristotle's teleology. There are forms of deontology that are not Kantian (Levinas); while, as already noted, philosophers such as O'Neill argue that it is the compatibilities between the ethical and deontological traditions that are more important than the oppositions.[10] But I have in mind here only a minimal difference between one approach (which I associate with the Aristotelian and neo-Aristotelian traditions of virtue ethics) that searches for some open-ended, quite general principles (not a comprehensive system) for evaluating practice upon which human beings at a particular place and time might come to agree, and another approach (that I associate with at least some versions of the Kantian tradition of moral philosophy) that continually searches for a comprehensive and systematic specification of moral rules that any rational being anywhere and at any time must find compelling.

Seeking to specify fully compelling rules for media practice is, in my view, hopeless once we consider the range of interlocutors required in such an inquiry: How can we possibly hope to find agreement between Christian, Islamic and secular traditions, for example, on what we are rationally required to do in relation to media? Each such tradition has different approaches to obligation and rationality itself (MacIntyre 1988: chapters 18–20). Does that mean that we should despair of developing a broader ethics, as MacIntyre's work (1988: Chapter 20) sometimes suggests? Not if the neo-Aristotelian tradition of virtue ethics provides tools for developing consensus in a different direction – that is, by prioritizing questions of the good, not the good in an abstract sense ('good' for any rational being) but the good 'for man' under common conditions that can be specified.

The positive basis for building such a neo-Aristotelian argument lies in our need, as human beings, to address certain shared questions and shared facts or conditions. Prioritizing the question of 'the good' – what it is to live well – does not rule out some eclectic borrowing from other traditions, whether some version of the Kantian principle of universalizability or Levinas' insights into the question of the Other. Indeed, both Kant and Levinas raise issues that can be drawn upon in our specification of 'virtues' within media practice, and the harms that, if embedded in daily practice, such virtues might minimize. But I will argue that the insights of Levinas and Kant work more effectively when translated out of the language of universal obligation (what Simon Blackburn once called in relation to Kant 'the mesmeric command...at the bottom of things' (1995: 42): cf. Geuss 2005: 20–21) and into the more flexible practice-based language of virtue ethics.

What might a neo-Aristotelian approach to media ethics involve?

A neo-Aristotelian ethics proceeds, Warren Quinn argues, by asking 'what...it would be good or bad in itself to do or to aim at' on the basis of 'what kind of life it would be best to lead and what kind of person it would be best to be' (Quinn 1995: 186).

Two questions – How should I live? and How should each of us conduct our life so that it is a life any of us should live? – can be posed to anyone. No assumption is made about the 'community' (if any) to which questioner and respondent belong: they could be any two individuals anywhere. A further question would therefore seem to flow automatically: How should we live together? An objection might be made against that further move: What if, from my perspective, a good or even tolerable life depends on your ceasing to live? If so, the question of how we live together would not arise. But to ask any philosophical argument to give us the resources to impose a dialogue between two parties determined to kill each other is hardly reasonable: creating a space for dialogue in such extreme circumstances requires means other than philosophical argument. Relying on the question, How should we live together? rests only on the minimal assumption that in some relevant respects the continued lives of each of us depend on our parallel use of common resources; no assumption of the necessity of mutual cooperation is required. Since media, distinctively, link people living parallel lives in multiple places into the same causal nexus, this point is crucial when we frame the first question of media ethics: How should any of us act ethically with and through media? All of us (whether media professionals or not) are potentially actors in relation to media resources in the digital age. But what if we lack even a framework within which agreed standards of media ethics can be assessed? Then debate about media ethics must address a preliminary question: From where (in the absence of an agreed concept of 'the good' in relation to media) can we start to build a framework within which such concepts might be formulated?

This is just the most basic sketch of the starting-points of a neo-Aristotelian media ethics. Underlying these questions is not Aristotle's particular view of 'human nature' – hardly acceptable today – but instead an account of the common conditions by reference to which any of us would start to answer the above questions. This minimal naturalism allows for a continuous rediscovery of what constitutes human 'nature': Why assume human 'nature' is fixed for all time? According to McDowell, human nature encompasses precisely the ability to live not only by certain fixed principles distinctive of the species (our 'first nature') but also within a reflexively and historically adjustable set of principles that he calls 'second nature' (Lovibond 2002: 25, discussing MacDowell 1994: 84).[11] This second nature includes the processes of reflecting on our accumulating history and our first ('fixed') nature. In such reflections, how can we avoid noticing the existence of media institutions and media platforms? Two decades ago, Hans Jonas pointed out that modern ethics faced a new type of problem from classical ethics, namely the long-term effects of human technology on physical nature; the scale of human environmental action cannot be understood except as global (Jonas 1984: 1). It is similarly implausible now to exclude from ethics the consequences that media messages have for a world audience even if its members, as I have insisted, may sometimes share very few moral values with the producers of those messages (O'Neill 1990: 176).

A neo-Aristotelian ethics asks what stable dispositions (or 'virtues') each of us needs to have in order to live well together in such 'natural' conditions.[12] Admittedly there is a dispute in interpreting Aristotle about whether he means by 'virtues' whatever dispositions might be discovered to help us live well together, or whether he draws his list of virtues from pre-existing conventions about how people should act

(Swanton 2003: 9, 87; cf. McDowell (1998)). But since Aristotle is quite explicit that his ethics is not grounded in isolation from everyday thought but rather seeks to clarify that thought's foundations, this point may be of secondary importance. A neo-Aristotelian virtue ethics, applied to media, would ask what virtuous dispositions can be expected to contribute to our living well together with and through media.

The notion of living well together is often expressed in the neo-Aristotelian tradition as 'human flourishing'. But the usefulness of this term is as disputed as the notion that human life is oriented to specifiable ends. Many would argue that the ends of human life are themselves now undecideable, since no consensual starting-points exist from which such a question can even be asked (Williams 1985: 53; Swanton 2003: 1–2). But that does not mean that other aspects of 'human nature' – what Foot calls 'essential features of specifically human life' (2000: 14) – are not stable and constraining enough to serve as starting-points for thinking about what is necessary, even if not sufficient, for a good life.

We do not need then to assume either a fixed human nature or a nature aimed at universally agreed ends in order to agree that humans have in key respects a 'characteristic way of going on' (Hursthouse 1999: 223) from which an evaluative framework can be built.[13] Bernard Williams, on whom I draw later, develops an account of the virtues of truthfulness via a 'genealogy' which 'is intended to serve the aims of naturalism' (2002: 22) without claiming that human nature is something either fixed or readily specifiable. And this is precisely the advantage of a neo-Aristotelian approach: that it can start a conversation about how we should live – for example, with and through media – without needing to specify fully the ends of human nature, and so without needing to foreground the disagreements that would no doubt emerge between us if we attempted such a full specification.

Accuracy and sincerity

What are the media-related virtues that might emerge from such a neo-Aristotelian perspective? Here Sabina Lovibond offers a helpful starting-point when she argues that at every stage of their history, humans have had 'natural interest in gathering correct information about their environment' (Lovibond 2002: 77), which requires them to rely on what others tell them about it. This suggests that there is a domain, broadly termed, of communicative virtue:

> if information about deliberatively relevant circumstances is (so far as it goes) a natural good, the lack of such information is equally a

natural evil and the benefit or harm we can incur from these sources brings communicative behaviour within the scope of ethics.

(2002: 78)

Williams in his book *Truth and Truthfulness* (2002)[14] explores this domain in detail, identifying through a complex argument two basic 'virtues of truth': accuracy and sincerity. The subtlety of his argument lies in insisting on the non-negotiable importance of these virtues for all human social life, while rejecting any assumption that particular embodiments and articulations of those virtues (and particular institutionally backed sanctions when we fall short of them) have an obligatory status for all historical periods. By non-negotiable, Williams means that in any plausible account of a sustainable human life, it has never been enough for people to pretend to care about telling the truth, since if that was all they did we would never have a stable basis for trusting them to tell the truth:

the reason why useful consequences have flowed [for humanity] from people's insistence that their beliefs should be true is surely, a lot of the time, that their insistence did not look just to those consequences but rather toward the truth.

(Williams 2002: 59)

It is only therefore if truth-telling is stabilized as a virtue – a disposition that humans can rely upon, because it is a reliable characteristic of virtuous people – that it contributes to the good collective life.[15]

Williams is not arguing that we must be truthful because we are obliged as rational beings to do so, as Kant did (Williams 2002: 106–107). He is arguing only (but this is already enough) that there is a plausible explanation why humans have come, over time, to hold each other to account for their truthfulness. Accuracy is the disposition not so much to always hit the truth (truth is too complex an achievement for that to be a plausible characteristic of anyone) but to make the 'investigative investment' (Williams 2002: 124) required for generally obtaining the truth. Sincerity, by contrast, is the disposition to make appropriate efforts to ensure, as far as possible, that what one says is consistent with what, more broadly, one believes.

To this point we have said nothing about media institutions as such, and the possibility that such general virtues of truthfulness might work differently where individuals or groups aim at truthfulness with or through the use of media. (By 'media' I mean institutionalized means of symbolic production, transmission and circulation.) Here we need to make a link to another philosopher who, while not exclusively writing within a neo-Aristotelian framework, had major influence in arguing for that framework's contemporary relevance: Alisdair MacIntyre. His concept of 'practice' is crucial in making the general notion of ethical 'dispositions' more specific. For him a 'practice' (1981: 175) is a coherent and complex form of cooperative human activity whose internal goods involve distinctive standards of excellence, which, if achieved, extend our wider notion of human excellence. Media are plausibly a practice in this sense.

MacIntyre's notion of practice gives bite in the media case to what might otherwise seem highly generalized virtues of accuracy and sincerity. If we agree that media – the set of institutional practices for circulating representations of common life – are integral to the life conditions that humans now encounter, that is, lifeworlds of complex interconnection across large scales (Beck 1992; Urry 2000), then media are plausibly part of the practices that contribute to human excellence. Conducting the practice of media well – in accordance with its distinctive aims, and so that, overall, we can live well with and through media – is itself part of human excellence. This affects not just individual journalists at a newspaper, or lone producers blogging from their rooms or tweeting from their phones, but also those proprietors and corporations that sustain the conditions for journalism and media practice more broadly.

How do such ideas work when they hit the ground in a newsroom or reporter pool? Recent studies reveal an alarming gap between the conditions under which journalists work in many countries and those under which ethical action, even ethical reflection, is possible. Let's ignore authoritarian states and concentrate on democracies where supposedly government/press relations work well. Nick Davies's extensive interviews with UK broadsheet journalists, press agency employees and freelancers (2007: 12, 28, 154) suggest that journalists in the UK 'work in structures which positively prevent them discovering the truth'. The problem is not that journalists have changed their values: they still aim to tell the truth. It is that the conditions under which they work are not ones where that value can be consistently or reliably acted upon. This may be because of direct interference by owners, or priorities set by editors (Phillips 2011), or because of the sheer speed of the production processes across multiple platforms in today's news production. In the digital age the newsroom has become congested to a degree which undermines ethical reflection. And yet was not a journalism oriented towards truth the original purpose of a free press? When media owners are not disposed to support the conditions of ethical production they can be asked: Do you not, by so acting, undermine the conditions for all of us living well together? This conflict becomes even sharper when we turn to questions of hospitality, or 'care' in media practice.

Hospitality or care

Communicating well involves considering the consequences of one's falsehood for distant others as seriously as the consequences for those close to us. As Sabina Lovibond notes, there is no ethical reason to distinguish one audience from another: 'only what is epistemically good enough for anyone is good enough for one's present audience' (Lovibond 2002: 84, added emphasis). Lovibond's argument is based on the common interest in the practice of truth-telling on any scale, rather than on an absolute obligation of truthfulness for all times and places (O'Neill 1996: 105). The general scope of truth-telling acquires particular importance in the era of digital media when communication for an intended local audience may suddenly and unpredictably be circulated to the largest possible global audience – for example, via *YouTube*.

Increasingly, global media present us with unfamiliar Others on a global scale, giving any discussion of the ethics of media an irreducibly global dimension. Roger Silverstone discusses the consequences in terms of a media obligation of 'hospitality'. Hospitality is normally understood as a virtue of the home, and as necessarily restricted in scope (O'Neill 2000). Clearly we cannot say that 'the world' is each media outlet's home, and equally hospitality involves some boundaries when strangers are invited into the home. Silverstone sidesteps these problems by drawing on a different notion of hospitality: Derrida's 'hospitality of visitation', not invitation (2002: 142). This acknowledges that media's 'home' is automatically affected by distant others who cannot avoid being affected by what media do. From the permanent porousness of the 'home' that media provide for their audiences, some broader notion of hospitality must, Silverstone argues, develop.

Silverstone's overall argument about 'media morality' is deontological, set within the Kantian and post-Kantian tradition. Paradoxically he uses the term 'virtue' when introducing 'hospitality', describing it as 'the first virtue of the mediapolis' (2006: 136).[16] But he tends to often write about hospitality in terms less suited to a virtue and more to an obligation, drawing on Rawls and Bauman (Silverstone 2007 147–148). But how can media professionals have a rationally compelling obligation to be hospitable to distant others, particularly if this clashes with their basic contractual obligations to their immediate audiences, including those who buy their newspapers or pay their channel subscriptions? And how can audiences have an obligation to pay attention to the distant Other presented through media ('an obligation to listen and to hear' others; 2000: 136)? Silverstone underpins his notion of an Other-directed obligation of hospitality by reference to Hannah Arendt's concept of 'space of appearance' (2006: 32–37). Important though that concept is, it is unhelpful here since media audiences (and media professionals) are precisely not visible to the distant Others represented in media, and media audiences' vision of those distant Others is limited to the view that media offers – quite different from the opportunities for open-ended mutual visibility that the Greek agora arguably offered its citizens.

Silverstone's argument places too much weight on the uncertain link between media and their audiences, displacing our attention from the process of producing media. The act of watching or listening, of itself, carries no opportunities to act upon the events to which one watches or listens: that depends entirely on other factors, including one's position in the social fabric. That, however, does not mean that media ethics should have nothing to say about 'audiences'. On the contrary, when a non-media professional sends an image to a broadcaster in the hope of its being used, s/he is already acting in the media process and the virtues of media practice are already relevant to evaluating that act.

A more flexible approach is to understand 'hospitality' precisely as a 'virtue' or disposition desirable in all those involved in the practice of media. Paul Ricoeur's late work *Reflections on the Just* offers a way forward. He attempts to reorient our conception of 'the just' away from the Rawlsian theory of justice or Habermas's focus on deliberative procedure towards a broader concern with 'politics in its root sense at the level of what we can call a willingness to live together' (Ricoeur 2007: 234, 248). As a form of life in the global era, living together necessarily involves media: we live together, irreducibly, in and through media. Ricoeur's broader strategy of bringing together Aristotelian ethics and Kantian deontology – indeed, deconstructing that division – has some similarities with Onora O'Neill's (1986). Its starting-point is, however, Aristotelian rather than Kantian, and its target is to reformulate our understanding of Aristotle's (1976: Book 6) overarching virtue of *phronesis* or practical wisdom (prudence). A key issue for prudence in Ricoeur's account is our unavoidable relationship with others. He approaches this through the notions of 'translation ethos' and 'linguistic hospitality'.

For him the issue of 'translation' addresses the problem of 'plurality in a world of dispersion and confusion' (2007: 28), providing a 'paradigm by which to expand the problematic of ethical thought' (2007: 29). To 'translate' in Ricoeur's extended ethical (not narrowly literary) sense is not to collapse the distance – and differences – between self and Other but 'to do justice to a foreign intelligence, to install the just distance from one linguistic whole to another. Your language is as important as mine' (2007: 31). This disposition can also be expressed in terms of 'linguistic hospitality' (2007: 116), grounded in an appreciation that 'it is always possible to say the same thing in a different way' because 'there is a stranger in every other' (2007: 116). The similarity with the work of Levinas (discussed earlier) is less here than might first appear, since Ricoeur makes clear that the 'solicitude' that underlies such hospitality is based on a care both for others and for the self (2007: 53), as part of living together.

Ricoeur's 'translation ethos' at no point refers to media as a distinctive practice with its own practical ethics. But the link can readily be made. Indeed, his notion of a 'translation ethos' – and his metaphorical notion of linguistic hospitality – is more useful than Silverstone's 'obligation' of hospitality. We have a choice. We might treat Ricoeur's reflections as a way of refining our grasp of how we relate to the 'Other in an abstract sense, drawing perhaps on writing in the broad poststructuralist tradition: Kristeva's call to become 'strangers to ourselves' (Kristeva 1991) or Maurice Blanchot's insistence on the need to interrupt and 'unsettle the construction of . . . any [communicative] order' (quoted in Pinchevski 2005: 98). Alternatively, we can follow Ricoeur's concern with prudence in an era of complex communication flows and apply his notion of 'solicitude' or care to any scale on which we communicate through media. As Jean Seaton put it beautifully, 'without news that is careful of us, how can we judge our situation, and know where we are?' (2005: xxiii).

It is good to be disposed to take care with respect to the effects of our media communications as they circulate, but this derives not from any notion of territory as 'home' (with its implied exclusiveness) but from the fact of our commonly experienced connectedness, the common fabric of a mediated world, which makes all of us vulnerable to each other. Misrepresentations (and the regular patterns or gaps in media representations) can always do harm. However much we disagree on specific moral issues and priorities, we may agree on one fact: that we inhabit a world connected by a common media fabric. Just as we need to show care in using the shared institution of language, so we need to be disposed to show care in our use of media, because through media we can harm each other, and in the long run harm the fabric of public life. Onora O'Neill (1996: 203), who has sought to overcome the artificial divide between ethics and deontology, similarly discusses (as a 'social virtue') 'the sustaining of the natural and man-made environments on which both individual lives and the social fabric depend'. Potentially this virtue of care through media is a principle around which neo-Aristotelian, Kantian and feminist approaches[17] to the normative questions raised by media might converge.

Conclusion

We can expect contradictions, certainly, between the media-related virtue of care and those of accuracy and sincerity. Imagine a UK journalist who, accused of using a rhetoric against asylum seekers that is inhospitable or at least carelessly aggressive, responds that he addresses the facts (about take-up of social services in particular locations and so on) as he, and his immediate readers, see them. But this is where a wider virtue of prudence becomes important in identifying the need to balance competing claims – the claim of addressing readers' immediate concerns versus the claim derived from the longer-term consequences of a dehumanizing rhetoric about asylum seekers that undermines peaceable relations between the groups and territories involved.

There is then no definitive answer to the following question: What should a journalist do? Journalists often face conflicted situations, where complex facts generate no easy answers. Recognizing the intractability of many ethical matters is an advantage of the neo-Aristotelian approach to ethics, what McDowell refers to as the 'uncodifiability' of ethics (1998: 73). At most we can hope to specify the disposition that would enable agents in the media process to find, more often than not, the appropriate balance between seemingly incompatible ethical demands. But this modest claim is already a great deal.

For all the modesty of its starting-points and claims, a neo-Aristotelian virtue ethics poses a challenge to every person who has responsibility for managing or using the resources or interfaces available for making media. If journalists increasingly work without the time, authority or resources to exercise any independent ethical discretion or choice, then they have no chance of contributing to a good life, and the media institutions in which they work risk undermining that good life. Certainly, (Onora O'Neill, Chapter 2 this volume) truth-telling is only one part of what media institutions exist to do: they also seek to entertain us. But why accept media institutions that are systematically reckless about their employees' chances of achieving, or even aiming at, truth? What sort of human collectivity is served by entertainment that regularly misleads people as to their conditions of existence? What counts as 'misleading' will, of course, often be the subject of fierce debate. Pretending that we don't care ethically about the conditions under which media get made is, however, not an option.

Notes

1. See Couldry (2006: 102–109).
2. For an example of how the force of Levinas' arguments depends on keeping the alternative of Enlightenment scepticism in play, see Levinas (1999: 7, 9). Compare Ricoeur's comment that Levinas confuses the old problem of self/other with the continuing and unavoidable questions of how we should act (Ricoeur 1992: 354).
3. Lovibond (2002); Ricoeur (1992; 2005); Taylor (1985).
4. I say 'closer to' because Bernard Williams rejects 'naturalism' as the formal basis of virtue ethics. However, Lovibond and MacDowell's historicist and reflexive account of 'nature' (on which, see later) is different from the original Aristotelian teleology to which Williams objects. See Hursthouse (1999: chapter 10) for helpful discussion.
5. Habermas's concept of 'postmetaphysical thinking' also aims to respond to modern moral complexity but depends on a dismissal of Aristotle (and any 'affirmative theory of the good life'; 1992: 50), exactly the mistake from which MacIntyre sought to rescue us.
6. For useful discussion of what distinguishes virtue ethics, see Oakley and Cocking (2001: chapter 1).
7. I leave out the third and, until recently, quite dominant alternative to deontology: utilitarianism. My reason, put crudely, is a belief that ethics must start out from broadly social considerations which any framework based in the optimization of individual good (conceived in terms entirely separate from social good) cannot provide. For useful discussion of the differences, and gradual convergence between, all three approaches, see Hursthouse (1999: 1–5) and Crisp (1996). For a classic diagnosis of the ethics/deontology fault-line, see Anscombe (1997) [o.p. 1958].
8. Other approaches to virtue ethics frame it differently in terms of common understandings about what count as good motivations in human beings (Slote 2001). In what follows I keep to the neo-Aristotelian approach. For discussion of this and other differences, see Oakley and Cocking (2001: 15–17).
9. Or, as Kant puts it more elaborately, what are the actions 'that I could also will [such] that my maxim should become a universal law?' (Kant 1997: 15).
10. The Kantian Barbara Herman goes further and argues that 'the canon that sorts all moral theories as deontological or teleological' is misleading in the case of Kant, whose ethics, she argues, is not deontological but based in the value of the 'good will' (1993: chapter 10). But I am only using

the ethics/deontology distinction to indicate a broad positioning of my argument; my main argument does not depend on that distinction.

11. For a similar argument about the necessary historical dimension to virtuous practice, see MacIntyre (1981: 180–181).

12. I will not consider here Swanton's (2003) attempt to develop a more inclusive virtue ethics, which allows various ways of grounding the specification of virtues, some based on human flourishing and self-fulfilment, and others based on appropriate responsiveness to certain types of situation.

13. Indeed Hursthouse argues that human nature is specifically 'non-teleological' (1999: 256), but this does not allow for the tiered notion of first and second nature proposed by McDowell and Lovibond.

14. The virtue of truthfulness is treated also by Onora O'Neill as one of a number of 'virtues of justice' along with fairness, toleration and respect for others (1996: 187).

15. A similar point emerges in Williams's argument against moral sceptics who doubt that truth-telling is generally in the individual's interest (2002: Chapter 5).

16. Silverstone echoes here a well-known sentence at the start of Rawls's *A Theory of Justice*: 'justice is the first virtue of social institutions' (Rawls 1972: 1).

17. Feminist ethics of care focuses on the need for *particular* practices of care (Held 2006). There is no contradiction, since the shared social fabric sustained by media is a particular object but one whose scale and scope is very general and wide.

References

Anscombe, E. (1997) [o.p. 1958] 'Modern Moral Philosophy', in R. Crisp and M. Slote (eds) *Virtue Ethics*. Oxford: Oxford University Press.

Aristotle (1976) *Nicomachean Ethics*. Translated J. Thomson. Harmondsworth: Penguin.

Beck, U. (1992) *Risk Society*. London: Sage.

Blackburn, S. (1995) 'The Flight to Reality', in R. Hursthouse, G. Lawrence and W. Quinn (eds) *Virtues and Reasons: Philippa Foot and Moral Theory*. Oxford: Oxford University Press, 35–56.

Cavell, S. (1972) *Must We Mean What We Say?* Cambridge, MA: Harvard University Press.

Cohen-Almagor, R. (2001) *Speech, Media and Ethics: The Limits of Free Expression*. Basingstoke: Palgrave.

Couldry, N. (2006) *Listening Beyond the Echoes: Media, Ethics and Agency in an Uncertain World*. Boulder, CO: Paradigm Books.

Crisp, R. (1996) 'Modern Moral Philosophy and the Virtues', in R. Crisp (ed.) *How Should One Live?* Oxford: Oxford University Press.

Derrida, J. (2002) *On Cosmopolitans and Forgiveness*. London: Routledge.

Durkheim, E. (1992) *Professional Ethics and Civic Morals*. London: Routledge.

Foot, P. (2000) *Natural Goodness*. Oxford: Oxford University Press.

Geuss, R. (2005) *Outside Ethics*. Princeton, NJ: Princeton University Press.

Habermas, J. (1992) *Post-Metaphysical Thinking*. Cambridge: Polity.

Held, V. (2006) *The Ethics of Care*. New York: Oxford University Press.

Herman, B. (1993) *The Practice of Moral Judgement*. Cambridge, MA: Harvard University Press.

Hursthouse, R. (1999) *Virtue Ethics*. Oxford: Oxford University Press.

Jonas, H. (1984) *The Imperative of Responsibility*. Chicago: Chicago University Press.

Kant, I. (1997) [o.p. 1785] *Groundwork to a Metaphysic of Morals*. Translated M. Gregor. Cambridge: Cambridge University Press.

Kristeva, J. (1991) *Strangers to Ourselves*. New York: Columbia University Press.

Levinas, E. (1999) *Otherwise than Being*. Pittsburgh, PA: Duquesne University Press.

Lovibond, S. (2002) *Ethical Formation*. Cambridge, MA: Harvard University Press.

MacIntyre, A. (1981) *After Virtue*. London: Duckworth.

MacIntyre, A. (1988) *Whose Justice? Which Rationality?* Notre Dame: University of Notre Dame Press.

McDowell, J. (1994) *Mind and World*. Cambridge, MA.: Harvard University Press.

McDowell, J. (1998) *Mind Value and Reality*. Cambridge, MA.: Harvard University Press.

Oakley, J. and Cocking, M. (2001) *Virtue Ethics and Professional Roles*. Cambridge: Cambridge University Press.

O'Neill, O. (1990) 'Practices of Toleration', in J. Lichtenberg (ed.) *Democracy and the Mass Media*. Cambridge: Cambridge University Press, 155–185.

O'Neill, O. (1996) *Towards Justice and Virtue*. Cambridge: Cambridge University Press.

O'Neill, O. (2000) 'Distant Strangers, Moral Standing and Porous Boundaries', in *Bounds of Justice*. Cambridge: Cambridge University Press, 186–202.

O'Neill, O. (2002) *A Question of Trust*. Cambridge: Cambridge University Press.

Phillips, A. (2011) 'Transparency and the New Ethics of Journalism', in P. Lee-Wright, A. Phillips and T. Witschge (eds) *Changing Journalism*. London: Routledge, 135–148.

Pinchevski, A. (2005) *By Way of Interruption: Levinas and the Ethics of Communication*. Pittsburgh, PA: Duquesne University Press.

Quinn, W. (1995) 'Putting Rationality in its Place', in R. Hursthouse, G. Lawrence and W. Quinn (eds) *Virtues and Reasons: Philippa Foot and Moral Theory*. Oxford: Oxford University Press, 181–208.

Rawls, J. (1972) *A Theory of Justice*. Oxford: Oxford University Press.

Ricoeur, P. (1992) *Oneself as Another*. Chicago: Chicago University Press.

Ricoeur, P. (2005) *The Course of Recognition*. Cambridge, MA: Harvard University Press.

Ricoeur, P. (2007) *Reflections on the Just*. Chicago: Chicago University Press.

Silverstone, R. (2007) *Media and Morality*. Cambridge: Polity.

Slote, M. (2001) *Morals from Motives*. Oxford: Oxford University Press.

Staten, H. (1986) *Wittgenstein and Derrida*. Lincoln: University of Nebraska Press.

Swanton, C. (2003) *Virtue Ethics*. Oxford: Oxford University Press.

Taylor, C. (1985) *Philosophy and the Human Sciences, Philosophical Papers vol 2*. Cambridge: Cambridge University Press.

Urry, J. (2000) *Sociology Beyond Societies*. London: Routledge.

Williams, B. (1985) *Ethics and the Limits of Philosophy*. London: Fontana/Collins.

Williams, B. (2002) *Truth and Truthfulness: An Essay in Genealogy*. Princeton: Princeton University Press.

Wittgenstein, L. (1958) *Philosophical Investigations*. Oxford: Blackwell.

4
Arendt on Media Ethics: Revisiting Traditions as the Heart of the Public Sphere

Ronald C. Arnett

This chapter examines the question of media ethics from the vantage point of tradition, an uncommon move in modernity. One modest presupposition about media ethics is that one must disclose the connecting communicative linkages that unite a given news event to explication in the public domain. Media ethics is the mediating fulcrum between an event and the public domain. Perhaps the first mediating function in the human condition is the notion of tradition, which, in the eyes of Hannah Arendt, mediates between past and future. This chapter examines the connections between these two mediating functions, media ethics and tradition. Media ethics within a modern context offers insight untainted by the local, the provincial and the traditional. This chapter offers an alternative perspective, relying upon the insights of Arendt's *Between Past and Future*, which provides a creative engagement of the notion of tradition as central to health in the public sphere from an established critic of modernity. This chapter frames media ethics within the notion of tradition as an alternative to a modern rendition of media ethics with a stress on the vitality of the public domain.

Media ethics in context

This chapter connects the question of media ethics to traditions. The explication of tradition in the plural follows the insights of Alasdair MacIntyre (1991) in *Three Rival Versions of Moral Enquiry: Encyclopedia, Genealogy, and Tradition*. He begins with the assumption that the Enlightenment ideal of universal rationality is a fractured project, giving way to multiple competing perspectives, with the Enlightenment ideal being but one of the competing and rival forms of moral inquiry. The notion of tradition assumes that there is an agreed upon set of practices that shape given perspectives in theory and action. Multiplicity of traditions acknowledges a postmodern moment of virtue and narrative contention. In modernity, the term that gets closest to 'traditions' is 'contexts'. Thus I will now examine the media ethics 'context' via significant scholars and ideas that give rise to a media ethics landscape composed of differing standpoints.

The confusion in ethics is reflected in the public response to the media. 'There is ample evidence to suggest that Americans at large no longer trust, if they ever did trust, the American media' (Cooper 2008: 25). The confusion in media ethics rests on both local and international soil with the increase in technological capability that opens the door to good, as well as its extreme counter, 'telecommunicated tragedy' (Cooper 1990: 13). Whenever media ethics is discussed, one major issue surfaces – 'pluralism' – in both content perspective and structure (Tehranian 2002: 79). To address the diversity of perspectives on media ethics I turn to a scholar who is arguably the standard bearer of media ethics, Clifford Christians.

Christians acknowledges MacIntyre's contention of rival moral enquiries, rejecting the Enlightenment hope of objectivity in gathering and disseminating news. He states: 'Defining news as objective information is too narrow for the complexities of a world understood in Habermasian, feminist, or communitarian terms' (Christians 2007: 126). Christians moves from a utilitarian view of individualism to a sense of the good attentive to the community. He (2007) offers a model of 'dialogic duty' that requires one to attend to the values of the community, 'identifying representative voices and communities rather than spectacular ones that are anecdotal and idiosyncratic' (p. 126). He offers dialogue with persons situated within a community, within a particular context, within a particular tradition, in order to advance understanding beyond the perspective of a solitary individual. We find ourselves in an increasingly oral culture; some are stating that we will lose our sense of ethical literacy. The dialogic alternative meets this challenge. Following Christians's lead, Plaisance (2005) supports an alternative to individualism with a stress on discourse that is attentive to the local without becoming captured by a locality alone. Additionally, the 'care-based ethics' of Vanacker and Breslin (2006) emphasizes an alternative to stress on the individual alone with attentiveness to the local in relationship with the 'greater community and resulting social and political policy' (p. 211). With the emphasis on the community and the local soil, there is an addition to the traditional view of media ethics of 'the voice of the One with the voice of the Many' (Hickey 2003: 62).

With the emphasis on community comes the necessity of public admission. Christians (2008) calls for a journalist who is responsive to the importance of 'theory' as a public blueprint for the why of given actions. Contrary to many assertions, we must take 'religious ethics' seriously when understood within the realm of theory. Without particular theories of particular religions, we cannot begin to understand numerous local and global religious disputes. Theory must accompany continuing examination of 'technology' – where it is needed and its displacement of previously agreed-upon assumptions. Such an examination invites a 'pragmatic objectivity' that understands the temporal and limited nature of our insights, which requires a 'philosophical mind' that embraces complexity of thinking. Theory permits one to acknowledge and respond to diverse practices that shape context, community and traditions that journalists cover and live within (pp. 4–12).

The insistence upon good theory takes Christians to a number of scholars outside media ethics to find theory that makes an impact upon the ground upon which we all walk. One such consideration is the scholarly insight of Agnes Heller, whose ethics fears totalitarianism and supports the practical counter of 'dissent' (Christians 2002: 414). It is in the act of dissent that one finds ethical hope, not in abstract codes and principles. Freedom, dissent and the demands to be a 'good person' cannot be separated from the study and the practice of ethics (Christians 2002: 414). Her work follows the pattern of Christians's interest in ethics, the 'unity of contraries' (Buber 1966: 111). 'If I abandon myself to another human being, I choose relative unfreedom (Heller 1987: 317)' (Christians 2002: 420). It is in the interplay between concern for subordination and relational concern that Heller frames a unique understanding of ethics with social and feminist interests that do not fully embrace the Enlightenment dream of full individual autonomy. Christians is interested in 'counter-Enlightenment' thinkers, from Giambattista Vico to Jean-François Lyotard, who do not abandon reason and, at the same time, reject the illusion of individual autonomy. He does not agree with all their presuppositions and questions the postmodern turn. However, he does not dispute the importance of engaging the interplay between the local and the universal or the normative and the universal (Christians 2000).

Christians (2005) acknowledges community and diversity with repeated calls for 'theoretical pluralism' (p. 12). However, with this pluralism he does not want to give up on the necessity of the universal.

He (2005) does not end with a stress on community and diversity; he unites community and diversity with temporal universals, 'protonorms' (p. 12). Christians's view of the universal is pluralistic as he considers protonorms that cut across multiple cultures. The key for Christians and Nordenstreng (2004) is to unite 'normative ethics' with a 'universal protonorm' of the 'sacredness of life' (pp. 21–24). They seek to move media ethics from codes to theoretical engagement and thinking about local and universal issues that frame ethics. They list the following aspects of a protonorm that attends to the sacredness of human life: i) 'respect for human dignity'; ii) 'truth-telling'; and iii) 'non-violence' (Christians and Nordenstreng 2004: 21–23). This push for theory and for the development of protonorms is difficult in an environment in which there is a 'need to prepare more researchers for advancing media ethics' (Lambeth, Christians, Fleming and Lee 2004: 250). There is a necessity for more journalism professors to have a philosophical education if ethics is to move beyond normative description and imposition of perspective. Lambeth, Christians and Cole (1994) lament the small number of essays on media ethics in refereed journals.

Ultimately, the test of media ethics rests in the strength and vibrancy of a public domain composed of multiple ideas that seek a hearing and following within the public domain. The public domain is companioned; we find this theme fundamental to Jürgen Habermas (1989) and Seyla Benhabib (1992). Habermas writes from a perspective of critical theory and Benhabib unites critical theory with feminist theory. Both of these scholars owe a significant debt to the work of Hannah Arendt. With an eye on the importance of the public domain, I turn not to Arendt's most famous book, *The Human Condition* (1958), but to *Between Past and Future: Eight Exercises in Political Thought* (1968). In this work, Arendt makes the case, through a series of essays, that the public domain does not live in an abstract ethereal space. Rather, it finds life from the reality of multiple traditions that influence and shape the public sphere.

Arendt *Between Past and Future*

Hannah Arendt (1906–1975) is a major foundational figure who championed the public domain and articulated its demise within modernity. In *Communication Ethics in Dark Times: Hannah Arendt's Rhetoric of Warning and Hope* (Arnett, 2013), I examine Arendt's ongoing critique of modernity as a form of 'dark times'. The theme of the collapse of the public domain in modernity is a central part of her larger project; a healthy public domain includes a multiplicity of opinions rising from a multiplicity of traditions.

Arendt begins this work with a quote from René Char (1907–1988), a French poet and writer, responding to the demands before France after liberation from the Nazis. *Notre héritage n'est précédé d'aucun testament* ('our inheritance was left to us by no testament') (Arendt 1977: 3). This quote from the conclusion of the Second World War fits today's world of crisis, with revolution, terrorism and economic collapse as common conversation in everyday media. Arendt (1977) calls attention to what happens when a society loses its 'treasure', meaning that holds together past and future – a live tradition (p. 5). Without this connecting link, according to her, we are 'stripped of all masks' to the point of paralysis; tradition gives us a focal point for continuity, change and necessary rebellion (p. 4). The reality of tradition makes Immanuel Kant's (1724–1804) notion of imagination possible. Kant (2006) understood 'imagination' as that which pushes off something real, with 'fantasy' responding to abstraction that has no genuine connection to the world before us (pp. 68–74). Without something concrete from which to respond, we are left wandering in obscurity, a phrase Arendt uses from Alexis de Tocqueville's (2000) *Democracy in America*. 'That this tradition has worn thinner and thinner as the modern age progressed is a secret to nobody. When the thread of tradition finally broke, the gap between past and future ... became a fact of political relevance' (Arendt 1977: 14). The treasure between past and future is tradition, but Arendt calls for traditions that are alive and responsive to change in the interplay of interpretation of a live past and unknown future.

Arendt contends that tradition requires 'leisure time' that is not contrasted with labour but with political life (Arendt 1977: 19). There is doing and serious play in leisure that is in stark contrast with 'recreation', which is tied to consumption (Holba 2007: 95). Leisure is a good model for understanding tradition in that leisure requires practices – such as playing a musical instrument – that move serious play into increasingly textured knowledge of a given task. There are multiple forms of leisure with each manifestation shaped by practices that are tied to serious play (Gadamer 1986). Arendt states that the 19th century is the locus of rebellion against tradition and, ironically, against leisure (Weber 2001), resulting in an increase in individualism.

Arendt states that the focus on 'individualism,' a term coined by Alexis de Tocqueville (2000), is a modern phenomenon in that one attempts to stand above all relational connections and all history. de Tocqueville (2000) states that individualism is a danger, a danger that is much greater than 'selfishness' (pp. 482–488). If one wants to be selfish, one must at least consider the impact on others because their reactions will have an impact on oneself. Individualism, on the other hand, ignores the social context, not unreflectively but by design. The first enemy of individualism is history, which Arendt states is a necessary part of tradition.

> History: For Arendt (1977), the classical understanding of history included the recording of 'wondrous deeds' and not the recording of great individuals (p. 41). The goal was to save these great deeds from oblivion. Greatness required history, the recording of great events and all those involved in the actions. History, in a classical sense, had 'impartiality' as a guiding action, in that one recorded great deeds, no matter who or what side in a given struggle participated and delivered great 'deeds' (Arendt 1977: 51). It is through this recording that 'immortality' was possible (Arendt 1977: 52). This view of life took a dramatic turn with the advent of Christianity. With this shift, history begins to move from the recording of great deeds that give rise to immortality to a linear detailing of the who, what and why of particular conflicts and developments in a society. The movement from great deeds to developments in a society responds to a view of life as frail, and the hope of lasting contributions resting with the recording of life within a particular place at a particular time.

The culmination of the impact of history on the modern world actually began in the 18th century with Georg Wilhelm Friedrich Hegel's (1770–1831) development of a metaphysics of 'history' and a firm situating of the modern understanding of progress within the march of history (Arendt 1977: 68). From Hegel we move to Marx and the view that one can make history. The shift is from recording great deeds, to detailing chronology of events, to forging a history that is not yet born. Out of this perspective comes a revolutionary view of history. This orientation does not begin with Marx, according to Arendt, but with the French Revolution (1787–1799). 'By pursuing their own aims without rhyme or reason men seem to be led by "the guiding thread of reason"' (Arendt 1977: 82).

Kant's thinking and reason stressed what to do, know and hope, which were all driven by contemplation that fuelled action. The shift in history begins with the turn from contemplation as the forerunner of action to reliance on action itself. Such action makes it difficult for one to discern the difference between 'meaningful' and 'meaningless' action (Arendt 1977: 87). Arendt's (1977) comment is that one of the ingredients that makes 'totalitarianism' possible is the move from thoughtful consideration to action that leads one to follow a herd without necessary consideration (p. 87). Without a sense of history, we lose that which is 'common to all' (Arendt 1977: 87). The loss of history moves us from imagination to fantasy and to a world in which comparison to previous demands and challenges is no longer possible, leaving one with a solitary question in the midst of difficulty: Why me? From the loss of history comes the loss of authority.

> Authority: The second loss in tradition, according to Arendt (1977), is authority (p. 28). We lose a place that we can turn to for imagination and for rebellion; authority calls for learning and responsiveness. The authority shifts from tradition shaped by doing and practices to autonomous reason that moves us from ground under our feet to the modern fascination with abstraction that tempts us to live life above all considerations except individual autonomy. It is against an 'egalitarian' world of 'persuasion' that 'authority' offers an alternative (Arendt 1977: 93). Arendt states that in a totalitarian government, authority comes from an external source; she contrasts this with authority emerging out of a given tradition. In the Roman Empire, authority was tied to foundations and growth was connected to the past, giving roots to authority. This is a dramatically different view of growth from what we have in a modern world tied to the notion of progress (Arendt 1977: 123). This perspective of authority connected to roots was extended by Augustine and later challenged by Martin Luther (1483–1546) during the Protestant Reformation. The irony of this view is that growth that only moves forwards actually puts at risk trust and belief in the future (Arendt 1977: 135). For Arendt, the Roman view of authority emerging from foundations is lost within modernity. 'Authority as we once knew it, which grew out of the Roman experience of foundation and was understood in the light of Greek political philosophy, has nowhere been re-established' (Arendt 1977: 141). Postmodern scholarship brings back the notion of foundations and origins.

The faulty assumption about postmodernity is that that perspective rejects all beginnings. This postulation is incorrect. Foundations lend to a given form of authority and a particular world-view. The key is that there is no one master foundation or perspective; rather, there are many.

The total disregard of foundation, origin or 'genealogy' (Foucault 2002: 119) lends back to the modern temptation that we can stand above any environment and engage in autonomous reason that does not need to attend to anyone but our own abstract sense of perspective. Arendt contends that if we engage history and authority, the public sphere is strengthened in acts of genuine freedom.

> Freedom: Arendt moves counter to a modern view of individualistic freedom that is both internal and psychological; she connects freedom solely to the public domain. It is within political life that one finds freedom in the public sphere. For her (1977), the experience of freedom requires 'liberation' to participate with the 'company of other men' in the public domain (p. 148). 'Without a politically guaranteed public realm, freedom lacks the worldly space to make its appearance' (Arendt 1977: 149). She states that the early Christian suspicion of politics put at risk both the public domain and the possibility of human freedom. Arendt (1977) details the human importance of 'I-know', 'I will' and 'I-can' (p. 160). The integration of these manifestations of the human ego occurs in the unity of acts of freedom in the public domain. This is the place of test for the possibility of freedom:

Public testing keeps the human being from thinking that one can become a self-appointed 'sovereign'. (Arendt 1977: 164)

> Hence it is not in the least superstitious, it is even a counsel of realism, to look for the unforeseeable and unpredictable, to be prepared for and to expect 'miracles' in the political realm. And the more heavily the scales are weighted in favor of disaster, the more miraculous will the deed done in freedom appear; for it is disaster, not salvation, which always happens automatically and therefore always must appear to be irresistible.
>
> (Arendt 1977: 170)

The possibility of what Arendt (1977) calls 'miracles' emerges out of real public demands – such is the hope that ever lingers within moments of 'disaster' (p. 170). It is the response to the demands of the historical moment, not to an abstract plea, that gives rise to freedom in the public domain. Arendt's tradition is framed by history, authority via foundations, and freedom within the public domain. One has much to push off of and respond to; it is this creative responsiveness that shapes multiple opinions within the public domain. She contends that the public sphere is put at risk in crises that function as defining markers within modernity: education, culture, the confusion of truth in politics and the loss of human stature. These crises emerge from a similar sense of abstract rootlessness that constitutes modernity.

Modernity in crisis: Arendt begins her assessment of crisis in modernity with a statement that challenges the relaxation of educational standards. The key to US education, for her, is its connection to opportunity and refusal to give power to an oligarchy that gives rise to meritocracy as a substitute for genuine work and achievement. To avoid such errors, authority must inform children about what is important; one must take the risk of adult leadership. Without the authority of adults, we open the door to the 'tyrannical authority' of the group (Arendt 1977: 181). Much of the key to education is the development of a 'habit of work and of not-playing' that keeps the demands for research and inquiry ever present in the actions of life-long learners (Arendt 1977: 183). She calls for a shift from extracurricular skills to those of the classroom and the curriculum. Again, she emphasizes the importance of learning and how those tied to families of 'darkness' can sometimes give the foundation for great achievement – darkness makes possible the recognition of real light (Arendt 1977: 186). Authority is the key in education; it is the task of a teacher to assist a student and to a have an environment of learning that makes the acquisition of knowledge possible. Authority keeps the public space of education possible; it is not the task of the student to provide the role of authority – such responsibility rests with the teacher (Arendt 1977: 196). Authority in the classroom that is attentive to history makes the public domain of diversity of opinion in education a reality, rendering a place where genuine freedom and advancement can be given birth to. Arendt contends that a similar crisis exists in culture that shapes modernity.

Crisis in cultural: Arendt (1977) asserts that a 'mass culture' is a 'contradiction in terms' (p. 197); a 'crowd psychology' cannot lessen 'loneliness' or 'isolation' (p. 199). We have moved to someone educated within a culture to an 'educated philistine', in which learning is viewed more as a 'commodity' or a form of 'entertainment' (Arendt 1977: 203–205). We have lost the impulse for learning and beauty that exceeds immediate needs, embracing a utilitarian and consumer-oriented society. In such a culture, we lose the connection between 'words' and 'deeds' (Arendt 1977: 218). The tendency is to fall into individual choice and private feelings without adherence to knowledge of public standards. '[T]he Romans – the first people that took culture seriously the way we do – thought a cultivated person ought to be: one who knows how to choose his company among men, among things, among thoughts, in the present as well as in the past' (Arendt 1977: 226). Culture in praxis permits one to discern and to make judgements in accordance with standards outside oneself. Without external commitment, history and authority, human freedom is put at risk. For Arendt, in such a modern culture there is a disconnect between truth and politics.

Truth and politics: Arendt reminds the reader that the perennial tension between truth and politics is an age-old dilemma. Power and truth do not always coincide, as Leon Trotsky (1879–1940) so aptly justified during the Russian Revolution. There has historically been concern about the ' truth-teller' and his/her inability to assist people in moments of complex and competing goods (Arendt 1977: 232). Such is the reason that James Madison stated that all governments live on 'opinion', not pristine truth (Arendt 1977: 233).

The challenge of truth and opinion is that the latter keeps the public domain vibrant and healthy and the former discerns one answer and excludes all others. The notion of 'philosophical truth' makes no sense once it enters the marketplace of ideas and is instantly transformed into opinions (Arendt 1977: 237). Pure philosophical truth is often one step from 'coercion' (Arendt 1977: 241). An 'enlarged mentality' (Arendt 1977: 241) requires that one attends to multiple and contrasting opinions that are never 'self-evident' (Arendt 1977: 247) but must be articulated with evidence that others must vet in the public domain.

Arendt (1977) makes a distinction between a 'traditional lie' of politicians and a 'modern lie' (p. 253). The former is directed at the 'enemy' and the latter is directed at the public domain, one's constituents and even oneself (Arendt 1977: 253). The modern lie is the deception of oneself to the point of viewing the statement as true, which constructs a large 'web of deceptions' (Arendt 1977: 255). She offers a more textured view of the truth-teller in the public domain as someone capable of aligning truth and reality, an ongoing act of reconciliation. The public domain does not live within the realm of pristine truth or within actions of lying to oneself in an effort to capture the public realm; the public realm flourishes with diversity of public opinions that require evidence and defence. The danger of pristine truth comes as we take ourselves too seriously. In Greek thought there was no assumption that the human is the highest being. We cannot ever reach an 'Archimedean point' in which one can objectively discern, inquire and judge with assurance of truth (Arendt 1977: 278). Human existence requires a place of difference shaped by histories, authorities and cultures that grapple with opinions that give us multiple traditions, the heart of the public domain. In terms of media ethics, the treasure that Arendt laments has been lost in modernity and returns only with a pragmatic humble gesture – making sure that multiple opinions supported by evidence and argument are co-present in the public domain. Arendt was ever wary of a pristine assumption that a metapublic domain is anything but an invitation for tyranny. Her understanding of the public domain is driven by multiplicity of traditions, ideas and opinions. Arendt's public domain is more akin to a collage of fabric than a quilt with a consistent pattern. The fundamental question for media ethics is how to alert people, readers, listeners and interactive participants to understand the importance of a vital public domain composed of multiple and contrasting traditions that give rise to difference and contrary opinions. For one answer of how we can nurture the tissue of the public domain without falling prey to the temptation of uniformity, I turn to the 18th-century insights of the Scottish Enlightenment. The key to this intellectual and practical movement was the manner in which it engaged differing opinions in the public domain, attending to the 'looking glass' propelled by 'sympathy'.

Opinion and the public domain

The insights of the Scottish Enlightenment and the connection to media ethics are outlined in a 2010 essay by Lawrence Souder, 'A Free-market Model for Media Ethics: Adam Smith's Looking Glass'. Souder (2010) returns us to the public domain through sympathy, which Adam Smith (1790) originally pens in his work *The Theory of Moral Sentiments*. He does so as a professor of moral philosophy and dean of faculty at the University of Glasgow in 1759. Souder begins his essay with a story about Bill Gates citing Smith's work in his address to the World Economic Forum in Davos, Switzerland. He ends with an assertion about Smith: it is his moral work that shaped health in the marketplace and permitted the shifting of class structure based on productivity, not accumulation of capital (Souder 2010: 63). Souder asserted that Smith cannot be used as a call for capitalism that is insensitive to persons and community. Rather, his entire project centred on trying to discern a practical way to contribute to the life of everyone in Scotland.

Smith framed understanding of a public marketplace on two major issues: i) sympathy and ii) a looking glass society. Sympathy is given a bad rap today; the modern assumption is that it is inferior to empathy. Sympathy is better understood as a premind/body dichotomy and precognitive act. The distinction between sympathy and empathy is laid out quite clearly by Edith Stein (1989); she gives a clear picture of this form of intersubjective connection that is prior to reflection. For instance, if one is walking next to another and the other falls, often one can literally feel the pain of the other. If one is sitting next to another who is going through papers and gets a paper cut, one grabs one's own finger as the other tries to stop the bleeding. We often feel strange sensations up our spines as we connect with another's difficulty. Smith understood the power of sympathy and how it connects one to another. His understanding of moral sentiments depends upon the intersubjective connecting power of sympathy. His understanding of capital had a face, including face-to-face interaction with one another. In such settings, sympathy can be counted on to temper and restrain one's working with others in the public marketplace. Smith understood that one cannot be at all places at all times, meaning that face-to-face interaction is not always possible. Thus he stressed a second form of constraint, a 'looking glass society.'

The looking glass conception assumes that there is diversity of individuals, and some form of constraint is necessary without simple reliance upon laws and police enforcement. Much of the heart of our interaction with one another cannot be policed or the intersubjective quality of our interaction dies. Yet, at the same time, we need a 'transparency' that permits us to look upon ourselves through the eyes of others, approval and otherwise (Souder 2010: 60):

> Smith in *The Theory of Moral Sentiments* offers many promising moral concepts for correcting this lack of transparency in the marketplace ... the looking-glass of society (1790, III.I.4) ... seems consistent with the notion of transparency and with Smith's 'philosophy of vision' (1790, III.I.44).
>
> (Souder 2010: 60–61)

Souder and Smith stress transparency in the public domain, which takes us back to the media ethics protonorms of Clifford Christians (2005: 12).

The basic and raw protonorm pointed to by Souder is the legitimacy of distrust. In a world of multiplicity of opinions, the protonorm of distrust necessitates a looking glass society of increasing transparency.

Together, Arendt and Smith point to protonorms. Arendt argues that modernity has not killed the reality of tradition; the protonorm is that traditions and multiplicity of opinions live within the fragile fabric of the public domain. Smith pointed to the reality of distrust when multiplicity is the recognized reality, multiplicity of opinions is the reality within which we live and engage in commerce. This recognition necessitates the enactment of a looking glass, transparency that adds assurance to the public domain. To protect the public domain, media ethics must understand the opinion-saturated diversity that constructs the public domain. Arendt reminds us that opinion does not come from abstract individuals but individuals committed to history, authority tied to history, and freedom that responds to the interplay of history and authority through acts of agreement and resistance that change the tradition before them. There are multiple traditions composed of differing histories, authorities and acts of freedom that comprise the public arena. The task of media ethics in response to this reality is not to limit one's task to reporting but to expand one's task to include learning and education. In an era of clashing traditions, the media ethics question is: How can the media assist in understanding multiple traditions through the complex interplay of history, authority and freedom that frames different traditions? If we are interested in a public arena shaped by media ethics that has an international and intercultural reach, then the focus on learning about what we do not know is central to the diversity of opinions in the public square.

Smith reminds us of sympathy that encourages a willingness to learn about diverse positions in the public square. Sympathy, however, does not work unless we can keep people turned towards one another. Sympathy assists in giving a reason for learning about difference, and the knowledge we gain about another, when understood in terms of real human faces, assists the power of sympathy. The looking glass gives us a chance to examine who and what is not near, ever impactful on those not at the table of conversation. The protonorm of media ethics in the 21st century is learning about difference – understanding histories, differing views of authority and contrasting acts of freedom that give rise to different traditions. Our desire to learn about such difference depends on our turning to one another in sympathy and to the Other with increasing commitments to transparency that gives insight and assurance to those not at a given place of decision-making. Media ethics in the 21st century centres on how we facilitate learning. The task is not one of reporting but the enactment of a protonorm – assisting in a desire to learn about traditions contrary to our own; such is the first step of media ethics in a world defined by narrative and virtue contention. On a final note, this commitment to the fragile fabric of the public domain constituted by multiplicity of traditions and opinions when connected with media ethics resembles Roger Silverstone's (2007) construct of 'mediapolis' (pp. 25–55). As he (2007) contends:

> The mediapolis is...the mediated space of appearance in which the world appears and in which the world is constituted in its worldliness, and through which we learn about those who are and who are not like us. It is through communications conducted through the mediapolis that we are constructed as human (or not), and it is through the mediapolis that public and political life increasingly comes to emerge at all levels of the body politic (or not). (p. 31)

The inspiration for his engagement with the public domain and this conception is akin to my impulse as well – the insights of Hannah Arendt are of vital importance as we recognize our increasing lack of confidence in modernity's efforts at amalgamation and unification.

References

Arendt, H. (1958) *The Human Condition*. Chicago, IL: University of Chicago Press.
Arendt, H. (1977) [o.p. 1968] *Between Past and Future: Eight Exercises in Political Thought*. New York: Penguin Books.
Arnett, R. C. (2013) *Communication Ethics in Dark Times: Hannah Arendt's Rhetoric of Warning and Hope*. Carbondale, IL: Southern Illinois University Press.
Benhabib, S. (1992) *Situating the Self: Gender, Community, and Postmodernism in Contemporary Ethics*. New York: Routledge.
Buber, M. (1966) [o.p. 1965] *The Knowledge of Man: A Philosophy of the Interhuman*. New York: Harper and Row.
Christians, C. G. (2000) 'Social Dialogue and Media Ethics', *Ethical Perspectives*, 2(3): 182–193.
Christians, C. G. (2002) 'The Social Ethics of Agnes Heller', *Qualitative Inquiry*, 8: 411–428.
Christians, C. G. (2005) 'Ethical Theory in Communications Research', *Journalism Studies*, 6: 3–14.
Christians, C. G. (2007) 'Utilitarianism in Media Ethics and Its Discontents', *Journal of Mass Media Ethics*, 22: 113–131.
Christians, C. G. (2008) 'Media Ethics on a Higher Order of Magnitude', *Journal of Mass Media Ethics*, 23: 3–14.
Christians, C. and K. Nordenstreng (2004) 'Social Responsibility Worldwide', *Journal of Mass Media Ethics*, 19: 3–28.

Cooper, T. (1990) 'Comparative International Media Ethics', *Journal of Mass Media Ethics*, 5: 3–14.

Cooper, T. (2008) 'Between the Summits: What Americans Think About Media Ethics', *Journal of Mass Media Ethics*, 23: 15–27.

de Tocqueville, A. (2000) [o.p. 1835–1840] *Democracy in America*, edited and translated H. C. Mansfield and D. Winthrop. Chicago, IL: University of Chicago Press.

Foucault, M. (2002) [o.p. 1966] *The Order of Things: An Archaeology of the Human Sciences*. London: Routledge.

Gadamer, H. G. (1986) [o.p. 1960] *Truth and Method*. New York: Crossroads.

Habermas, J. (1989) [o.p. 1962] *The Structural Transformation of the Public Sphere: An Inquiry into a Category of Bourgeois Society*, translated T. Burger. Cambridge, MA: MIT Press.

Heller, A. (1987) *Better Justice*. Oxford: Basil Blackwell.

Hickey, H. G. (2003) 'A Masochist's Teapot: Where to Put the Handle in Media Ethics', *Journal of Mass Media Ethics*, 18: 44–67.

Holba, A. (2007) *Philosophical Leisure: Recuperative Practice for Human Communication*. Milwaukee, WI: Marquette University Press.

Kant, I. (2006) [o.p 1798] *Anthropology from a Pragmatic Point of View*. Cambridge: Cambridge University Press.

Lambeth, E. B., C. Christians and K. Cole (1994) 'Role of the Media Ethics Course in the Education of Journalists', *The Journalism Educator*, 49(3): 20.

Lambeth, E. B., C. G. Christians, K. Fleming and S. T. Lee (2004) 'Media Ethics Teaching in Century 21: Progress, Problems, and Challenges', *Journalism & Mass Communication Educator*, 59: 239–258.

MacIntyre, A. (1991) *Three Rival Versions of Moral Enquiry: Encyclopedia, Genealogy, and Tradition*. Notre Dame, IN: University of Notre Dame Press.

Plaisance, P. L. (2005) 'The Mass Media as Discursive Network: Building on the Implications of Libertarian and Communitarian Claims for News Media Ethics Theory', *Communication Theory*, 15: 292–313.

Silverstone, R. (2007) *Media and Morality: On the Rise of the Mediapolis*. Cambridge: Polity Press.

Smith, A. (1790) [o.p. 1759] *The Theory of Moral Sentiments*, 6th edn. London: A. Millar.

Souder, L. (2010) 'A Free-market Model for Media Ethics: Adam Smith's Looking Glass', *Journal of Mass Media Ethics*, 25: 53–64.

Stein, E. (1989) *The Collected Works of Edith Stein: On the Problem of Empathy*, 3rd vol, translated W. Stein. Washington, DC: ICS Publications.

Tehranian, M. (2002) 'Peace Journalism: Negotiating Global Media Ethics', *The International Journal of Press/Politics*, 7: 58–83.

Vanacker, B. and J. Breslin (2006) 'Ethics of Care: More Than Just Another Tool to Bash the Media?', *Journal of Mass Media Ethics*, 21: 196–214.

Weber, M. (2001) [o.p. 1904] *The Protestant Ethic and the Spirit of Capitalism*, translated S. Kalberg. Chicago: Fitzroy Dearborn.

5
Anthropological Realism for Global Media Ethics

Clifford G. Christians and Stephen J. A. Ward

This chapter puts forward a form of moral realism which we call 'anthropological realism'. We argue that this is an important tool in the construction of a global ethics, and a global media ethics.

The chapter provides the theoretical basis for a new form of realism as a response to a philosophical stalemate in moral theory between forms of realism and anti-realism. Current understandings and presentations of the issue, such as in theory textbooks, tend to divide positions into the duelling camps of moral realism and moral anti-realism, ignoring the rich possibilities of hybrid theories between the polarities. Realism is pitted against anti-realism: or realism is said to be incompatible with invention, constructionism and pluralism. Moreover, we believe that existing forms of moral realism are not adequate for the proper understanding of global ethical principles. One regrettable characteristic of varieties of realism is that these theories cannot properly account for, let alone recognize, the central ethical phenomena of variety and change in moral beliefs, and the idea of ethical construction. Hence too often these theories, while affirming universal principles, become absolutist and overly rationalistic. Therefore anthropological realism seeks to be a theory between the polarities. It is a form of universal realism that avoids simplistic dualisms in moral theory. It shows how we can conceive of universal values, with realism the primary theoretical term, yet still acknowledge the role of human interpretation and construction in ethics.

Construction of anthropological realism is important because meta-ethical ideas, such as our views about the nature of human values and moral claims, influence our ethical beliefs on a more practical level, such as beliefs about the possibility of a global media ethics. Scepticism about a global ethics in any field is often based on the meta-ethical view that moral universalism is impossible. This scepticism is based, consciously or unconsciously, on a strong anti-realism assumption which holds that since moral values are plural and are socially constructed, no moral principles can be universal or 'global'. Instead, anti-realism implies a relativism concerning moral principles that, if true, defeats any hope of a global ethics. Therefore the construction of a global ethics of any kind requires inquiry into the varieties of realism, and the relationship of moral universalism to ethical plurality.

Moral realism

Philosophical realism

In philosophical realism, reality is independent of our conceptual schemes, our beliefs and our empirical observations. Entities exist in their own terms; humans do not invent them but discover their properties. The material world, mathematical numbers and moral categories are independent of the human mind. 'Realism in philosophy refers to a family of theories developed from antiquity onward.... For the realist, there exists an independent, external world containing an immense number of objects, properties, relations, facts, and law-like behavior which await correct description' (Ward 2011: 146; cf. Alston 1996: 5–6). If ice covers the North Pole, this reality is independent of whether anyone believes it to be true or has perceived it. In realist terms, morality has an explicit character that belongs to its own existence. Physics, chemistry and biology do not tell us what has the most value or how humans should live.

Philosophical realism is contrasted with philosophical idealism. In metaphysics, idealism is the view that the ideal or the spiritual are central to the constitution of the world and to our understanding of experience. Idealism asserts that reality, or reality as we can know it, is mentally constructed – that is, reality is fundamentally immaterial. Some forms of idealism hold that reality exists essentially as spirit or consciousness; other idealists focus on abstractions and laws as being more fundamental than the sensate world. Modern idealism not only asserts the existence of ideas (and the minds or consciousness whose ideas they are) but thereby places a restrictive claim on the nature or composition of reality as a whole.[1]

Moral realism

Debates over idealism and realism continue, though idealism is a form of monism that was easier to defend in a Newtonian cosmology of unchanging order. The issues regarding the nature and plausibility of philosophical realism need ongoing attention, but most realists defend a certain kind of realism. Although historically it was typical to accept or reject realism across the board, today it is more common for philosophers to be selectively realist or non-realist about various topics. Thus it is plausible to be a realist about scientific phenomena and their properties, and be a non-realist about morals. Metaphysical realism faces the most straightforward dispute with idealism. The latter suggests a view of life in which the predominant forces are spiritual. Metaphysical realism allows for a supernaturalism in which natural kinds and substances exist by divine creation. This form of realism carries the foremost responsibility today in confronting idealism, rather than a generic philosophical realism confronting a generic idealism.

This chapter on realism and global ethics defines and defends the subcategory moral realism. While attending to the philosophical disputes between generic realism and idealism, moral realism requires a focus on the specific issues within its own domain. For moral realists, the propositions of ethics are independent of any beliefs that humans have about them. Moral predicates (such as right and wrong) refer to moral properties (such as rightness and wrongness) so that moral statements (such as 'temperance is good' and 'slavery is unjust') express propositions that are true, or approximately true or largely false. Most of us think of the following statements in realistic terms as moral propositions: 'The Tutsis ought not to have killed 800,000 Hutus in the Rwandan genocide'; 'Sexual abuse of children is wrong'; 'Human beings should not be kept as slaves'; 'Moral realism is a cognitivist point of view which defends a moral domain that can and should be acted upon.'

Moral anti-realism is the denial that moral properties, facts, objects and relations exist independently of the mind. Moral non-cognitivism and moral error theory are two ways of demonstrating that moral properties do not exist. These two specific forms of moral anti-realism need to be critiqued for moral realism to serve as the basis for a global ethics.

In moral non-cognitivism, moral judgements may be used to express emotion (feelings of disapproval), to voice commands (stealing is wrong) or to express a wish (would that no one would steal). Non-cognitivism sees these possibilities in terms of what moral language is used for, not as a matter of the meaning of moral language.[2] 'Right' and 'wrong' are similar to 'unicorn' in that these words do not apply to the real world. Moral statements express non-cognitive attitudes, such as desires and approval or disapproval. A.J. Ayer in 1971

[1936] made the first clear statement of moral non-cognitivism. As a logical positivist, he considered all meaningful statements to be either analytic or empirically verifiable. Moral utterances appear to be neither, so Ayer 1971 [1936] concluded that they were not meaningful statements; they should be understood as ways of expressing one's emotions and issuing commands. Therefore it is not possible to speak of ethical reasoning because ethical sentences do not express propositions that are true or false.

The second standard type of moral anti-realism has been called 'moral error theory', following its founder, John Mackie, who coined the term in 1977. Moral error theorists contend that although moral judgements aim at the truth, they systematically fail to secure it. Realist discourse in general is infected with error. When we say, for example, that 'murder is wrong', we are asserting that the act of murder entails the property of wrongness. But, in fact, in making this assertion realists presume that a moral domain instantiates the property and thus the utterance concludes with its premise. Such concepts as moral obligation, moral value and moral desert make unwarranted connections between cause and result, confuse discourse with the empirical, and misconstrue ought and is.

In considering moral anti-realism as a whole, not just its two specific forms, David Brink (1989) argues that it bears a prima facie burden of proof. 'We begin as (tacit) cognitivists and realists about ethics.... Moral realism should be our metaethical starting point, and we should give it up only if it does involve unacceptable metaphysical and epistemological commitments' (23–34). 'Poisoning the water supply is wrong' appears to be self-evident. We certainly think we are saying something true here, and it seems correct to think that way. Most people are naïve realists. Agreeing with Brinks' prima facie burden of proof, it is our judgement in this chapter that anti-realism has not developed arguments strong enough to overcome this methodological handicap.

Moral realists face a number of intellectual challenges in explaining how the moral order, natural reality and mental processes are related. But the realist–anti-realist dualism draws up the terms of the debate in confusing ways. The moral landscape is too complicated to be contained in this dichotomy. Rather than be trapped in meta-ethics, continuing to work with moral realism while dealing with the intellectual issues surrounding it enables us to develop a normative ethics that fuses moral realism with global ethics, and applies to media ethics as an exemplar of a wider normative ethics.

Anthropological approach to moral realism

The approach to moral realism taken here is anthropological. In that sense, moral realism gives priority to the necessary and sufficient conditions of being a member of the human species. The conceptual framework for moral realism is decidedly anthro-ontological. Anthropological moral realism is built from the characteristics that are both common and unique to human beings as such. Ethics is situated fundamentally in the creaturely rather than in abstract conceptions of the good.

From this perspective, *Homo sapiens* is defined as cultural being. 'We are language-using and culture-incorporating creatures whose forms of experience, conduct, and interaction take shape in linguistically and culturally-structured environments and are conditioned by the meanings they bear' (Schacht 1975: 229). This is an integrated view of humans as whole beings who create and maintain through language the value-centred world we call culture. A cultural definition escapes the reductionistic and static view of humans as rational beings, while establishing our humanness in common and therefore universal terms. We are born into an intelligible and interpreted universe, and we use these interpretations creatively for making sense of our lives and institutions. The ethicists' primary obligation is getting inside the way humans arbitrate their presence in the world, and therefore the character of human existence is the centrepiece of a global ethics.

An anthropological understanding of moral realism stands in contrast to the epistemological and metaphysical approaches to moral realism, which have dominated the field. In the epistemological approach to moral realism, moral propositions are true or false regardless of our moral reasoning or intuitions, and some such properties are in fact true. Moral truth is discovered, not invented.

In the metaphysical approach to moral realism, there is an ultimate reality that exists independently of the mental. Philosopher Hilary Putnam is a well-known critic of metaphysical realism, and consequently has been branded an 'anti-realist' although his position escapes clear categorization as metaphysical anti-realism or strong anti-realism. Putnam (1981) defines metaphysical realism as the view that a fixed domain of external things and sets of things exists in its own terms. There is one and only one true description of the way the world is (102) In its supernaturalist version (inspired by Leibniz), moral kinds and substances exist as they do ultimately by virtue of divine creative activity. God being omniscient always commands us to do what is right.

The epistemological version involves intellectual disputes over the nature of truth and the essence of the external world, though Russ Shafer-Landau's *Moral Realism: A Defence* (2003) is a credible argument for this kind of moral realism. Metaphysical moral realism requires a substantive defence on this side of Darwin, Einstein and Freud, and William Alston (1996: Chapter 5; 2002) provides a vindication of it, especially in dealing with Hilary Putnam's formidable opposition.

However, neither the epistemological nor the metaphysical approaches are an adequate substitute for an anthropological moral realism as a robust framework for global ethics. The epistemological version has generally assimilated moral realism into the subjective–objective dualism. Moral realism is thus understood as a contemporary form of moral objectivism, and that articulation inevitably leads to intellectual impasses over the subject–object dichotomy.

Metaphysical moral realism generally entails a prescriptivist understanding of ethics – abstractions, imperatives and rules. Anthropological moral realism is 'anthropological' in looking for universal values in the primordial experience of being human, in all of our human complexity, rather than seeking to ground universal ethics on one aspect of being human, such as the ability of reason to affirm certain abstract principles. Anthropological realism locates the heart of ethics in the human community. Our moral obligations are not invented by individuals but they are situated within the social worlds that we enter and within which we live. A conception of the good as abstract imperatives does not square with our actual moral experience.

Advantages of anthropological moral realism

There are several advantages of bringing moral realism into global ethics. Recasting it around philosophical anthropology frees the concept of moral realism from metaphysical and epistemological debates, and enables the idea to serve as an intellectually productive framework for global ethics. Three advantages are the most obvious.

First, moral realism allows the ordinary rules of logic to be applied directly to moral statements. The concept of moral realism affirms that moral beliefs are justified or contradictory, in the same way as we would conclude in scientific realism that a factual belief is true or false. Moral realism enables us to say that malnutrition in sub-Saharan Africa is unconscionable, and that the city's mayor has integrity. The concept of innocent non-combatants in war needs to be understood across borders so that Red Cross vehicles can travel safely, and moral realism promotes that in principle. The subordination of women can be judged to be contrary to someone's religious values. Realism defends standards of logic so that a system of moral values is declared incoherent or internally inconsistent. Moral realism contradicts moral scepticism and gives credibility to the idea that criteria can be established by which to evaluate differences between cultures rather than consider all practices equally justified.

A second advantage of moral realism is that it serves as an alternative to moral intuitionism. In making judgements on particular cases, or assessing degrees of punishment, moral realism has the capacity to resolve moral disagreements. When conflicts over humane and inhumane practices arise in assessing the treatment of prisoners, for example, a rationale can be presented rather than following one's intuitions which themselves are conditioned by personal experience. In intercultural conflicts, if ethical statements are understood to represent cognitions, one can distinguish self-interest and communal good. In both intra- and intercultural circumstances, propositions can be translated from one setting or language to another and be intelligible.

Third, moral realism makes work on moral universals credible. It enables us to distinguish moral universals from absolutism, for instance. Overall, the normative theory developed in this chapter is systemic, and, to be defensible, moral universals must be integrated into the system, and a realist framework promotes that. The specificatory global media ethics is not independent of moral universals, nor of the more fundamental moral realism, but, in fact, grounded in it. We can unreflectively presuppose, but if the presuppositions of ethics are true, there is strong antecedent probability that the substance of ethics is also true. Moral realism makes such reflection credible. In moral realism, practices and moral claims are articulated to the presuppositions on which they are based.

Construction and relativism

So far this chapter has laid the theoretical basis for reconceiving moral realism. The realism on offer incorporates the fact of ethical variety and change into the core of the theory. This section explains how anthropological realism achieves this integration of perspectives. We clarify how we use the words 'pluralism' and 'construction', and describe the fact of ethical change. Then the chapter shows how the fact of ethical change can be incorporated into realism by using the ideas of 'levels of ethical thinking' and the 'multiple realization of basic values'.

These findings have direct implications for global media ethics. If we can correctly conceptualize the relationship of the universal and the particular in ethics per se, we can use that understanding to explain how global media ethics can be both universal in its basic principles and compatible with cultural change and variation.

Pluralism and monism

Pluralism has many meanings in philosophy, politics and ethics. In metaphysics, it is the belief that reality consists of many different kinds of things, as opposed to the view that there is one type of thing, such as matter or spirit. Culturally, pluralism refers to the fact that a society contains many types of ethnic group, religious tradition, language and conception of the good life – and groups may have conflicting interests. Politically, pluralism refers to a society where two or more states, groups or sources of authority coexist and share power. In ethics, pluralism is the belief that there are many independent and non-reducible sources of moral value that come into tension. There is no one uniquely correct moral system for all humans and all situations. Instead, there are contending values that humans need to prioritize in general and in specific situations. In theory, there may be several equally good ways to rank (or prioritize) basic values. Ethical reasoning, then, is weighing conflicting values in a holistic manner.

Ethical pluralism is contrasted with ethical monism. The latter believes that sources of moral value are reducible to one supreme moral principle, such as happiness or one uniquely correct set of moral values, such as the Ten Commandments – what Philips (1994: 89) calls a 'supercode'. Kekes (1993: 8) describes monism as 'the view that there is one and only one reasonable set of values. This system is the same for all human beings, always, everywhere.' Monism regards differences in moral belief as either variations on a common morality or the result of mistakes in moral belief.[3] Human lives are good to the extent that they conform to this one system of objective general values. There is a unique and correct ranking among ethical values.

Monistic views of ethical reasoning attempt to show how values and standards, where valid, are deducible or justifiable by reference to one supreme principle, such as utility or the categorical imperative. If basic values conflict, the pluralist prefers a flexible approach that seeks to identify which action best balances the conflicting basic values. The monist seeks to identify the action that honours (or maximizes) the one supreme value or supercode. For example, Mill's utilitarianism reduces ethical issues to questions about the greatest happiness for all those affected.

The central issue is what approach to value – monism, relativism, pluralism – best advances a good life. The central belief of pluralism is that 'good lives require the realization of radically different types of values. both moral and non-moral, and that many of those values are conflicting and cannot be realized together' (Kekes 1993: 11). There are diverse sources of ethical value such as the good, duty, personal ideals, love, loyalty, justice and human rights. Humans are also motivated by non-moral values, such as pursuing a career, creativity, playfulness, adventure and style. We experience conflict not only within morality but between morality and other dimensions of life, such as politics, aesthetics, intimate personal relationships and reasonable self-interest. Values come into conflict and we must choose among them. To achieve a good life, humans seek a 'coherent ordering' of their values. But the possible orderings are themselves plural and can come into conflict, as when I decide to live a life of monastic devotion to prayer over a life devoted to developing my artistic talents. Humans need to integrate their plural values across a lifetime and across a moral system.

For Kekes (1993: 12), pluralism's central evaluative claim is that despite the conflicts of values, pluralism enriches the likelihood that we live good lives. Pluralism increases our freedom and self-control, and enlarges the 'repertoire' of conceptions of life that we regard as good. Monists want humans to conform to one morality – to achieve what all individuals ought to want to achieve. Pluralism wants people to make a good life for themselves through different orderings of values.

Constructive realism embraces a pluralism similar to that of Kekes. It affirms the plurality of basic values and the plurality of their possible rankings in living a morally good life. Yet it thinks that pluralism is compatible with a system of universals embedded in the ethics of being. So the approach of this chapter is monistic and universalistic in advocating a set of universal protonorms that provide a common ethical framework. It is pluralistic in acknowledging the many ways in which those values can be realized and combined to live good moral lives and to create varied communities. We will return to this important point later.

Construction and invention

Talk of choices and rankings lead naturally to the topic of human construction in morality. Pluralism assumes that humans are, and should be, involved in working out the integration of their values as they seek a morally worthwhile life. Theories of ethical construction examine how such integrations are created. Construction goes beyond changing one's ranking of values to include creating new values and reinterpreting existing values. Construction means the improvement or reformulation of ethical concepts as humans confront new ethical issues and new social conditions.

Ethical construction is the work of the human imagination and emotion. But it is not an arbitrary, subjective construction, free from any rational or real-world constraints. It is not a construction ex nihilo. Any construction must have materials from which it works. In the case of ethics, the materials consist of existing values and moral traditions, rigorous moral reasoning and facts about the world. Ethical invention is a form of conceptual creativity that occurs in other areas, such as science, technology, politics and art.

Across history, new ethical notions have been introduced to cultures by insightful thinkers and remarkable individuals. Consider the following such ethical and humanistic inventions: the apostle Paul's notion that Christ's message was not just for Jews but also for Gentiles; the ancient Stoic notion of a universal humanity; the movement against slavery in the 19th century; and Ghandi' s idea of non-violent resistance. Pluralism and the need for construction imply ethical change. With pluralism, the possibility of tension between norms opens up. This is stimulus to debate, introspection and ethical change.

The fact of ethical change

Jose Ortega y Gasset (2000), a Spanish philosopher, wrote: 'The good is, like nature, an immense landscape in which man advances through centuries of exploration' (37). For Ortega, history and human activity are crucial to the search for the good. The metaphor of searching across a landscape is directly applicable to the human activity of doing ethics. Following Ortega, we can conceive of ethics as a dynamic exploration of aims, principles and responsible conduct that is open to the future. The idea of ethical exploration is nonsensical (or misguided) if ethics is a monolithic, absolute system of principles fixed once and for all. Understanding ethical change across 'centuries of exploration' is central to ethical theory.

What is the fact of ethical change? It is a fact about ethics as a human phenomenon. Anyone who reads history and travels beyond his/her parish is confronted with the variety of different norms embraced by different cultures in different eras. Slavery was once acceptable: now it is considered a great moral wrong. For some cultures, child labour is acceptable, for others, it is unethical exploitation. Ethical change also occurs when citizens come to believe that some activity, once considered outside ethics, is a legitimate area for ethical concern. As a result the scope of ethics widens. In our own time, the scope of ethics has enlarged to include new (or insufficiently developed) subjects, such as environmental ethics, the human treatment of non-human species, and gay and feminist rights.

For our theory, one type of force for change is especially relevant: the impact on ethics of new social conditions and new technology. For instance, in medical science, the development of powerful technology to keep humans alive raises questions about when doctors should refuse, limit or stop using such technology. The technology challenges our philosophical understanding of concepts such as the quality of life and respect for life. To take another example, the exposure of traditional cultures to global media may change social attitudes concerning sexual behaviour, the role of women and the authority of religious leaders. Tensions arise within a culture and prompt citizens to consider whether ethical change is needed.

The fact of ethical change does not entail that one ethical theory is right and another is wrong. The moral relativist, pluralist and monist all agree that people hold a variety of moral beliefs. Where they differ is how they explain the variety of moral belief. Some theories react to ethical variety by advancing an absolute monism as a bulwark against extreme relativism. Variation from the one correct set of moral beliefs is due either to ignorance or imperfect moral character. Below the shifting variation are absolutes or universals. Other ethicists think ethical change and variety show that there is no universal ethics – that is, ethics is local or parochial.

Constructive realism and ethical change

Constructive realism is compatible with the fact of ethical change, in the form of a variety of moral systems and beliefs. It explains the variety not as an 'appearance' but as a reality closely connected to the existence of universals. Variation in ethical norms is due to different cultural expressions of underlying presuppositions that express our humanness. Those 'expressions' show how the universal is immanent in human existence.

Two ideas help us to understand how universals are expressed in a variety of ways – the idea of multiple realizations and that of levels of ethical thought.

Multiple realizations and levels of ethics

The idea of multiple realizations of a phenomenon plays a central role in many theories, from natural science and linguistics to ethics.

In linguistics, Chomsky's theory of universal grammar suggests that there are universal features of language – grammatical forms innate to the human mind – that receive multiple expression (or realization) in all languages. In the philosophy of mind, theorists influenced by the rise of computers and cognitive science have talked about the mind not as a mysterious mental substance but as a collection of functions – remembering, paying attention – that can be realized in numerous ways in terms of material substrate. The functions of memory and computing can be realized by neurons, silicon chips and other materials. Moreover, different parts of the brain can carry out one and the same brain function if one of the parts is damaged.

In the philosophy of journalism, Ward has argued (cf. 2011) that different media cultures realize and understand differently the basic moral terms, such as social responsibility. There is enough common meaning among media cultures to ensure that journalists are talking about the same concept, but enough difference in the understanding and application of the concept to suggest multiple realizations of one and the same idea. For example, social responsibility in the US may mean the willingness to be accountable and to explain one's journalism. Social responsibility in a more communitarian society or developing country, such as Singapore or South Africa, may mean something stronger in terms of practice – of not writing stories that would gravely embarrass or weaken the government. In Europe, social responsibility may refer primarily to the mandate of public broadcasting, as an alternative to commercial news media (Christians and Nordenstreng. 2004). In the social sciences, 'glocalization' theories leave open the possibility of local and indigenous cultures 'appropriating' and giving different expression to global practices. Rao (2009) has shown, for example, that in India, glocalization means that global forms of media production and practice are adapted to local conditions. The idea of 'investigative journalism' or 'news' may be imported from the global media world, yet how news is done has a distinct Indian realization. In human development theory, Martha Nussbaum (2006) holds that the universal capabilities that a person has for developing a decent life are realized by people in different ways in different societies.

We can adopt the same view towards the universal protonorms or presuppositions that form the heart of anthropological realism. Protonorms in morals are similar to the protonorms of language. They are capable of being expressed in a variety of forms across cultures. Anthropological realism expects universal norms to be realized in many ways.

The idea of multiple realizations also allows us to adopt a realist perspective on construction and invention in ethics. From this view, construction in ethics is the task of applying the universals of constructive realism to particular professions and situations. Ethical invention is guided normatively by universals. The basic materials of construction are the presuppositions of humanness. Pluralism is not the enemy of realism. Pluralism and construction signify the human activity of expressing universals in different forms.

This idea of moral multiple realization assumes that there are levels of ethical thought, and ethical change does not necessarily occur on every level. Constructive realism believes that universal protonorms are an unchanging basis for ethical discourse. However, the ways in which we realize such norms through specific standards, protocols for practice and codes for specific professions may indeed be altered as social conditions change. Constructive realism does not agree that construction and invention occur at every level of ethics. Instead it sees construction and invention occurring at the level of precepts and principles of professions and other areas of human endeavour. Construction does not occur at the level of universal presuppositions and protonorms.

Realism and relativism

Anthropological (or constructive) realism agrees with monism that the basis of ethics is a set of universals. Both constructive realists and monists are universalists. However, constructive realists disagree with monists that there is only one uniquely correct moral system for all cultures and all humans. Moral systems, where valid, are seen as cultural expressions of universal protonorms. The protonorms may receive a number of valid moral realizations. Constructive realism disagrees with extreme relativists that any moral system is as good as any other. Constructive realism believes that there are universal values that restrain the range of acceptable moral systems.

Relativists have long been committed to certain universals, if only to the universal generalization that all truth is relative. Many relativists base their scepticism of realism on a belief in what Ward calls 'factual universals' (2010: 174), such as certain universal features of human life or social existence. The sophists in ancient Greece posited, as universal, the fact of normative variance among cultures. Moral sceptics also assume factual universals, such as the belief that all humans are motivated by self-interest. Therefore the issue between realists and relativists is not the assumption of universals per se but whether we also need to assume normative universals.

Nuanced relativism: Wong

Extreme relativism is a bold and unsophisticated theoretical position. It asserts that all moral beliefs and moral criteria are relative to the person or society who holds them and there is no higher ground upon which to evaluate between differences in moral belief or between conflicting moral criteria. As a consequence, all moral beliefs or moral systems are equally valid since all are equally subjective and relative. In recent years a more nuanced form of moral relativism, what we might call 'moderate relativism', has been developed to which universalists need to respond. Moderate relativists help themselves to factual universals, especially knowledge from social evolutionary theory, neuropsychology and theories about the origin of social cooperation. They use these facts to bolster their claim that morality is a product of social evolution and that its function is to adjudicate among conflicting interests. Like constructive realists, moderate realists seek to avoid both absolute monism and extreme relativism. They claim that there is no one uniquely correct supercode, but there is a universal or objective way to rationally evaluate between moral systems (or principles). Not all moral systems are adequate or good.

An example of this approach is the 'pluralistic relativism' of David Wong (2006). Another example is Michael Philip's (1994) theory of 'ethics as social artifact'. Ethics as social artifact means that 'moral standards are justified to the extent that they promote a reasonably valued way of life'. Morality evaluates ways of life by considering 'the concrete goods and evils they promote and protect us against' (Philips, 1994: 5). Both Wong and Philips are pluralists. Philips does not call himself a relativist but his theory seems to lead to a relativism like Wong's insofar as the reasonableness of moral beliefs appear to be relative to the reasonableness of the larger moral system of which they are a part.

Philips sees morality as a 'tool' that society uses to address common social issues such as homicide, sexual relations, property rights and the education of citizens. A society that successfully addresses these issues creates a social space for individuals to live good lives. For both writers, societies may develop different ethical rules and policies for addressing such problems. Any set of rules is evaluated by how well it performs the stated functions. There are, as Wong says, 'universal criteria' by which to evaluate moralities based on basic human needs, social facts, human biology and the requirements of social cooperation. Therefore Wong and Philip are pluralists in denying that there is a supercode for all societies. As Wong notes, some societies will stress a communitarian approach to social issues that privileges social solidarity and respect for authority. Other societies will privilege the rights of individuals. Some moralities will be deontological, stressing the duties that people have with respect to others, while others will be consequentialist, stressing the primacy of the overall good.

Both Wong and Philips maintain that there could be more than one adequate morality for a society and more than one adequate morality for humans. Wong states (2006: 6): 'a plurality of different cultures could provide legitimate satisfaction and sustenance to human beings, and in that sense be worthy of respect'. Philips (1994: 89) comes to the same conclusion: there are no universal moral standards, and no necessity to posit one optimal code for any society.

What is interesting about these two theories is that, in their appeal to common needs and functions, they suggest that there are common values, such as resolving conflicts of interest or living valued lives. But neither of these writers wants to move from this point to a monistic position that behind these commonalities is a supercode. Our view is that such a move cannot be avoided. Our anthropological approach to ethics makes no quarrel with the ideas of pluralistic realizations of standards, as discussed by Wong and Philips. However, our realism does not consider this sufficient grounds for concluding that nuanced relativism is correct. Pluralism does not entail relativism. We argue that their 'common function' approach is best completed (or understood) by reference to a common set of moral values grounded in our humanness. Therefore we would add to the constraints on an acceptable morality, as provided by Wong and Philips. We would add that moral systems should honour and realize the protonorms and presuppositions of anthropological realism.

Conclusion

We have constructed an anthropological, constructive realism that recognizes universal values grounded in an ethics of being yet also finds a significant place for ethical variation and ethical construction.

Anthropological realism is a distinct view in moral theory in at least two ways. First, it combines realism and constructivism. Second, it is a pluralism that rejects relativism. Anthropological realism moves beyond the traditional polarities of realism and anti-realism, realism and constructivism, realism and human invention (and meaning-making).

One motivation for constructing an anthropological realism is the need for global ethics and global media ethics. Any ethics must be able to do two things.

First, let us take the case of general morality. General morality must be universal in having basic principles that apply equally to all humans. It must provide a vocabulary of basic moral values by which to adjudicate disputes and conflicts that occur within societies and across borders.

The main issue is not so much the claim that morality needs a core of universal principles but rather what those principles might be and how they relate to different cultures.

Second, a global media ethics must be able to recognize, as genuine and fundamental, moral change and moral differences within and across cultures. Otherwise, global ethics becomes an intolerant, imperialistic enterprise whereby, in the name of global ethics, thinkers or practitioners from a certain culture seek to impose a supercode on others.

Both factors apply to a global media ethics. The possibility of such an ethics requires i) the identification of plausible universal principles to guide the problems and conflicts that arise for a global media and ii) an interpretation of those principles that recognizes moral change and differences across media cultures.

Our realism seeks to adequately satisfy both requirements of a global ethics. It does not flinch from talking about universal values, and it constructs a pluralistic view of how such universals are realized that is consistent with the fact of ethical change. Our theory rejects extreme relativism and responds to recent forms of moderate relativism. The implication of our work is not that any construction in ethics will do. Construction must be normatively guided. Like Wong and others, we seek to limit the range of acceptable moralities. We want to acknowledge decent moralities that advance human flourishing (Ward 2010). A morality is to be judged by how well it expresses our universal values.

This chapter has provided a basic orientation and some basic concepts. It is now up to scholars of global media ethics to develop the framework and to test its assumptions with new research and critical philosophical analysis.

Notes

1. For classical idealism, see Berkeley (1734) and Bradley (1930).
2. For more on speech act theory as a form of realism, see Searle (1969) and Austin (1962).
3. Gert (1998: 4; cf. 2004), in arguing monistically for a 'common morality', says that he prefers to see differences in moral beliefs, which can be significant, as variations of the one common morality, or as a different morality based on a 'common framework'.

References

Alston, W. P. (1996) *A Realist Conception of Truth*, Ithaca, NY: Cornell University Press.

Alston, W. P. (2002) *Realism and Anti-Realism*. Ithaca, NY: Cornell University Press.

Austin, J. L. (1962) *How to Do Things with Words*. Oxford: Clarendon.

Ayer, A.I. (1971 [1936]). *Language, Truth and Logic*. Harmondsworth: Penguin.

Berkeley, G. (1734) *A Treatise Concerning the Principles of Knowledge*. London: J. Tonson.

Bradley, F. H. (1930) [o.p. 1893]. *Appearance and Reality: A Metaphysical Essay*. Oxford, UK: Clarendon.

Brink, D. (1989). *Moral Realism and the Foundations of Ethics*. Cambridge: Cambridge University Press.

Christians, C. and Nordenstreng, K. (2004) 'Social Responsibility Worldwide', *Journal of Mass Media Ethics*, 19(1): 3–28.

Gert, B. (1998) *Morality: Its Nature and Justification*. Oxford: Oxford University Press.

Gert, B. (2004) *Common Morality*. Oxford: Oxford University Press.

Kekes, John (1993). *Morality and Pluralism*. Princeton, NJ: Princeton University Press.

Mackie, J. L. (1977) *Inventing Right and Wrong*. Harmondsworth: Penguin.

Nussbaum, Martha C. (2006) *Frontiers of Justice*. Cambridge, MA: Belknap Press.

Ortega, Y Gasset, J. (2000) *Meditations on Quixote*. Translated Evelyn Rugg and Diego Marin. Urbana and Chicago, IL: University of Illinois Press.

Philips, M. (1994) *Between Universalism and Skepticism: Ethics as a Social Artifact*. Oxford: Oxford University Press.

Putnam, H. (1981). *Reason, Truth and History*. Cambridge: Cambridge University Press.

Rao, S. (2009) 'Glocalization of Indian Journalism', *Journalism Studies*,10(4): 474–488.

Schacht, R. (1975) *Existentialism. Existenz-Philosophy and Philosophical Anthropology*. Pittsburgh, PA: University of Pittsburgh Press.

Searle, J. (1969) *Speech Acts. An Essay in the Philosophy of Language*. Cambridge: Cambridge University Press.

Shafer-Landau. Russ (2003) *Moral Realism: A Defence*. Oxford: Clarendon Press.

Ward, S.J.A. (2010). *Global Journalism Ethics*. Montreal: McGill-Queen's University Press.

Ward, S.J.A. (2011) *Ethics and the Media: An Introduction*. Cambridge: Cambridge University Press.

Wong, David (2006) *Natural Moralities: A Defense of Pluralistic Relativism*. Oxford: Oxford University Press.

Part II
Interfaces

6
The Culture of Blogging: At the Crossroads of Narcissism and Ethics

Joanna Zylinska

June 08, 2007

It's no secret that I've been having a hard time of it lately. You don't even need to click back through the archives, you can just scroll down the screen to witness that I'm out looking out at the abyss. For the past week I've been trying to figure out where I screwed up, how I can pinpoint the exact moment I made the wrong decision. I'm a big believer in taking responsibility for your life and I've been trying to take responsibility for mine – and now Will's – to figure out how to get out of the financial and career mess that I've gotten myself into. 'I have to contribute' is the mantra that's on eternal repeat in my head, playing faster and faster, and louder and louder until the pressure starts building and I can feel the pinpricks of the migraine beginning to jab at the back of my eyeballs. I scan job boards, send out resumes, make follow-up phone calls and try to get a temp agency to even give me the time of day, as Los Angeles has a glut of unemployed overeducated workers all scrambling for the ten-buck-an-hour temp job.

(*The Slack Daily*, http://www.theslackdaily.com/)

Numerous critical accounts of blogs and social networking portals, such as *MySpace, Facebook, LiveJournal and Blogger*, position these newly emergent media forms as clever market devices, through which naïve,

This article is an abridged version of Chapter 3 from my 2009 book *Bioethics in the Age of New Media* (Cambridge, MA: MIT Press). I am grateful to the publisher for granting us non-exclusive permission to reuse the material here.

91

self-indulgent and narcissistic users provide international conglomerates with precious marketing data and thus fulfil the neoliberal imperative for individualized productivity. Offering an alternative reading of such online media, I will argue that they can facilitate the development of a new form of media ethics, an ethical framework for being with others in global or transnational media spaces. I will also suggest that blogging and social networking enable the self to establish an active relation to its own life and the processes of its management. This is why I propose to describe this form of media ethics as bioethics – not in a medical sense but rather in the sense of an ethics of life, relating to both political and material aspects of life (i.e. what Aristotle termed *bios* and *zoē*). The argument of my chapter is organized around one key question: What if Foucault had had a blog?

The ethics of the self

Before I get to this question, I would like us to take a closer look at Foucault's conceptualization of ethics (although I have to warn you that I will eventually part ways with Foucault in my ethical wanderings). The subject of ethics does not feature explicitly in any of Foucault's major works: it is only in short articles and interviews, gathered in the volume *Ethics: Subjectivity and Truth* (1997), and then in the series of lectures given at the Collège de France in 1982 and published as *The Hermeneutics of the Subject* (2005), that Foucault addressed the issue of power and resistance through the ethical processes of self-fashioning and self-creation. Foucault understands ethics in terms of 'ethos', which stands for practice, embodiment and a style of life. It is a practice of freedom derived from the game of truth (see Rabinow 1997: xxv–xxvii). Its origins lie in the twin imperatives of ancient philosophy – 'know thyself' and 'care for thyself' – which in Christian times underwent a transformation into the principle of asceticism. The care of the self has a critical function in this relationship between self-knowledge and attention to the self, as it not only enables one to 'unlearn' bad habits and cast away false opinions but also can play a curative role. Ethics thus becomes a vocation focused on developing a free relationship of the self to itself, and on arriving at a 'subject of desire' responsible for creating new forms of pleasure. The ethics of the care of the self, especially in its Greek incarnation, is also a communal task, where subject formation is to benefit others.

While in ancient Greece the care of the self was the consequence of a statutory situation of power exercised by individual Others (2005: 36), Foucault explains that in Roman times, particularly in Epicurean and

Stoic philosophy, it was repositioned as a permanent task to be taken up by every individual throughout his life – although there, of course, remain both political and individual limitations to this universalism. Significantly, ethics arising from the 'care of the self' principle does not rest on any prior rules of conduct but rather on the sense of obligation and duty that imposes itself, in a direct and often uncomfortable way, on us. Foucault writes: 'The care of oneself is a sort of thorn which must be struck in men's flesh, driven into their existence, and which is a principle of restlessness and movement, of continuous concern throughout life' (2005: 8). He also points out that in Hellenistic and Greco-Roman culture, the principle of taking care of oneself was a very powerful concept, which entailed constant working on oneself, and was thus very different from 'the Californian cult of the self', where you are supposed to discover your true self (see Foucault 1997: 269–271). The notion of truth is vital for Foucault, but he speaks about 'particular truth' to be created by each self as a relationship to what is not in it, not a pre-existent general truth already in place, waiting to be discovered.

This idea of a particular truth to be arrived at and a particular way of life to be created foregrounds one of the most significant aspects of the ethics of the self: the absence from it of any prior codification or instructions on how to live. It is the ethical activity itself, 'vigilant, continuous, applied [and] regular' (2005: 84), which is important rather than the fulfilment of any particular commandments. The 'transformation of one's self by one's own knowledge' and the elaboration of new, beautiful ways of life are of primary importance in this ethical project (1997: 131). Foucault's ethics thus has a strong aesthetic dimension. In his discussion of non-normative sexualities he goes so far as to compare an imperative 'to create a gay life. To become' (1997: 163) with the creation of works of art. This process does not occur in vacuum: we cannot just become who we want to be as our very self-knowledge about our wishes and the direction of our transformation need to remain subject to a critical scrutiny. We are also bound by the power of institutions and social relations, and by their disciplinary and constraining effects. As power for Foucault is a strategic rather than just an oppressive relation (Lazzarato), power can also be productive, creating the possibility of agency for the subject on the way to its desire and truth.

In this project the self is established as a subject through 'techniques of the self' (also translated into English as 'technologies of the self'),

which permit individuals to effect by their own means, or with the help of others, a certain number of operations on their bodies and

souls, thoughts, conduct, and way of being, so as to transform themselves in order to attain a certain state of happiness, purity, wisdom,
perfection, or immortality.

(1997: 225)

Amongst these technologies Foucault lists dream interpretation, 'taking
notes on oneself to be reread, writing treatises and letters to friends to
help them, and keeping notebooks in order to reactivate for oneself the
truths one needed' (1997: 232). It is his focus on letter writing and diary
keeping that is particularly relevant for my attempt to assess to what
extent social networking portals such as *LiveJournal*, *MySpace* and *Flickr*,
as well as blogs, could be read as facilitating the very care of the self that
Foucault analyses in Greco-Roman culture, and perhaps even enacting a
new ethical way of being in the world.

Foucault is keen to emphasize the long-term scope of the care of the
self project.[1] He argues that 'the general Greek problem was not the
tekhnē of the self, it was the *tekhnē* of life, the *tekhnē tou biou*, hot to
live' (1997: 260). Getting to the heart of his own biological and medical
rhetoric, he goes so far as to insist that 'Permanent medical care is one of
the central features of the care of the self. One must become the doctor
of oneself' (1997: 235). I would like to suggest that his ethics of the self
can be interpreted as a different form of bioethics. By bioethics I mean
a performative ethics of life which both enacts new practices of living
and looks after the life of its agents who are always on the way to their
selfhood/health. The ethics of the self must not be understood as an
attempt on Foucault's part to promote a selfish or, worse, delusional
individualism under the guise of his 'how to live' techniques. The Stoic-
inspired withdrawal from the affairs of the world is to be interpreted
instead as a better, more prudent preparation for being in the world,
and for relating to people, things and events. As well as becoming an
art of (whole) life, the care of the self principle makes life better: it is
said to have a curative and therapeutic function (1997: 97) and thus, as
indicated earlier, remains in 'kinship with medicine' (2005: 125–126).
While in Plato the art of the body is clearly distinguished from the art of
the soul, in the Epicureans and Stoics 'the body reemerges very clearly
as an object of concern so that caring for the self involves taking care of
both one's soul and one's body' (2005: 107–108).

This 'Foucauldian bioethics' presents a very different model of
bioethics from the dominant one, in which the self is most often positioned as an object of medical procedures and political interventions.
It provides us with a new way of thinking about what it means to live

an ethical life, a healthy life, and how to care about one's life, without relying on predefined values or legal frameworks.

Life on the web

I would like now to focus on one particular domain of contemporary media culture – blogs and social networking portals, such as *LiveJournal* and *MySpace* – where millions of users are drawing on a daily basis on what Foucault described as technologies of the self. The aptly titled *LiveJournal* is one of the most popular sites where users keep their blogs, pre-dating such popular networking websites as *MySpace* (which in April 2007 had 185 million accounts) and *Flickr* (a photo-sharing site).[2] The ambition and scope of these online portals should not be underestimated: they aim to create the experience of 'total life' by building intricate systems of connections between online and offline spaces, personae and narratives. According to Adam Reed, 'The updating quality of weblogs is what for [bloggers] makes this text feel "alive" ' (2005: 227).

It seems that one way of managing the novelty and rapidity of development of these social networking sites is by commenting on them in terms of old, already known technologies. Blogs then are seen, on the one hand, as a megaphone for the already existing but silenced or little-heard voices; they amplify thoughts and passions already in place and help to build communities of like-minded people: be it cat lovers or anti-globalists. They are also seen as a way of 'empowering the little guy' (Hall 2008: 114–15) On the other hand, blogs and social networking function as 'a full consensus-creating machine', where the work of the digital proletariat can be exploited. The argument goes that if we do not get on *MySpace* soon we will all become obsolete, unnecessary and disposable (Hall 2008: 114–15).

This narrative of the exploitation of the individual by the (techno)system has been accompanied by another offshoot of the Marxist and, more broadly, modernist critique of popular culture: that concerning the alleged banality of its practices and the narcissism of its participants. As Kris R. Cohen explains, 'Bloggers are said to be narcissists because they persist in publicizing their boring lives.' Cohen identifies an interesting contradiction in the public perception of bloggers: they are seen as occupying a position that is simultaneously too public (i.e. they are too easily noticed by peevish critics, or too easily thought of as pretentious by other bloggers) and not public enough (with the blogger just speaking to him/herself, or worrying about losing the audience when their hit count drops). '[T]he absence of a "real" audience leaves the blogger seeming to stare at herself while thinking she is staring at others – pathetically deluded like Narcissus' (Cohen 2006: 164).

So how can we get out of this dialectical impasse in thinking about blogging and social networking online? How, in other words, can we think about these new media practices without immediately valorizing them as good or bad, productive or useless, resistant or oppressive? To do this I want to develop what might initially seem like a negative thread which I have picked up from Kris R. Cohen, and entertain for a moment the idea that blogging and 'hanging out' on *Facebook* are perhaps indeed intrinsically linked with narcissism. I do see these practices as a reinforcement of the ego-ideal users construct of and for themselves, and then painstakingly attempt to achieve. Even the recognition of personal failures – from 'Why did he dump me?' to 'Why did my paper get rejected by an academic journal?' – seems to provide a way of reinforcing the ego on its way to self-fulfilment and closure. For example, many academic and professional blogs function as veritable 'brag-spaces' in which one just lists one's achievements – the notable invitations one has received, the publications one has had accepted this year. And yet there is a generous side to both academic and non-academic blogging, where blogs and other social sites function as spaces through which one 'gives' and 'shares' interesting notices or funny comments with others. The *Delicious* website – originally independent but now owned by Yahoo – is one example of such 'sharing sites' on which users can store, exchange and discover one another's web bookmarks.[3] Both of these types of activity – the crafting of the self according to the ego ideal and the sharing of the (data) gifts one has amassed – are narcissistic: the former as a manifestation of one's exaggerated investment in one's image (as a lover, music fan or professional), the latter as an attempt to gather the whole world 'in my image' and then give it to others. Blogging can thus perhaps be jokingly described as a delirious activity in which the self attempts to be with others, while also recoiling from the wounds that the other (blogger) inflicts on them.

May 31, 2007

Today is the day where nobody is returning my phone calls or emails. I have left phone messages for at least eight people without being called back. I've also emailed several of these people to tell them to check their messages and to call me back. Eight people, I kid you not. If I have either called or emailed you today, please call or email me back either tonight or early tomorrow, because you are all giving me a massive complex.

(Clublife, http://www.standingonthebox.blogspot.com/)

The media culture of narcissism

You may now perhaps wonder whether I have not just come up with another dismissive account of blogging and social networking which inscribes itself in the negative strand of narratives about new media in general and blogging in particular. This would be the case if we were to take narcissism as a negative phenomenon, a cultural or personal pathology which has to be overcome for social relations to be established. However, I want to suggest that narcissism is inevitable, or even necessary, for sociality; and, indeed, to use Derrida's words, that 'There is not narcissism and non-narcissism; there are narcissisms that are more or less comprehensive, generous, open, extended' (1995: 199). Derrida goes on to argue that what is referred to as non-narcissism is only a more welcoming, hospitable narcissism, one that is much more open to the experience of the other as other. He explains:

> I believe that without a movement of narcissistic reappropriation, the relation to the other would be absolutely destroyed, it would be destroyed in advance. The relation to the other – even if it remains asymmetrical, open, without possible reappropriation – must trace a movement of reappropriation in the image of oneself for love to be possible, for example. (199)

It is in this sense that an act of reaching to the other (through an online posting, a link to someone else's site or a fantasy of, and desire for, multiple readers) is narcissistic, but also that narcissism is revealed as necessary to establishing this relationship.

Drawing on Derrida's playful account of the ambivalences of our psychic economy, let me thus suggest that this desire for (the death of) the other manifested by bloggers and other online social networkers is actually a condition – even if not a guarantee – of an ethical way of being with others. If we define ethics after Lévinas and Derrida as openness to the infinite alterity of the other (leaving aside for a moment the Foucauldian thread developed so far in this chapter) (see Lévinas 1969, 1989), narcissism is revealed as an inextricable part of ethics. There can therefore perhaps be 'good' and 'bad' narcissism, where 'good' and 'bad' do not stand here for moral categories sanctioned by predefined philosophical or religious positions but rather for conditions of our sub-jectivity, our psychic health. The blogger's delirium, manifesting itself in the constant checking of the site's counter, in comparing him/herself with other bloggers or in instantiating flame wars in comment boxes, can be read as an attempt to construct a self. This is a much more seri-ous and difficult project than one focused on merely expressing oneself or even on performing one's identity, whereby one either attempts to convey to oneself and others what one is 'truly' like, or draws on the set of available props and identitarian positions (a white middle-class boy, a suburbanite housewife from Dallas, a dog) to enact a self or play a role. The narcissist's 'delirium' is rather like the Nietzschean rapture, a positive condition of the ethos of becoming that we can also find in the work of Deleuze and Foucault.

What is so interesting and promising about Nietzsche's state of rapture is precisely its reaching to the outside – to what or whom it desires – which 'draws the subject out of itself' (Ziarek 2001: 39). This 'attrac-tion of the outside' can also be located at the heart of the Foucauldian ethos, a suggestion which offers a possibility of rapprochement between Foucault and Lévinas. Foucault himself is less concerned with the onto-logical conditions of this outside (which ultimately imposes a limitation on his ethics) than with the self's breaking out of the congealed, fixed forms of being in an attempt to imagine and create some new ways of life.[4] But this drive towards an outside already establishes a relation to what is not in the self (even if Foucault's own concern will remain with the self's process of becoming rather than with the forms of alterity that make the emergence of this self possible). This rapture or delirium in which the self cannot be contained within its own boundaries can thus perhaps be interpreted as the blogger's enactment of what I term 'good narcissism' – a reaching towards the other (blogger, reader, hacker), the material effects of whose online presence are constantly calling the blogging self into being. This is also a way of countering what Craig Saper describes as 'b-logocentrism', 'a neologism in which the extra b stands for banal narcissism, suggest[ing] how blogs can intensify the appearance of a self-present speaker instead [of] a de-centered subject in hypertextual webs' (2006: non-pag.; added emphasis).

Returning to the dialectical new media narratives sketched out ear-lier through which blogging and social networking are usually analysed (good/bad, resistant/oppressive), I want to suggest that to read these practices in terms of the Foucauldian ethics of becoming is not to negate the possibility of interpreting them as political practices, in which cit-izenship is recognized at the microlevel and in which 'little guys' are given the voice. But neither is it to subsume these practices under the recognizable framework of democracy, political participation or even friendship, because doing so would mean reducing the ethical possibility of both the self and the technology with which it remains in a dynamic relationship. Nor is it to deny that banality, boredom and self-obsession constitute part of the experience of blogging or hanging out on *Facebook*. It is precisely in this tension between many users' sense that these portals are merely mirroring the banality of their own and others' lives, and the possibility that they may contribute to the reworking of life forces and establish a new relation to one's life (on – and offline) that the ethical potential of live web lies. Interestingly, Foucault associates the practice of self-writing precisely with an ethos of life, as the keeping of individual notebooks and memory books focused on the recollection of the past, or capturing the already said, or what one has managed to hear or read, is for him 'a matter of constituting a *logos bioēthikos* for oneself ... an ethics quite explicitly oriented by concern for the self toward objectives defined as: withdrawing into oneself, getting in touch with oneself, relying on oneself, benefiting from and enjoying oneself' (1997: 211). This phrase *logos bioēthikos* provides a key for my rereading of bioethics as a practice of good life, always on the way to becoming a good life. But Foucault has in mind something much more material and direct than just a story about one's life and how it should be lived: this practice of self-writing is said to produce 'a body'. Drawing on Seneca, Foucault claims that 'writing transforms the thing seen or heard into tissue and blood'. From this perspective, diaries, blogs and online profiles are not just commentaries on someone's life, already lived to this point, but also somehow more 'real' outside its narrative; rather, they are materializations of it. Digital writing and linking is therefore a form not only of cultural but also of corporeal production; it literally produces the body by temporarily stabilizing it as a node in the network of forces and relations: between multiple servers and computers, flows of data, users' eyes, fingers and sensations, particles of electricity and so on.

There is, of course, no guarantee that such 'delicate ethical work' will be undertaken, or that the work on the self – be it in the form of blog postings, *MySpace* links or *Flickr* community activities – will be ethical rather than banal or solipsistic. Even though the care of the self becomes coextensive with life (which means that, say, john23's blog is always already john23's life, not just an account of, or a secondary reflection on, his life, while his offline activities are somehow more real), Foucault recognizes that this practice of the self which is 'theoretically' open to everyone will only be realized by a few (2005: 113). He lists the lack of courage, strength or endurance, the inability to grasp the importance of the task and see it through, and the unwillingness to listen as limitations to the universality of this ethics of the care of self. It is perhaps not surprising that a great number of blogs and individual profiles on social networking portals present themselves to many media and cultural critics as boring, replicating the most fixed ideas and values (although we cannot, of course, rule out critics' own intellectual and cultural preferences and values reflected in these judgements). However, to say that the care of the self is indeed a 'universal practice which can only be heard by a few' (2005: 120), and that what we can call 'the event of ethics' will therefore be very rare, is to assert something else than just that 'every site will find its fans' or to argue that only popular sites with the most hits have managed to embrace this ethical potential of the medium. Popularity (or its lack) has nothing to do with the care of the self, on or offline. I therefore want to suggest something that perhaps goes against the grain of more typical media and cultural studies interpretations of blogging and its users. Rather than see *LiveJournal* or *Flickr* as being primarily about exchange, with bloggers expecting to be read, responded to or at least tagged and thus acknowledged in one way or another, I propose to read blogging as being as much about experiencing and enacting the simultaneous difficulty and necessity of relationality as a condition of being in the world. This interpretation seems more plausible in the light of the fact that most blogs and online profiles have very few readers: in most cases, the blogger him/herself.[5] Social networking sites are thus a testing ground for enacting the dramas and (inevitable) failures of sociality.

But even if what we might call 'the event of ethics' in the blogosphere is indeed very rare, the enactment of the technology of the self through the techniques of writing and linking makes the blogosphere a privileged space for analysing the emergence of the practice of the care of the self. Naturally we could explore the enactment of this ethics through the technologies of the self in such cultural practices as dieting, bodybuilding or reading self-help manuals. And yet there is something very particular about how this ethics of the self takes place through writing, especially the writing that involves new media, because of the kind of self and the kind of life that are performed in this process. It could be argued that in blogging and online networking an enactment of a more embodied, aware and 'lively' relationship of the self with technology takes place, and that 'life' is thus revealed as always already technological. Foucault himself, when commenting on the coming into vogue of notebooks to be used for personal and administrative purposes in Plato's time, foregrounds the technological aspect of all writing that needs to be taken account of. Providing an interesting gloss to the current debates on the novelty of technology and 'new media', he argues that in ancient Greece 'This new technology was as disrupting as the introduction of the computer into private life today. It seems to me the question of writing and the self must be posed in terms of the technical and material framework in which it arose' (1997: 272).

Social networking sites thus provide an experiential space for actively taking on, rather than merely acting out, the trace of technology in the human self. Recognizing that media users' attention is usually focused on the content of the technology rather than its machinic or formal qualities, Mark Poster states that 'Whenever individuals deploy media, they are in the midst of a system of power relations that remains out of phase with their conscious mind' (2006: 38). This leads to a reconfiguration of the subject–object distinction into what he calls 'the humachine' (36). Even if it is the intuitive and unconscious embracing of technology (as this process itself is simplified through the use of templates, etc.) that precedes the self's attempt to connect with others, blogging and social networking return agency to this process of being in the technoworld, of living with technology. This goes some way towards interpreting media culture as a productive apparatus of power, a network of nodes and temporary stabilizations of forces, where the self is neither entirely 'free' and singular nor entirely and permanently subjugated. Rather, it emerges from this network as technological, or 'humachinic', and does so not just through its writing and linking activities but also through the construction of its life – past, memories, dreams and desires – as technological traces. For Bernard Stiegler, any technical instrument registers and transmits the memory of its use (1998). For example, a carved stone used as a knife carries a record of an act of cutting and therefore acts as a form of memory. Technology becomes for Stiegler a condition of our relationship to the past, but it also works as a kind of compass, positioning the self in the temporal network from which the linear sequence of events can be distinguished – precisely by the identification of technological traces (cuts on the knife's blade, rearrangements of the online template).[6]

And it is precisely as the leaving of traces that Stiegler interprets human existence, an existence that is for him always already technological. He argues that what Heidegger calls *Besorgen*, more recently translated as 'taking care' (rather than the earlier 'concern'), is also 'beyond the mere activity that survival requires, the will to be, that is to say to exist, to be in the sense of ex-isting, and therefore of marking, leaving a trace' (2003: 161). Existence, or life, for humans means the use of language, or writing, which in *Of Grammatology* Derrida interprets as precisely the leaving of traces, or marks. The 'delete' function on one's keyboard or screen also lets users remove, or at least obscure, their traces, and to experiment with ways of narrativizing their life – and death. The *MyDeathSpace.com* site, which provides an archive of deaths of selected *MySpace* members (but is not officially affiliated to *MySpace*),[7] allows for dead members' profiles to be kept 'alive' by comments and mementoes posted by one's 'friends'. Of course, this can all be a hoax. To paraphrase an old adage: on the internet, no one knows you're a ghost.

The nodes of power in the web of life

Blogging and social networking enable the self to establish an active relation to its own life and the processes of its management. It is the taking up of this challenge that I describe as bioethics, that is, an ethics of life whereby the (always emergent) self takes responsibility not just for its own health but also for life as such. Bioethics can thus be understood as an ethics of becoming and self-creation. The impetus for this process, I would argue – contra Foucault – always comes from the alterity 'before me', in both a temporal and a spatial sense. Foucault positions his ethics as response and resistance to the organized forms of power and its historical structuration. Situating it in the context of the relationship with, and pleasure of and for, the Other, he defines ethics as 'an experiment with the possibility of going beyond' the limits imposed upon us (quoted in Ziarek 2001: 41). Ewa Ziarek argues that Foucauldian ethics limits otherness to the endless variations on the plane of immanence, as a result of which it cannot accommodate an obligation to the Other or respond to an external claim (6). It is in Lévinas's ethical call as coming from the always already anarchic and primordial alterity of the Other that, I believe, we can locate a more convincing ethical framework. The Lévinasian supplement to the ethics of becoming should not, however, be seen as a one-way shift from immanence to transcendence but rather as a different, pragmatic resolution of the question of ethical injunction – that is, this drive that pushes the self to self-create, to forge life, to become. It is also a way of ensuring that alterity or difference does not get reduced to a mere resource for the self.

This ethics of life I am outlining is therefore situated in, or even arises out of, the tension between bad and good narcissism, between the Foucauldian relationship to the self and the Lévinasian response to the alterity of the Other, and, last but not least, between self-creation as neoliberal imperative for individualized productivity and an ethical injunction for continuous restlessness and movement. This tension is not a permanent suspension between two sets of equally valid options: it entails a need for a decision, to be taken, always anew, in a singular way, in an undecidable terrain. The possibility of the imperative of the care of the self turning into bad narcissism, b-logocentrism or moral dandyism, and of self-creation becoming a neoliberal project in which the self is seen as the ultimate value that needs protecting, has to be kept in place precisely as a guarantee of the ethicality of this project. Were we to eliminate this possibility (or even danger) in advance, we would be turning our bioethics into a technicized schema for the improvement of the world, predefined and carefully designed by 'ethics experts'. Technology does serve an important role in this ethics of life – not as a threatening other which needs to be overcome for the protection of life or as a set of calculation procedures worked out in advance, but as a container for the tensions between bad and good narcissism, between self-creation and reaching out to alterity. The bioethics I am proposing is thus always already technological, in the sense that it is predicated upon the acceptance of the technicity of life as its condition of being.

To answer the question that frames my chapter – What if Foucault had had a blog? – I think he would have been a narcissist, but what I have described here as a good, or ethical, narcissist. As mentioned before, 'good' does not stand here for an a priori universal valorization but rather for the recognition of narcissism as an inevitable condition of an ethics of the self, and of the self's being with others. So, are bloggers narcissistic? Absolutely, but also inevitably. Are they ethical? Possibly, but also, perhaps, rarely.

Notes

1. As Foucault puts it, 'Care of the self becomes coextensive with life' (2005: 86).
2. Other examples of popular social networking websites include *Facebook, Open Diary* and *MyDearDiary.com, Blurty, Xanga, DeadJournal, Blogger* and *DiaryLand*. Perhaps appropriately, I used *Wikipedia* (http://www.wikipedia.org) – a free online encyclopaedia edited (and constantly re-edited) by users themselves but also a form of online community in itself – to develop some of the definitions presented in the main body of the chapter.
3. Academic blogs have also been described as 'experiments in digital scholarship', or a testing ground for research in progress (see Saper 2006). Melissa Gregg's article, 'Feeling Ordinary: Blogging as Conversational Scholarship' (2006), provides an excellent justification for the use of blogging as a form of scholarly exchange and an alternative scholarly practice.

4. Because it bears a relation to the outside, which is the experience of the limit of social regulation and thus of the historical constitution of the subject, the experimental praxis cannot be simply reduced to a goal-oriented activity. On the contrary, the outcome of such an experimental praxis aiming to surpass the historical limits of bodies, language and sexuality cannot be predicted in advance because it opens up a relation to a future that can [no] longer be thought on the basis of the present... Foucault's invention of the improbable stresses the radical futural dimension of praxis beyond the anticipation of the subject.

(Ziarek 2001: 41)

5. The American internet entrepreneur Alan Levy is rather explicit about the status quo: 'The blogosphere is a world of haves and have-nots. Frankly, about two bloggers out of every million have meaningful traffic and readership' (Hall 2006: 34).
6. I am indebted to my ex-PhD student Federica Frabetti at Goldsmiths for her discussion of the relationship between memory and technology in Stiegler.
7. I found out about *MyDeathSpace.com* from Cortney Heimerl's presentation at the Homelands: Spaces of Inclusion/Exclusion, Spaces of Power/Security graduate conference at NYU Steinhardt on 10 November 2006.

References

Cohen, Kris R. (2006) 'A Welcome for Blogs', *Continuum: Journal for Media & Culture Studies*, 20(2) (June): 161–173.

Derrida, Jacques (1995) ' "There is No *One* Narcissism" (Autobiophotographies)', in Jacques Derrida, *Points...Interview, 1974–1994*. Elisabeth Weber (ed.). Stanford University Press: Stanford.

Foucault, Michel (1997) *Ethics: Subjectivity and Truth*. (ed.) Paul Rabinow. Allen Lane: London.

Foucault, Michel (2005) *The Hermeneutics of the Subject: Lectures at the Collège de France 1981–82*. (ed.) Frederic Gros and Francois Ewald. Palgrave Macmillan: Basingstoke.

Gregg, Melissa (2006) 'Feeling Ordinary: Blogging as Conversational Scholarship', *Continuum: Journal for Media & Culture Studies*, 20(2) (June): 147–160.

Hall, Christian (2006) 'An Interview with Alan Levy', *net*, 157 (December): 34–36.

Hall, Gary (2008) *Digitize This Book!: The Politics of New Media, or Why We Need Open Access Now*. University of Minnesota Press: Minneapolis.

Lazzarato, Maurizio (n.d.) 'From Biopower to Biopolitics', Trans. Ivan A. Ramirez. Available at http://www.geocities.com/immateriallabour/lazzarato-from-biopower-to-biopolitics.html. Accessed on 31.05.2007.

Lévinas, Emmanuel (1969) *Totality and Infinity: An Essay on Exteriority*. Trans. Alphonso Lingis. Pittsburgh, PA: Duquesne University Press.

Levinas Emmanuel (1989) 'Ethics as First Philosophy', in *The Levinas Reader*, Sean Hand (ed.). Blackwell: Oxford.

Poster, Mark (2006) *Information Please: Culture and Politics in the Age of Digital Machines*. Duke University Press: Durham and London.

Rabinow, Paul (1997) ' "Introduction" to Michel Foucault', *Ethics: Subjectivity and Truth*. (ed.) Paul Rabinow. Allen Lane: London.

Reed, Adam (2005) ' "My Blog Is Me": Texts and Persons in UK Online Journal Culture (and Anthropology)', *Ethnos*, 70(2) (June): 220–242.

Saper, Craig (2006) 'Blogademia', *Reconstruction*, 6(4). http://reconstruction. eserver.org/064/saper.shtml.

Stiegler, Bernard (1998) *Technics and Time, 1: The Fault of Epimetheus*. Trans. Richard Beardsworth and George Collins. Stanford University Press: Stanford.

Stiegler, Bernard (2003) 'Technics of Decision: An Interview with Peter Hallward', Trans. Sean Gaston. *Angelaki*, 8(2): 151–168.

Ziarek, Ewa Plonowska (2001) *An Ethics of Dissensus: Postmodernity, Feminism, and the Politics of Radical Democracy*. Stanford University Press: Stanford.

7
Facing the Image: Towards an Ethics of Seeing

Roy Brand and Amit Pinchevski

> – Suppose that there is a kind of vision which is not like ordinary vision, but a vision of itself and of other sorts of vision, and of the defect of them, which in seeing sees no colour, but only itself and other sorts of vision: Do you think that there is such a kind of vision?
>
> – Certainly not.
>
> Plato, *Charmides*

In a dialogue that concerns moderation and self-knowledge, Plato suggests that there could be a way of seeing that does not observe the object but focuses on our ways of seeing it. More accurately, Plato seems to suggest a vision of vision itself, a way of facing that makes what is seen into a mirror that returns the vision to itself. At the centre of the following discussion is the duality of facing the image: an image that we face and an image that faces back at us. We usually look at images for what they are, and examine what they represent or how they affect us. But we can also make the image look back by describing its capacity to awaken in us a way of seeing that is more reflexive, that places us as the agents of sight and hence as implicated by what we see.

It is customary to criticize images as promoting an attitude of detached observation. Our photographic culture and the proliferation of images everywhere seem to create a sense of passivity or frustration in the face of the represented. Can we learn to look otherwise, or can we describe images that function like a face – that look back at us? And how can we describe the ways in which an image addresses us as if it were a face? These questions are informed by the philosophy of Emmanuel Lévinas, and their trajectory leads to engagements with corresponding questions raised by Roland Barthes, Judith Butler and Giorgio Agamben.

Lévinas proposed the concept of the 'face' to describe the way alterity appears and is approached beyond and despite its appearance and representation. In what follows, we consider what might be called a Lévinasian perspective on photography: the way the photographed face might not only appear but also address, and hence make an ethical claim in and through mediated form.

Performative iconoclasm

In *Precarious Life*, Judith Butler (2006) takes up Levinas's ethics of the Other to bear specifically on media's use of the figure of the face. Her discussion takes issue with the way humanization and dehumanization are often linked with the question of representation. The intuitive claim is that those who gain representation, especially self-representation, have a better chance of being recognized and humanized, while those who suffer from misrepresentation or under-representation might not be recognized, let alone recognized as human. Following her reading in Lévinas, Butler unsettles the intuitive relationship between representation and humanization, claiming that 'personification does not always humanize... personification sometimes performs its own dehumanization' (p. 141). At issue here are the ways in which the media produce the face as a marker of evil – the faces of bin Laden, Arafat or Saddam Hussein, which are all framed as faces devoid of humanity. Such forms of personification devoid of humanity are widespread. For example, the bare faces of Muslim women were foregrounded in US media as a banner of newly found liberty, a face that celebrates the victory of American cultural assumptions but conceals the suffering and agony of war, and in that respect effaces the human. According to Butler, these and other images tend to suspend the precariousness of life, the fragility exposed by the face of the Other. Rather than expressions of the human, these images are 'the spoils of war and the target of war' (p. 143). If the Lévinasian idea of the face is of an otherness that exceeds representation, the faces marshalled on the media are representations that defeat otherness, that efface precisely what is human in the face – that is, its irreducibility to representation.

Butler proceeds to consider the conditions of possibility for the face to appear as bearing an ethical demand:

> For Lévinas, then, the human is not *represented by* the face. Rather, the human is indirectly affirmed in that very disjunction that makes representation impossible, and this disjunction is conveyed in the

impossible representation. For representation to convey the human, then, representation must not only fail, but it must *show* its failure. There is something unrepresentable that we nevertheless seek to represent, and that paradox must be retained in the representation we give. (p. 144)

Thus according to Butler, for representation to carry and convey the ethical mark of the face, it must somehow undo itself, not simply by failing to capture its referent but by performing that failure. Put differently, for the face to appear as what exceeds any representation, it must somehow display how it destroys its representation. The face appears beyond any form of containment, thereby revealing the human precisely as what surpasses any attempt to confine the human in an image. Representing the human, along with Butler, would be possible only by means of a performative iconoclasm, which serves to make manifest the impossibility of manifestation. This gestural act operates along the lines of the Kantian sublime: it is the failure of representation itself that invokes the idea that there is the unrepresentable. Performative failure showcases the paradox of representation: its 'success' is achieved by displaying its 'failure'.

Butler has been able to demonstrate the implication of Lévinas's ethics outside the realm of the face-to-face, where it is usually placed, while importantly rethinking, through Lévinasian philosophy, the relationship between representation and humanization. However, in highlighting performative failure as the condition of possibility for the face's signification, Butler misses the complexity of Lévinas's reflection on the face. Her reading seems to implicitly assume a divorce between the Other and its image, as if the Other exists independently and outside the realm of appearance – and comes to appear only by destroying its appearance. In the following we attempt to draw attention to a more complex and nuanced understating of the concept of the face as drawn from Lévinas. Following this reading, we propose the face as the locus of two incompatible yet necessary dimensions – image and address – and claim that it is precisely through this incompatibility that the face issues a demand, which is viable both ethically and visually.

Suspicion about appearances is undoubtedly a common theme in Lévinas's philosophy (Jay 1994; Keenan 2011; Van de Vall 2003). Indeed, it is possible to detect in Lévinas's writing a consistent doubt and distrust in sight, image and representation. His critique of Western philosophy can be read as a critique of the Enlightenment and of rationalism, a critique directed against the ethos of 'bringing to light' or of 'rendering visible'. Thus reading Lévinas as taking the Second Commandment – prohibiting graven images – to its ultimate severity is the typical, orthodox approach to his work. However, recent interpretations suggest a more complex discussion of his treatment of the visible (Davis 1993; Taylor 2006; Vasseleu 1998). According to these and other accounts, there is in Lévinas's thought an integral and constitutive tension between alterity and its incarnation, a tension marking not only their incommensurability but also their profound interdependency. Since full explication of this tension is beyond the scope of the present discussion, we would suffice with following only one thread which concerns the visibility and invisibility of the face.

While being critical of appearances, Lévinas often resorts to visual terms in order to explicate the relation to the Other. This apparently paradoxical approach – describing that which is not properly visible in terms of the visible – serves Lévinas in implicating vision with an ethical sensibility. As he writes, 'ethics is an optics. But it is a "vision" without image, bereft of the synoptic and totalizing objectifying virtues of vision' (Lévinas 1961/1988: 23). Recasting vision away from the imperial, panoptic gaze seeking possession of its object, Lévinas seems to suggest a radically different way of seeing – seeing without object identification, seeing through what is seen; or better, not seeing the seen so as to see the unseen. This kind of seeing is not properly ocular: the eye does not merely watch, it is an 'eye that listens' (Lévinas 1974/1998: 31). By confounding the optical and aural, Lévinas ascribes seeing with attributes not normally assigned to the realm of vision: passivity, sensitivity, duration and responsiveness. The eye is therefore not only a lens but also a cornea, not only the source of gaze but also the interface of address.

Face and address

The word 'face' reveals a conceptual duality. As a noun, it connotes not only the physiognomic appearance but also, and more generally, frontage, façade or surface. As a verb, it connotes standing opposite, in front of, but also the act of confronting, encountering and contending with, as well as accepting, admitting and acknowledging. Derived from Old French, its Latin source, *facie* ('appearance', 'form'), is probably related to *facere* ('to make', 'to do'). The French *visage* comes from *vis* (related to *vivre*, 'to see') and is the source of *vis-à-vis*, meaning both face-to-face and in relation to; its Latin root *videre* is found in many words relating to sight ('vision', 'view', 'visitation' and 'voyeur'). In Greek the word *prosopon* (literally, 'what stands before the eyes') means both 'face' and 'person' and is akin to *prosopopoiia*, 'the putting of speeches into the mouths of others'. Related to *prosopon* is the Latin *persona*, which captures most figuratively the face's internal split, denoting a 'facial mask' but also the composite *per-sonare*, 'to sound through', as in a mask through (*per*) which resounds (*sonare*) the voice of the actor. In Hebrew the word for face is *panim*, which shares the same root with *pniya*, 'to turn towards so as to address'. These semantic variations serve to demonstrate the double-faced nature of the face: a concept that includes both an appearance and a relation with what shows itself through the appearance. For the face upholds an internal split: one side of the face is an image, semblance, surface; the other side is relation, interaction, interface. One side is tied to the realm of appearance and as such is amenable to representation, reproduction and dissemination; the other is fixed in the face-to-face and the here-and-now, singular, unrepeatable, temporal and dialogical. The face carries the incommensurability of singularity and duplication, of difference and repetition, of a unique individuality and a universal humanity. Like Janus's head, the two sides face opposite directions but are inextricably linked.

Lévinas's choice of a concept so graphic and visual such as the face to signify the elusiveness of the Other's alterity is already telling of the inherent contradiction within face, already betrays its double-face. An often cited description of the face from *Totality and Infinity* (1961/1988) reads: 'The way in which the other presents himself, exceeding *the idea of the other in me*, we here call the face...The face of the Other at each moment destroys and overflows the plastic image it leaves me.' Here the face is cast as that which transcends what is necessarily plastic in appearance, reiterating Lévinas's choice in a concept that simultaneously connotes what is first encountered in the Other and what escapes the self's grasp of the Other. But within the face there teems the inexorable tension between what is seen and what forever remains out of sight. Hence the Other is not pure transcendence defying incarnation and form – the Other has a corporeal existence, a concrete appearance, a 'plastic image'. That the Other has an image is not inimical to his or her own transcendence; the transcendence is not of the face but immanent to the face. It is through and beyond its image that the face makes its ethical claim: 'Thou shall not kill.'

And yet the face does not ultimately manifest itself by its visible qualities, even if we understand the visible in the Lévinasian sense of sensitivity and responsiveness. Its primary modality is that of expression: the face expresses itself, it addresses, as Lévinas states: 'Face and discourse are tied. The face speaks. It speaks, and it is in this that it renders possible and begins all discourse' (Lévinas 1985: 87). The face does not merely resist its image; its resistance is actualized in addressing, which is how it comes to signify through and beyond its image. It is in this sense that face and address are linked: the face addresses in facing, the face faces by addressing. To quote Lévinas again, 'The face, still a thing among things, breaks through the form that nevertheless delimits it. This means concretely: the face speaks to me and thereby invites me to a relation incommensurable with a power exercised, be it enjoyment or knowledge' (1961/1988: 198). The face calls for a relation other than appropriation or exploitation. Indeed, it calls to be seen otherwise, seen but not completely grasped in seeing. In facing, the face addresses itself, exposed, as alterity that subverts representation, and as singularity that underpins universality.

Thus neither properly image nor properly speech, the face appears by not appearing completely, emerging precisely through the gap between seen and unseen; likewise the face speaks beyond mere words, by approaching through speech. The face retains an excess that is convertible neither to sight nor to sound. What the face exposes is exposure itself, and what the face addresses is addressability itself. One finds oneself taken by the face, called to responsibility, even if one turns away from it, for turning away already presupposes that there is someone to be shunned. The face has a hold, even if it does not have the power to hold: 'I cannot escape it in its forsaken nakedness, which glimmers through the fissures that crack the mask of the personage or his wrinkled skin, in his "with no recourse," which we hear as cries already cried out toward God, without voice or thematization' (Lévinas 1998: 71).

In a late interview, 'On Obliteration', Lévinas commented on a series of human sculptures, some of which had obliterated faces:

> there are different ways of being a face. Without mouth, eyes or nose, an arm or a hand by Rodin is already a face. But the napes of the necks of those people who wait in line at the entrance gate of the Lubyanka prison in Moscow – in order to deliver letters or packages to parents or friends arrested by the GPU, as we find in Vasily Grossman's *Life and Destiny* – those napes which still express anguish, anxiety and tears to the people who see them, are obliterated faces, though in a very different manner.
>
> Lévinas (1989: 38)

This passage demonstrates the complexity of Lévinas's thinking of the face. Rather than the face-to-face, here Lévinas entertains the possibility that the face may have other manifestations, including artistic representations, such as a sculpted hand or a literary portrait of napes waiting in line. To be sure, Lévinas is still reluctant to consider the work of art as containing a face per se – that threshold is never crossed – yet there are arguably some works that bear something of the face's signature, something of its inspiration, even if in the form of its obliteration. Indeed, the negative condition – that is, what effaces or obliterates the face and bars it from facing – is more easily approached conceptually and perhaps also aesthetically. This is because the dimension of address can never be properly thematized and represented, for if it were it would no longer be an address but a representation of an address. It must therefore retain its alterity in the event of its appearance, which is what Lévinas calls 'epiphany'. But this does not mean that the face is beyond the visual. The face calls for a seeing rather than looking, the difference between the two being that seeing is always conscious of its action, seeing itself in seeing; looking, on the other hand, is a passive visual encounter, a gaze that is forgetful about itself.

Face and trace

Roland Barthes (1981) famously distinguished between the studium and the punctum of photographed portraits. The studium is the informative element, the aboutness of the photograph, which is always culturally determined. It serves a function: 'to inform, to represent, to cause to signify, to provoke desire' (p. 28). The punctum disrupts the studium; it is the contingent and disharmonious element that stabs and punctures: 'A photograph's punctum is that accident which pricks me' (p. 27). While one studies the photograph in order to access its studium, one is taken by, even taken aback by, the punctum: 'it is the element which rises from the scene, shoots out like an arrow, and pierces me' (p. 26). The punctum manifests itself as the detail that stands out and reaches out, or, as Jacques Derrida noted, it is the detail that 'seems to look only at me. Its definition is that it addresses itself to me' (1998: 264). One is addressed by something concrete yet intangible within the photographed referent; moreover, one recognizes oneself as the one seeing precisely by virtue of being addressed. To be sure, it is not the referent itself that addresses but precisely its reproduced trace: the photograph does not bring to us the referent as such, does not present or re-present it. What it brings to us, rather, is a singular moment, a once-only configuration, a contingency, which is capturable only under the conditions of technical reproduction. In other words, it brings to us the singular repeatability (or repeatable singularity) of its referent. And it is only under these conditions that we can be addressed by, let alone conceive of, what Barthes identifies as the punctum.

Later in the book, Barthes develops a second version of the punctum, focusing on the temporal structure of the photograph. What the photograph refers to, what is its photographed referent, is captured by a conjunction of the present and the past: 'it has been here, and yet immediately separated; it has been absolutely, irrefutably present, and yet already deferred' (p. 77). The photograph brings us evidence of presence (evidence in the sense of its Latin root, *evidentem* ('clear' and 'obvious')). The referent has been there to leave its singular mark through the lens and onto the reproduced image, reaching us, to use Susan Sontag's metaphor, like the delayed rays of a star that might be long gone. Hence every photograph brings with it a touch of death, the kind of death that haunts every living moment, the future as well as the past. The punctum comes out most acutely in Barthes's discussion of a picture of a death convict awaiting execution: 'The photograph is as handsome, as the boy: that is the studium. But the punctum is: *he is going to die*. I read at the same time: *This will be* and *this has been*; I observe with horror an anterior future of which death is at stake' (p. 96). Thus the photograph summons a clash between two temporal orders: between past in the present and past in the future – this was, and has been, as is seen now in the picture, but by the time we see it, it is already gone, in the past. The present of the photograph, its 'this has been', announces the collision between past anterior and future anterior. 'Whether or not the subject is already dead,' concludes Barthes, 'every photograph is this catastrophe' (p. 96).

Between developing the two kinds of punctum, Barthes tells about a photograph of his mother he discovered shortly after her death. The photograph shows her as a child with her brother, standing together at the end of a wooden bridge in a glass conservatory. Barthes does not include this photograph in his book, assuming that the reader will not be affected by it: 'at most it would interest your studium: period, clothes, photogeny; but in it, for you, no puncture' (p. 73). As Derrida notes, this intermezzo can be seen as the punctum of the whole text, the punctum of a photograph we never see but somehow reaches us through Barthes's rendering. Yet is the punctum addressing Barthes, interpelating him as its exclusive addressee, not already a form of facing? Moreover, is its referentiality not a special kind of facing, one that is impossible to achieve when facing face-to-face? Barthes is facing his mother otherwise and for the first time: 'During her illness, I nursed her, held the bowl of tea she liked because it was easier to drink from than from a cup; she had become my little girl, uniting for me with that essential child she was in her first photograph' (p. 72). The photograph performs a reversal by which Barthes faces in retrospect his mother as his own child and, having not procreated himself, as the child he never had.

Barthes's speculations on the punctum might be read alongside Lévinas's conception of the face, particularly when understood as a trace. Lévinas conceives the face as emerging from an anterior temporality, one which lacks synchronicity with the present – the time in which things are re-presented. 'A face is a trace of itself, given over to my responsibility, but to which I am wanting and faulty' (Lévinas 1974: 91). The face is never fully present, like Barthes's photo of his mother; it is coming from an impossible temporality, from a past that is 'older' than any past. When Barthes observes his mother at an age before he was born, she is already dead. It is a past that, properly speaking, was never a present and hence cannot be recollected or recalled by memory, cannot be re-presented. This is the time from which the face issues its call to responsibility, its address: always beyond the present, addressing me as failing in my responsibility. Thus the trace, like the face, signifies otherwise, not like a sign that operates within the system alongside other signs but as an originary signification, outside context and rupturing any context.

Following this analysis, we can find a structural similarity between Barthes's punctum and Lévinas's face. The punctum and the face seem to share the same formal structure of both trace and address. This is not to say that the face *is* a punctum or vice versa. Rather, the two have corresponding modalities of signification: something in the photographed face operates as an anterior address, the 'this has been' that pricks and stabs precisely as a trace and only as a trace – a trace of a face; and something in the face stretches out and touches beyond and through the portrait, addressing from behind and before the image. One might object to equating the two temporalities at work here, namely the 'past that was never present' of Lévinas's trace with the 'this has been' of Barthes's punctum. It can be argued that the time of the punctum was at some point a present moment – that is, a moment that existed to be caught by the camera's lens. Yet is it not also the case that such a moment, rather than experienced in the present, is accessible only through its trace, only as a technologically frozen moment? No static moment was ever truly present. We never smiled that way outside the flux of time, and the horse never hovered frozen in mid air. That moment was too fleeting to be fully 'in the present', it passed before it could be experienced as such. In this sense, the photographic moment, the 'this has been' could be said to be 'a past that was never a present,' and at the very least as a moment that is produced as past already in the present.

What is never fully present is precisely what haunts the present. Mythologies and folklore tell us about a past when people were haunted by non-present voices, spirits and ghosts. Nowadays, these stories seem absurd, relics of past civilizations. Yet it seems that in our time images have come to take a similar role, functioning as a contemporary form of haunting. In *Regarding the Pain of Others*, Susan Sontag (2003) makes the following claim: 'Narratives can make us understand. Photographs do something else: they haunt us' (p. 89). Haunting is a form of visitation that is rarely invited; that which haunts is a paradoxical presence, not entirely present and not entirely absent, both seen and unseen, retuning and escaping. Sontag finally calls upon photographs to keep visiting: 'Let the atrocious images haunt us. Even if they are only tokens, and cannot encompass most of the reality to which they refer, they still perform a vital function' (p. 115). The photographed image is the apparition of our age. This haunting is important because it retains the possibility of being addressed by what we cannot fully see or understand. It is as if images look back at us, seeing us seeing, and keep looking even after we have looked away.

Total image

There are images that inflict on us an awareness that goes further than any information we can skim from their surface. They do not simply prompt understanding or compassion but call upon us, or awaken in us, a sense of responsibility. There is a clear sense of uneasiness in the face of these images. We have followed Levinas in calling this ethical dimension that of address, and by analogy sought to extend this logic to a way of looking at images such that the look is returned. Thinkers from Barthes to Butler try to render this tension explicit: Barthes, by adopting a temporal modality that explains the presence of what is absent in the image; Butler, by performing the failure of representation as what suggests its beyond. While acknowledging their motivations, our intention here is to resist interpretation. Facing the image as both image and address, and allowing for the tension between these two forms of seeing, is precisely what constitutes the ethical stance. But there are other, more detrimental, ways of resolving this tension, most callously by eliminating any beyond and ascribing total value to the image. If in Butler and

Barthes the image addresses by virtue of what it lacks, the more regular use of images nowadays produces them as fully real, as if touching and embodying the event in the flesh. This form of positive dogmatism not only misses but altogether precludes the ethics of facing the image.

Giorgio Agamben (1998) has developed the concept of bare life to indicate life devoid of its normative protective shield – that is, life outside the protection of the law, language and society. The notion has its roots in Aristotle's distinction between *zoē*, the life common to all living beings, and *bios*, the life that is proper to humans. Agamben makes use of the concept to underscore the peculiar logic of the political that includes bare life only by way of excluding it. Thus what was traditionally left outside the political order – bare life – reappears on the inside in the form of exception: 'Bare life remains included in politics in the form of exception, that is, as something that is included solely through an exclusion' (p. 11). Agamben provides a few paradigmatic examples of bare life. The most horrifying is the 'muselmann': the name given by the inmates in the Nazi concentration camps to those who were on the verge of death – living corpses, walking dead – whose impossible sight was unbearable even to other inmates. Agamben mentions a film shot in Bergen-Belsen shortly after the camp's liberation in 1945 in which the camera lingers on piles of corpses, but when capturing for a short moment a group of what appears to be muselmanners, the camera quickly turns away, as if unable to stand the picture of the ghostly creatures. What lies at the centre of Agamben's analysis of bare life, then, is an image of an impossible seeing – a paradoxical vision of life as it is bare (cf. Bernstein 2004).

Agamben's analysis steers clear of any engagement with the mechanisms of producing images and has little to say about whether and to what extent the media is also implicated in the modern production of bare life. And yet, not only is Agamben's notion of bare life relevant to analysing contemporary media but it is in the media that we might find a corresponding mechanism of rendering life bare. To an increasing degree, the media today attempt to penetrate life – that is, divulge all its secrets and present it as immediately and utterly legible. Take, for example, television shows like *CSI*: in traditional detective genre, criminal investigation proceeded through interaction and interpretation – that is, through a discursive engagement with suspects, witnesses, bystanders, law officers and so on. In *CSI*, investigation is reduced to the scientific production of evidence, thereby extracting detective work from the social altogether. In this case there is no reason to engage the situation discursively: there is no question of motivation and interpretation, of assumption and procedural achievement of truth. Objectivity is asserted in its most radical form: the evidence is already the proof and the verdict. A similar penetrating procedure is evident in makeover shows, such as *The Swan*, where participants' bodies are shown in their most gruesome, surgical detail. Bodies are nothing but soft tissue brought under the chisel of an apparatus that makes and remakes images. Here, too, the presentation circumvents the person and shortcuts into the flesh, as if transformations can be achieved directly by the manipulation of life, or life as an image. In both cases the fascination is with an image that leaves nothing out of sight, an image that becomes a presenting of facts and which displays life only insofar as it is exposed to unmitigated violence.

It is in such instances that we find the participation of the media in the making of life bare: the abandoning of life through its total exhibition, the exclusion of life precisely through its flagrant exposition. The image of Saddam Hussein's dental examination provides another example of the attempt to penetrate the 'Other': to strip his life bare, a destructive fascination with capturing the 'Other' beyond image, beneath the skin and without the complexities of the face. The enemy is not reduced to a mere mask of evil, as per Butler's analysis, nor is it made into a symbol; here the enemy is broken into and examined as bare life. This form of representation intensifies the image so that it becomes life outside the human order – biological life in itself. It is in this respect that the media participates in the attempt to capture bare life, precisely to capture life as bare. Such is the impossible image of life without death, of life without image, hence the repetition of such scenes over and over again: a televized 'repetition compulsion', acting out the impossibility of seeing through the incessant broadcasting of pictures. It is the fascination with rendering life visible without the burdens of representation – a promise that is as captivating as it is crippling.

It now appears that we have come full circle: an uncanny thread seems to run through Butler's account on the face, Agamben's account of bare life, and also some of the media's current fascination with images of horror and violence. Implicit in all of this is a radical divorce between the face's two faces: image and address. There are different modalities to this divorce: opting for pure address without an image or for a total image that lays life bare. The disambiguation of the face drains its potential to invoke ethical engagement.

This is of particular significance with respect to recent discussion about 'distant suffering' – the mediated suffering of individuals and collectives from Third World countries as represented to television audiences in the West. Integral to this moral situation is the inability to act directly to alleviate suffering, hence the opening for a politics of pity, which replaces shame and guilt for the inability to actively engage with what is seen (Boltanski 1999). Also integral to this condition is fixating the image of the Other as sufferer, making suffering the ultimate predicate of the distant Other. The Other is visualized as the picture of suffering. If for Butler the media dehumanize the face by using it as a marker of evil (bin Laden's face as the face of terror, etc.), we might find a parallel form of dehumanization in the media's use of the face as a marker of pain and suffering. In both cases the image is stripped of the possibility of an autonomous address. While in the case of evil we are expected to abhor the face, in the case of suffering we are expected to feel for it. The media's reduction of the face transports us to a domain where a transcendental demand is heard – to pity the Other – a demand that sidetracks or outtakes the address. Our empathy is increased in proportion with our helplessness, and it seems that the less we can do, the more intensely we feel. But this almost pornographic revelation of the pain of the Other leaves us without resources. The total image is too real, too shocking or too mesmerizing. Its call is not an address that awakens us but a silent shout that captivates and cripples us.

It is customary to refer to morality rather than ethics in cases where the demand is emanating from a purely transcendent source. Morality is about what one should do in all cases irrespective of his/her concrete life circumstances. The moral law – for example, in Kant – binds categorically, which means that it legislates over all rational beings in all instances and for eternity. Ethics, on the other hand, traditionally concerns the 'good life' – that is, the life that is at each and every moment my own. Following this distinction it is possible to suggest that the double reduction of the face into *either* pure address *or* total image ends up in a curious situation where the moral claim is elevated at the same time as the ethical claim diminishes. And if the media is a principle site for the divorce between image and address, it is possible to speculate whether and to what extent the media's engagement with the face tends to over-moralize and de-ethicize such representations. The difficult duality of the face is indeed what makes ethics so hard to maintain, both in theory and in practice. It may be that this inherent ambiguity is what the media finds hard to tolerate; the same ambiguity that those who opt for pure address are tempted to transcend. But, to paraphrase Kant's famous assertion, an image without an address is blind, and an address without an image is empty. It is within this incompatibility and irresolvable tension, between the two faces of the face, that a new perspective for an ethics of representation awaits further elaboration.

References

Agamben, G. (1998) *Homo Sacer: Sovereign Power and Bare Life*. Stanford: Stanford University Press.

Bernstein, J. M. (2004) 'Bare Life, Bearing Witness: Auschwitz and the Pornography of Horror', *Parallax* 10(1): 2–16.

Boltanski, L. (1999) *Distant Suffering: Morality, Media and Politics*. Cambridge: Cambridge University Press.

Butler, J. (2006) *Precarious Life: The Powers of Mourning and Violence*. New York: Verso.

Davis, P. (1993) 'The Face and the Caress: Levinas's Ethical Alterations of Sensibility', in David Michael Levin (ed.) *Modernity and the Hegemony of Vision*, 252–272. Berkley and Los Angeles: University of California Press.

Derrida, J. (1998) 'The Deaths of Roland Barthes', in Hugh J. Silverman (ed.) *Philosophy and Non-Philosophy Since Merleau-Ponty*, 259–297. New York: Routledge.

Jay, M. (1994) *Downcast Eyes: The Denigration of Vision in Twentieth-Century French Thought*. Berkley and Los Angeles: University of California Press.

Keenan, H. (2011) 'Facing Images After Lévinas', *Angelaki,* 16(1): 143–159.

Lévinas, E. (1961/1988) *Totality and Infinity*. Pittsburgh, PA: Duquesne University Press.

Lévinas, E. (1974/1998) *Otherwise than Being, Or Beyond Essence*. Pittsburgh, PA: Duquesne University Press.

Lévinas, E. (1985) *Ethics and Infinity*. Pittsburgh, PA: Duquesne University Press.

Lévinas, E. (1989) 'On Obliteration', *Art & Text*, 33 (Winter): 30–41.

Lévinas, E. (1998) *Of God Who Come to Mind*. Stanford, CA: Stanford University Press.

Sontag, S. (2003) *Regarding the Pain of Others*. New York: Farrar Straus and Giroux.

Taylor, C. (2006) 'Hard, Dry Eyes and Eyes that Weep: Vision and Ethics in Levinas and Derrida', *Postmodern Culture*, 16(2), http://muse.jhu.edu/journals/pmc/v016/16.2taylor.html.

Van de Vall, R. (2003) 'Touching the Face: The Ethics of Visuality between Levinas and Rembrandt Self-Portrait', in Claire Farago and Robert Zwijnenberg (eds.) *Compelling Visuality: The Works of Art in and out of History*, 93–111. Minnesota, MN: University of Minnesota Press.

Vasseleu, C. (1998) *Textures of Light: Vision and Touch in Irigary, Levinas and Merleau-Ponty.* London and New York: Routledge.

8
The Predicament of (Journalism) Ethics as Seen in the About-to-Die Image: Lévinas's Subjunctive Mood and the Third

Piotr M. Szpunar

Entrance

Mohammed Bouazizi was an unemployed Tunisian youth who attempted to earn some money by selling fruit on the streets of Sidi Bouzid. Lacking a permit, he was repeatedly targeted by police, who would confiscate his produce. On 17 December 2010, after a series of such incidents, the cumulative humiliation led Bouazizi to set himself ablaze. His final days in hospital were captured in a photo (Figure 8.1) taken and released by the Ben Ali government, the very government ousted by a movement which used Bouazizi's sacrificial act to mobilize Tunisians. The image presents Bouazizi bandaged from head to toe with only one visible opening for a ventilator, one of several machines keeping him alive. At the foot of the hospital bed stands the then Tunisian president, Zine El Abdine Ben Ali, flanked by doctors and other political figures. This image is not one of death but one in which Bouazizi is about to die – the text that accompanied the image often explicitly stated the fact of his death. This particular type of image, the 'about-to-die image', which implies what could be rather than what is (Zelizer 2010), highlights well the nature and predicament of operationalizing a journalism ethics steeped in Lévinasian philosophy (Figure 8.1).

In Lévinas's discussion of ethics as pertaining to a complex social environment, journalists were given a crucial if not fundamental role:

> you know the prophets of the Bible, they come and say to the king that his method of dispensing justice is wrong. The prophet doesn't

do this in a clandestine way: he comes before the king and he tells him. In the liberal state, it's the press, the poets, the writers who fulfil this role.

Lévinas and Mortley (1991: 19)

However, applying Lévinas's 'first philosophy' in service of a journalism ethics, while maintaining the 'essence' of Lévinasian ethics, is no straightforward task. His work must be read against the Other. This involves positing the basic ethical relation as triangular rather than dyadic (I–Other is replaced by I–Other–Third), thus directing my responsibility to and for the Third, a responsibility that, while established passively, invites and requires action. Such a reading highlights the predicament of ethical action in a complex social environment characterized by triangular relations: an ethical action to and for the Third is carried out at the expense of the Other, and this very distinction is characterized by uncertainty and risk. Ultimately, these considerations take the subjunctive elements of Lévinasian philosophy (i.e. a past so past it is irrecoverable; an absolute responsibility that remains even if it

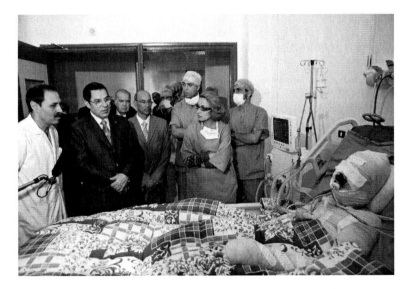

Figure 8.1   Former Tunisian President Zine El-Abidine Ben Ali (second left) visits Mohamed Al Bouazzizi (right) at the hospital in Ben Arous near Tunis on December 28, 2010. Source: Handout from Tunisian Presidency of Zine El-Abidine Ben Ali
Source: Getty/AFP.

is impossible to fulfil) and turn them towards the future, establishing an ethics of position rather than content. Using the about-to-die image not as an example of an ethical image but as an illustration of the theoretical and operational issues of journalism ethics, this chapter provides a journalism ethics that is concerned with opening up spaces in which the Third can 'speak' and maintaining an environment in which meaning cannot be consolidated. In other words, the ethics here seeks to establish a community of interruption concerned not with, in the first instance, prosecution or diagnosis but with the next moment.

Responsibility to and for the Other?

The Other is the centre of Lévinas's ethical universe. I am commanded to be responsible to the Other 'without deliberation, and without the compulsion of truths in which commitments arise, without certainty' (Lévinas 1998, 120) and in a way that exceeds rather than simply meets social norms (Pinchevski 2005a: 74): 'to-be-for-another . . . is to take the bread out of one's own mouth, to nourish the hunger of another with one's own fasting' (Lévinas 1998: 56). This responsibility is 'unlimited' (10) and does not depend on the presence of, or my desire for, reciprocity; 'reciprocity is his affair' (Lévinas and Nemo 1985, 98). Lévinas states this asymmetrical relation another way: 'Each of us is guilty before everyone for everyone, and I more than the others' (Dostoyevsky cited in Lévinas 1998: 146).

This responsibility stems from an encounter in a past so past it is irrecoverable (Lévinas 1998); a relation 'beyond' 'the Said' – the material language that upholds the signifier, signified, referent relationship and 'proclaims and establishes "this as that" ' (Lévinas 1998: 35). In this experience – one that is a priori to any experience (Lingis 1998: xxviii) – I encounter the Other in her radical alterity and thus acquire my subjectivity. Lévinas asks: 'Where is my uniqueness? At the moment when I am responsible for the other I am unique' (Lévinas and Poirié 2001: 66). This foundational alterity cannot be thematized in the Said (Lévinas 1998: 3, 24; Lévinas 1969: 194). This subjection to the Other 'beyond essence' is what makes the Other our primary ethical concern and because the difference between me and the Other is irreducible (Pinchevski 2005a) the 'Other is not a mere object to be subsumed under one of my categories and given a place in my world' (Wild 1969, 13: Introduction to *Totality and Infinity*).

This relation 'beyond' material language (the Said) is the basis for Lévinas' (1969) ethics as 'first philosophy' (304); an ethics that is preontological, anterior to intuition and reason, and precedes any 'existential base' (Lévinas and Nemo 1985: 95). However, one can 'experience' this in a world dominated by the Said because, for Lévinas, language cannot be reduced to the Said. There exists what he refers to as 'the Saying', that which goes beyond or overflows the thematization of the Said (Lévinas 1998: 37; Lévinas, 1969: 51); it is a modality of approach, a proposition (Pinchevski 2005a: 81–82) that does not 'consist in giving signs' (Lévinas 1998: 48). This approach is found in the 'face' of the Other. This face is itself not physical but straightaway ethical, though it does appear in an ever-unfaithful form in the Said (Lévinas and Nemo 1985: 85–86). This provocation establishes my responsibility not through what it states but through 'the very fact of its address' (Pinchevski 2005a: 77). The 'face' of Mohammed Bouazizi is represented in the Said (i.e. made plastic through its representation in image and text) – analogously, his physical face is in bandages – and yet it 'speaks' to us, it unsettles the reader, disrupting her complacency in being.[1] This is precisely the 'essence of Lévinasian ethics in a world dominated by and dependent on the Said: 'Ethics does not have an essence, its "essence," so to speak, is precisely not to have an essence, to unsettle essences…Ethics is precisely ethics by disturbing the complacency of being' (Cohen 1985: 10; Introduction to *Ethics and Infinity*). Thus 'interruption' (Pinchevski 2005a; 2005b) – the puncturing of the Said by the Saying – is central to ethics. Ethical action is thus established through renouncing all imperatives 'except for the two words ending Jacques Derrida's text on Lévinas: "Interrupt me"' (Derrida 1991, cited in Pinchevski 2005a: 101). Thus ethics in this formulation requires us to be open to interruption, to be called out of our complacency, and about-to-die images, such as the Bouazizi photograph, are powerful examples of this.

Reading Lévinas against the Other

The above imperative captures the radical passivity of Lévinas's responsibility. For Lévinas the 'approach of the other is an initiative I undergo. I am passive in regard to it' (Lingis 1998: xxiii, 62). One is commanded by the Other, and thus responsibility is not an act of intent.[2] Using Babenco's *Kiss of the Spider Woman*, Zizek (2005) provides a cogent starting-point in illustrating the problematic nature of applying an absolute and passive ethics to society:

A high Gestapo officer explains to his French mistress the inner truth of the Nazis, how they are guided in what may appear brutal military interventions by an inner vision of breathtaking goodness. We never learn in what, exactly, this inner truth and goodness consist; all that matters is this purely formal gesture of asserting that things are not what they seem (brutal occupation and terror), that there is an inner ethical truth which redeems them.

(Zizek 2005: 184)

In this scenario the passive imperative and an absolute responsibility to an Other does little to foster ethical action. The problem lies in the above imperative's focus on a dyadic relationship (the I–Other relation) characterized by passivity. In order to avoid the pitfalls that the above parable intimates, two conceptual manoeuvres are required. First, the Third – the Other's Other – must be conceptualized as 'always-already here'. Second, an active imperative, one dependent on its passive counterpart, must be flushed out of Lévinasian responsibility and its consequences considered.

The Third is not a straightforward concept in Lévinas's work (Szpunar 2012). Here the Third is not the 'thirdness' that appears in the face of the Other (i.e. humanity; see Lévinas 1969) but rather an individual who 'is other than the neighbor, but also another neighbor, and also a neighbor of the other, and not simply his fellow' (Lévinas 1998: 150, 157; see also Szpunar 2012). This Third is, however, secondary in Lévinas's philosophy. Lévinas states that the Third calls into question one's unlimited responsibility to the Other and transports us into the realm of the Said (Lévinas 1998; Pinchevski 2005a; Simmons 1999). She 'enters' or 'troubles' the I–Other relation and 'introduces' problems. Though Lévinas admits that 'We are not a pair, alone in the world, but at least three', he goes on to posit this as 'Two plus a third' (Robbins 2001: 193) – that is, he reasserts 'that everything begins as if we were only two' (Lévinas et al. 1988, 170). Zizek (2005) counters this and claims that the primary ethical act requires us to acknowledge the Third as 'always-already here'[3]: 'Instead of pairs, there are at least triangles' (Dayan 2007: 120). This ethical situation is captured in the Bouazizi image. The relation is fundamentally triangular: I–Other–Third or, specifically, reader–Ben Ali–Bouazizi.

Zizek (2005), however, does not make the distinction between the temporality of ethics characterized by the I–Other relation (the primary sensation of subjectivity) and the temporality of justice characterized by the social I–Other–Third relation. Therefore the Third, as in Lévinas's work, remains the central concern of justice rather than ethics. However, Lévinas can be read against the Other even in the temporality of ethics. His focus on a dyadic relation in the preontological 'experience' of subjectivity is largely arbitrary apart from Western philosophy's long tradition of employing dualisms. Lévinas is read against the Other by positing the ethical relation as triangular; a move that maintains his ideas concerning responsibility, difference, passivity and, most importantly, the essence of his ethics.

In such a triangular ethical relation, all three parties are irreducibly different and the difference between the parties is not established by reason or knowledge; it is anterior to the Said. There is no reason to suppose that if we accept Lévinas's I–Other distinction as an irreducible difference, this move to add a third is implausible or counter to other fundamental Lévinasian concepts. In this experience I am not approached by the Other but by the Third – why this is not simply a semantic distinction I will deal with below. I remain passive, and this experience prior to all experience remains an 'initiative that I undergo'. However, in the Third's approach, that which establishes the I's absolute responsibility to her, the Other is left out. This exclusion is not one dependent on knowledge, thematization or material language; rather, it is a fundamental and inextricable dimension of the Third's approach. This exclusion does not suggest intent on the part of the I; the approach remains the primary sensation of subjectivity but one that includes this dimension of exclusion.

Babenco's parable illustrates this relation – albeit in a different temporality – and the exclusive dimension within it. Subsequently, it highlights that the passive imperative is inadequate for fostering ethical action in a social situation; one must act and, thus, there is a need for an active imperative. In fact, this active imperative is both implied in the passive and requires it. Lévinas hints at this when he states: 'I am another for others' (Lévinas 1998: 158) who commands (Lévinas 1969) and who is responsible for the Other's responsibility (Lévinas and Nemo 1985). Responsibility for the Third, established passively, subsequently requires one to act – that is, to actively interrupt (Szpunar 2012): the prophet must tell the King that he is wrong. This triangular relation acknowledges that just as the about-to-die image requires the reader to 'complete' the image (Zelizer 2010), the face of the Third, while I am passively disrupted by it, requires me to act, and this action often requires me to step over the Other, to smash the face of the Other – the French mistress must smash the 'face' of the Gestapo officer.

Counter to Lévinas, it is this need for action that brings us into the realm of the Said rather than the figure of the Third. The simple presence of the Third does not require judgement, but action does, and this action requires us to distinguish parties from one another, something that can only be done within the Said. In Babenco's scenario above, one requires knowledge and signification to distinguish the Third (the Jewish people) from the Other (the Nazis) in order to act ethically; this need for distinction does not emerge from the mere presence of a third party, but from the I's need to fulfil its responsibility to the Third, who has interrupted its complacency in being. The resulting ethical act requires us to 'smash' the face of the Other. The face of Bouazizi interrupts me and calls me to ethical responsibility that requires me to step over the Other (Ben Ali); the reader must smash the face of Ben Ali for Bouazizi.

This reconceptualization is consequential. Positioning responsibility as to and for the Third is not simply semantic because it acknowledges the exclusionary dimension of ethics and draws out a schadenfreude-esque quality in ethical action. Counter Lévinas's conceptualization of justice as a primary violence, this violence is now hinted at in the preontological ethical relation and is a part of the I's subjectivity. Moreover, in the necessary act of ethics – which stems form the passive imperative and brings us into the Said – this violence is illustrated: the ethical action, par excellence, requires one to step over or smash the face of the Other, for the Third, adding a new dimension to Lévinas's claim that we are all guilty.

Journalism ethics: From essence to practice

The essence of ethics continues to be the disruption of essences, interrupting one's complacency in being (Lévinas 1998: 14). However, this essence now includes the admission that this interruption is done at the expense of another. Moreover, ethical interruption is no longer only characterized by a passive openness to interruption but includes an imperative to actively interrupt. In a complex social environment, populated by a multitude of Others (whose relations to one another are varied), journalism is often our only avenue through which to come into proximity (in the Lévinasian sense) with far-off faceless Thirds. In such a milieu, one couched and dependent on the Said, journalistic practice is central to the ethical effort of reducing 'the said to the saying' (Lingis 1998: xxxvii). Journalism ethics here is centred on actively living this effort. Thus the problem of operationalizing the ethics outlined above for journalistic practice is centred on the problem of fostering interruption via Saying, on creating a space in which the face of the Third can speak.

To operationalize this ethics, the concept of the Said must be pluralized. While Lévinas refers to the Said as material language, he also conceptualizes it as something produced by the state, medicine and philosophy (Pinchevski 2005a: 86). In this sense it is clear that to the Said purported by these institutions there are obvious challengers. While a Said cannot be faithful to an addressing face, the use of another Said – that is, a different way of speaking – while also unfaithful to any addressing face, can play the role of Saying insofar that it interrupts the original Said. A Said here does not act as a face of the Third. It is only in the subsequent fissure or tension caused by this interruption, this collision of Saids, which provides a space or moment where the face of the Third may make an entry. Applied to media that use a combination of image and text, the ethical act formulated here is one of creating a space for the Third's face to speak, in fostering interruption. Consequently, neither a single image nor a text is conceptualized as bearing the 'face' of the Third; rather this face, that which interrupts me, emerges only from the fissure caused by using one Said to interrupt another. While both image and text independently contain a potential for fostering interruption, the interest here is the use of both concurrently in journalistic practice to convey a Said and create a fissure.

The Ben Ali government initially issued the Bouazizi image in an attempt to stave off dissent by consolidating the meaning of Bouazizi's self-immolation and denying that there was a Third-Other distinction to be made. The image, however, was quickly reappropriated and couched in another Said: one which posited Bouazizi as a martyr and as the catalyst for the Jasmine Revolution (in both English and Arabic-language news media and blogs). This usage established a Third–Other distinction and interrupted the Said purported by the Ben Ali government. In this process the journalist actively interrupts for the Third and does so at the expense of another. Here the journalist creates a fissure which facilitates the possibility of the Third coming into proximity with me, the reader/viewer, and calls me to be responsible.

This is a possibility. The potential for fostering interruption is not equal across images or texts, or across combinations of them. This potential depends on the qualities and content of the Said against which images and texts (and the Said they convey) are juxtaposed as well as the openness, position and reading of the reader/viewer. There is no measurement of potentiality or possibility; interruption is an art rather than a science, and one that can fail. Operationalizing the ethics outlined above for journalism is focused on the potentiality of using these modalities of communication in order to actively interrupt a Said, create a fissure and allow for the possibility – a possibility that is never guaranteed – of providing the reader/viewer with the experience of being interrupted by the face of the Third. The very possibility, the very potential of this type of ethical action, lies in the nature of image and text, a nature that is clearly displayed in the about-to-die image.

Zelizer (2010) explains that the about-to-die image portrays 'what could be' rather than 'what is'. Bouazizi is about to die; he is not dead yet. The image is subsequently couched in text, which informs the reader of this fact and fills in what the image leaves out. The Bouazizi image was couched in a discourse that formulated the event surrounding the image as an injustice, one that was a direct consequence of the actions and policies of Ben Ali and his regime. While such images, couched in words, are presented in order to further particular interests – the image above was originally given to the press by the Ben Ali government – they highlight particularly well the inability of any image to be complete. While the subjunctivity of any image is a matter of degree (Zelizer 2010), there is no image, and no text for that matter, that can provide a complete closure of meaning. It is the very fact that there is an opening, an incompleteness that allows for ethical action in a complex social environment. Also, and perhaps counterintuitively, often the more an image is couched in words, the more it is open to interpretation and reappropriation (Zelizer 2010: 174), the more available it is for the practice of interruption. This incompleteness allows the image to be reappropriated in the service of another Said, creating the potential for a space in which the 'face' of the Third can 'speak' to me.

The predicament of ethics

The very source of the possibility of ethical action – that is, the impossibility of closure – is also the source of the predicament of ethics. This predicament comes into focus once the fact that any such engagement with this opening is characterized by emotion, imagination and contingency (Zelizer 2010: 14). Thus the ethical act performed at the expense of the Other begs the question: How does the reader distinguish between the Other and the Third? Lévinas acknowledges this predicament:

> What then are the other and the third party for one another? What have they done to one another? Which passes before the other? The other stands in relationship with the third party, for whom I cannot entirely answer, even if I alone answer, before any question, for my neighbor.
>
> (Lévinas 1998: 157)

The ensuing predicament can be outlined by a series of propositions: if we live in a complex social environment populated by a multitude of Others; and if our experience of interruption – that comes through the active disruption caused by a journalistic practice that utilizes both image and text – which puts us into proximity with the Other's face (in an ever-unfaithful form) is a pure address; and if ethical action in such an environment requires an active response; and if the response that such an image compels is characterized by emotion, imagination and contingency; then distinguishing the Other from the Third is not obvious, nor does it have a single outcome that can be praised by an ethics of journalism. The about-to-die image illustrates this remarkably.

The about-to-die image on its own is ambiguous and 'invitational' (Zelizer 2010: 313). While this openness is what allows for ethical experience, it is an environment that is characterized by contingency. Zelizer (2010: 269) states clearly that 'blending impulses of presumption, possibility, and certainty with a reliance on emotions, the imagination, and contingency', the 'as if', offers a variety of groups and individuals the chance to use an image for their own purposes. In analysing the frame captures of a young Palestinian, Mohammed al-Dura, killed by the Israel Defense Forces in 2000, Zelizer (2010: 202) shows that such images can accommodate diametrically opposed interpretations. The Bouazizi image is no different. After the Jasmine Revolution of 2011unfolded in Tunisia, it may seem obvious to whom we owe our responsibility. However, the point remains that initially, in the fog of a nascent uprising, this is anything but clear. In fact, the Bouazizi image is one released by the Ben Ali government in an attempt to curb dissent – that is, to state that there was no Other–Third distinction to be made. The point is that even though the image was quickly picked up by blogs, news outlets and Tunisians in support for the ouster of Ben Ali, the image itself accommodates both readings. This predicament places the media practitioner in a complex situation characterized by uncertainty. While the Bouazizi image may provide us with an 'obvious' scenario long after the event itself, at the moment this event is happening, when events surrounding it are unfolding, it is never so clear.

The challenge this poses to media practitioners is daunting. The practice of interruption and an openness to being interrupted places any media practitioner in an uncomfortable situation: one of contingency and uncertainty. The status of prophet comes with heavy responsibility. Thus presented here is not an ethics of content but one of position. Key to any media practitioner is a sense of distrust – a distrust of her sources, those she is reporting on, those for whom she is opening up a space to speak (the Third) and even herself (so that she remains open to being interrupted as well). Such distrust should be viewed as vital to a community of interruption; a community in which the journalist states: 'I do not trust you all.' Based on Lacan's idea of the universal and its constitutive exception, Zizek (2005) uses historical examples, such as Nazi ideology, to show 'that universal love for humanity always led to the brutal hatred of the (actually existing) exception, of the enemies of humanity' (183). Consequently, rather than a statement of universal love, only ' "I do not love you all" ... [can be the] foundation of "there is nobody that I do not love" ' (183) as this opens up an environment in which each party must necessarily be permitted to speak – if one does not trust the party who approaches her, this requires that she makes room for others to speak. Thus 'I do not trust all of you' becomes the foundation of 'there is nobody that I do not trust.'[4] This is not objectivism, nor is it a statement of content (of whom one trusts and whom one does not trust). Rather, it is a position of openness and suspicion that requires the journalist to interrupt but also allows for her to be interrupted (the latter requires the former: Lévinas's edict remains). What this ethic does is position the journalist in a way that places upon her an important role in fostering a community of interruption while acknowledging the exclusionary dimension of her ethical actions; often we come face-to-face with others only through the news media, but we come into proximity with one at the expense of another. Given the uncertainty that characterizes this position – in my act for the Third at the expense of the Other, I may err – the environment in which it operates must necessarily remain incomplete. In this milieu, what is fostered above all else is the next moment regardless of how uncertain, ambiguous and risky this next moment may be; in other words, it is a position that requires an environment that maintains the possibility of interruption.

Ethics of the next moment: The subjunctive mood in Lévinas

The ethics outlined above, while reading Lévinas against the Other, maintain key tenets of his ethical philosophy. The Self's subjectivity still originates in a relation; responsibility is maintained; the passive imperative is far from negated as is the '(non)concept' of the face (Pinchevski 2005a: 76, fn 5); there continues to be no guarantee of reciprocity; and most importantly, the ethics above maintains the spirit or 'essence' of Lévinas' ethics – to unsettle essences. Nowhere in his works is Lévinas concerned with an ethics that praises or sanctions particular actions or representations (through image and text); rather, his is an ethics that can be read as being concerned with the 'next moment' (Sheil 2010), an ethics of what 'could be' rather than what is or what 'ought to be'. This becomes evident in tracing the subjunctive mood in Lévinas, and how this mood translates onto the triangular ethical relation and the active imperative that comes out of the passive and brings us into the Said.

Lévinas does not explicitly use the concept of the subjunctive. However, the concepts he utilizes – concepts maintained in positing the fundamental ethical relation as triangular – highlight a subjunctive mood throughout his thought. Lévinas's ethical philosophy, contrary to ontology, does not seek to 'establish the structure of reality by the exploration of "what is"' (Pinchevski 2005a: 72). He formulates ethics as 'otherwise than being', as 'beyond essence' and as anterior to reason. To establish absolute responsibility he posits an 'irrecuperable, unrepresentable' past (Lévinas 1998: 47). This temporality is that primary sensation of subjectivity and highlights what Sheil (2010) refers to as a highly subjunctive mood: 'something appears to be aimed at, but this thing is just as uncertain as the aiming itself... [and] in contrast to ordinary subjunctives which do point to an eventual state of affairs and have some congress with the indicative, highly subjunctive moods... do not' (153–154). Furthermore, once we enter into the Said, into social relations, Lévinas states that the ethical edict of responsibility – 'without deliberation, and without the compulsion of truths in which commitments arise, without certainty' (Lévinas 1998: 120) – remains even if it is impossible to fulfil (Simmons 1999). That is, as stated above, Lévinas stresses that even in a world where we are at least three, 'everything begins as if we were only two' (Lévinas et al. 1988: 170).

Lévinas's thought does lend itself to thinking about living out one's responsibility despite its impossibility – as if it could be. As outlined above, the passive imperative implies an active counterpart. In order for me to fulfil my responsibility to and for the Third, I must act. The focus of ethics here is flipped. The responsibility that stems from an 'irrecoverable past' – but one that we should act on as if it was – subsequently requires us to act (on our responsibility) and this requirement, in turn, refocuses our sights on the future, a future so futuristic that it will never be (see: Sheil, 2010). Just as the subjunctive about-to-die image presents what could be and invites the viewer/reader to fill in the next moment, the subjunctive mood in Lévinas, once the active imperative is acknowledged as central, turns ethics towards the next moment; responsibility invites us to act and then turns us towards a distant horizon – one we cannot clearly make out.

What remains in a philosophy that is not concerned with prosecuting or diagnosing (Sheil 2010: 192) in a world of multiple Others is interruption. In contrast with some readings of Lévinas (e.g. Silverstone 2007), this does not require one to ignore all particularity and attempt to act in an absolute way to an Other, the evils of which both Zizek's use of the *Kiss of the Spider Woman* and an uncritical acceptance of the Bouazizi image as presented by the Ben Ali government highlight well. Rather, ethics is constituted in a dynamic interest in the next moment (Sheil 2010: 134). This focus on an ethical position that fosters interruption and maintains an incomplete environment is made all the more important once the Third is considered as always-already there. Ethics in this formulation acknowledges that such action is uncertain and risky; attempts could fail, errors might be made. Determining who is the Third and who is the Other – whose face you are to smash – is not a science but a precarious art, thus the focus of ethics is necessarily processual. What becomes important is the maintenance of a process that allows for multiple voices and challenges – a community of interruption.[5]

An environment where a Said could be used to interrupt another in service of the face of the Third establishes the 'community of interruption' that Pinchevski's (2005a: 96–100) reading of Lévinas seeks to foster – though one that includes an active ethical imperative alongside the passive of 'interrupt me'. This community of interruption is concerned with maintaining an incomplete environment, preventing any Said from transforming the social world into impermeable plastic. This is especially important given that in my ethical act for the Third at the expense of the Other, I may err. Here ethics takes on a subjunctive quality in that it is concerned with what 'could be' and not 'what is'. My responsibility stems from a past so past that it has never had a present and, because it requires me to act, is directed at a 'future so futuristic that it will never be present' (Sheil, 2010: 154); here ethics lies in fostering the next moment.

No exit

In a world of multiple others, one in which the relations between them are complex and can be characterized by hostility, fraternity, ambivalence, indifference and so on, and one in which we are exposed to Others through media texts and images, any journalistic ethics that can be operationalized is wise to, in its formulation, admit that an ethical act towards one is often done at the expense of another. This is captured by positing the fundamental ethical relation as triangular: I–Other–Third. This places the journalist in a much more complex social environment dominated by material language and yet, as outlined above, there is a way to envision an ethics faithful to the 'essence' of Lévinasian ethics – fostering a 'community of interruption'. If 'all one can do is live this effort to reduce the said to the saying' (Lingis 1998: xxxvii), then to interrupt a Said with another Said, and within the subsequent fissure perhaps allow for the face (of the up-to-then faceless Thirds in the shadows) to make an entry, is perhaps the ethical act par excellence, even if it is done at the expense of another face. This scenario highlights the subjunctive mood of Lévinasian ethics, the focus on the 'could be' and the next moment.

The about-to-die image, 'open, suggestive, porous, generalizable, and ambiguous', and accommodating of oppositional interpretations (Zelizer 2010: 313), highlights the predicament of ethics, the uncertainty of the I–Other–Third relation. It is this very uncertainty that requires an ethics of position rather than content. Interruption, the address of the face of the Third, just as the about-to-die image, invites and coaxes the reader into action. However, this engagement is characterized by imagination, contingency and emotion – precisely what allows it to occur in the first instance – and thus I may err in my ethical action for the Third. Thus what a journalism ethics needs to be concerned with is the maintaining of this openness, with the creation of fissures in which the face of the Third can speak, with the subjunctive next moment, with what 'could be'. This active imperative – to which a passive imperative is central – brings us into the Said and requires one to smash the face of an Other. In this ethics lies a call to politics. Ethics *qua* ethics exists within political action rather than only in a temporality above or beyond it, a political action that not only prevents the consolidation of meaning but actively works to open up spaces in which the ethical experience can emerge in the next moment.

Notes

1. As I will show below the 'bearing of the face' is a more complex phenomenon.
2. The fact that the Self's subjectivity is based in the Other highlights that his relation occurs before intentionality as the Self's experience of the Other is simply in relation ('inter-esse' means here 'between being' or 'relation') (in Robbins 2001, 150); the experience of the Other does not occur because the Self wills it, but rather, is *a priori* to such intentionality.
3. Zizek's critique is not as anti-Lévinasian as he makes it out to be (see: Szpunar 2012).

4. Zizek's posits a triangular relation between love, hate and indifference. While an attractive philosophical approach, in applying this to news media, this 'indifference' comes far too close to being 'Objectivism'. Instead to complete the triangle in which I have placed trust and distrust and to overcome the coldness and 'inactivity' of objectivism, 'openness' provides a fruitful starting-point. It allows for the active imperative highlighted above and acknowledges the impossibility – and ethically undesirability – of indifference.
5. For example, rather than focusing on the content of representation, the focus becomes preventing the consolidation of meaning through representation (see Szpunar 2012).

References

Cohen, R.A. (1985) Translator's Introduction. In *Ethics and Infinity*, Ed. E. Levinas and P. Nemo, 1–15. Pittsburgh, PA: Duquesne University Press.

Dayan, D. (2007) 'On Morality, Distance and the Other: Roger Silverstone's *Media and Morality*'. *International Journal of Communication*, 1: 113–122.

Derrida, J. (1991) Des tours de Babel. In *A Derrida reader*, Ed. P. Kamuf. Translated J. F. Graham. New York: Columbia University Press.

Lévinas, E. (1969) [o.p. 1961] *Totality and Infinity: An Essay on Exteriority*. Translated A. Lingis. Pittsburgh, PA: Duquesne University Press.

Lévinas, E. (1998) [o.p. 1974] *Otherwise Than Being, Or, Beyond Essence*. Translated A. Lingis. Pittsburgh, PA: Duquesne University Press.

Lévinas, E. & Mortley, R. (1991) Emmanuel Lévinas. In *French Philosophers in Conversation*, Ed. R. Mortley. London: Routledge.

Lévinas, E. & Nemo, P. (1985) *Ethics and Infinity*. Translated R.A. Cohen. Pittsburgh, PA: Duquesne University Press.

Lévinas, E. & Poirié, F. (2001) [o.p. 1986] Interview with Francois Poirié. In *Is It Righteous to Be? Interviews with Emmanuel Lévinas*, Ed. J. Robbins, 23–83. Stanford, CA: Stanford University Press.

Lévinas, E., Wright, T., Hughes, P., & Ainley, A. (1988). 'The Paradox of Morality: An Interview with Emmanuel Lévinas', in *The Provocation of Levinas: Rethinking the other*, Ed. R. Bernasconi and D. Wood, 168–180. London: Routledge.

Lingis, A. (1998) Translator's Introduction. In *Otherwise Than Being, Or, Beyond Essence*, Ed. E. Lévinas, xvii–xlv. Pittsburgh, PA: Duquesne University Press.

Pinchevski, A. (2005a) *By Way of Interruption*. Pittsburgh, PA: Duquesne University Press.

Pinchevski, A. (2005b) 'The Ethics of Interruption: Toward a Lévinasian Philosophy of Communication', *Social Semiotics*, 15(2): 211–234.

Robbins, J. (2001) *Is It Righteous to Be? Interviews with Emmanuel Lévinas*. Stanford, CA: Stanford University Press.

Sheil, P. (2010) *Kierkegaard and Lévinas: The Subjunctive Mood*. Farnham: Ashgate.

Silverstone, R. (2007) *Media and Morality: On the Rise of the Mediapolis*. Cambridge: Polity.

Simmons, W.P. (1999) 'The Third: Lévinas' Move from An-archical Ethics to the Realm of Justice and Politics', *Philosophy and Social Criticism*, 25(6): 83–104.

Szpunar, P.M. (2012) 'Journalism Ethics and Lévinas' Third: Interruption in a World of Multiple Others', *Social Semiotics*, 22(3): 275–294.

Wild, J. (1969) Introduction. In *Totality and Infinity: An Essay on Exteriority*, Ed. E. Lévinas, 11–20. Pittsburgh, PA: Duquesne University Press.

Zelizer, B. (2010). *About to Die: How News Images Move the Public*. New York: Oxford University Press.

Zizek, S. (2005) 'Neighbors and Other Monsters: A Plea for Ethical Violence', in *The Neighbor: Three Inquiries in Political Theology*, Ed. S. Zizek, E.L. Santner and K. Reinhard, 134–190. Chicago: University of Chicago Press.

9
Liberal Ethics and the Spectacle of War

Lilie Chouliaraki

War as a paradox of in/communicability

In his moving account of the First World War, Sir Philip Gibbs, war correspondent for the *Daily Telegraph*, describes the difficulty that journalists faced in communicating their battlefield experiences to those back home:

> Those young men who had set out in a spirit of adventure went back to Fleet Street with a queer look in their eyes, unable to write the things they had seen...Because there was no code of words which would convey the picture of that wild agony of peoples, that smashing of all civilised laws, to men and women who still thought of war in terms of heroic pageantry...
>
> (1920: 4)

It is this in/communicability of war that concerns me, here. There is, on the one hand, Gibbs's absence of a whole 'code of words' about war that turns its professional storytellers into 'mute witnesses' of the unspeakable horrors of the battlefield (Hood 2011: 40). And yet, on the other, Gibbs did write about the battlefield, not only as a correspondent but also as an author of five books about the Western Front. Indeed, stories about his war, and others since, abound today: photojournalism, television news, films, poetry, novels, paintings, games and comics are only some of our public practices of storytelling that mundanely confront us with the realities of war. Together they constitute what we may call a 'war imaginary' – a configuration of popular genres through which the war is regularly imagined as a taken-for-granted part of our public life. How, then, might we explain this paradox of in/communicability about war that defines our public life? How can traumatic silence and celebratory eloquence coexist in the war imaginary of modernity?[1]

The paradox of the war imaginary, I argue, reproduces another paradox in the nature of the moral order of modernity. Drawing on the 18th-century culture of sympathy, modernity construed a predominantly humanitarian imaginary, which was based on benevolence and civility and, hence, on the denaturalization of violence as primitive evil – 'a predicament of the past, governed by prejudice, irrationalism ... and considered an illegitimate product of modernity' (Huppauf 1997: 12). While, as I have shown elsewhere, the humanitarian imaginary has been instrumental in establishing an unprecedented culture of solidarity in Western modernity (Chouliaraki 2012), there is a constitutive complicity between humanitarianism and violence that should not be ignored. If anything, violence historically emerges as an inherent dimension of the humanitarian imaginary, both negating and confirming humanity in and through war; in and through 'the deliberate infliction of suffering and death on other people' (Bourke 2008: 370). My focus on war, then, draws attention to a crucial aspect of our public culture that cannot be captured by a focus on the benevolent sensibilities of modernity, and it explores the distinct ways in which violence has been equally instrumental in creating modern moral sensibilities and collective bonds – what Frazer and Hutchings (2011) call 'virtuous violence'.

What the in/communicability of war reflects, in this sense, is more than the muteness of war correspondents. It reflects a deeper tension in the liberal spirit of modernity itself, namely that its defence of humanity can only be achieved by means of inhumanity: 'What conclusions are we to draw,' Howard asks, 'from this melancholic story of the efforts of good men to abolish war, but only succeeding thereby in making it more terrible?' (2008: 130). Eloquently put in this quote, the paradox of liberalism has been explored in Howard's historical account of post-18th-century warfare, where he argues that this paradox consists in the failure of liberalism, a political ideology resting on the vision of perpetual peace, to safeguard its vision without resorting to violence. Following, in particular, the unprecedented 20th-century terrors, war now emerges not as primitive evil, but as integral to modernity – not an interruption but a rearticulation of its ethics of humanity: 'in that very attempt to instrumentalise, indeed universalise, war in pursuit of its global projects of emancipation, the practice of liberal rule itself becomes profoundly shaped by war' (Dillon 2008: 4).

Yet, even if this awareness of the complicity between humanity and inhumanity in liberal modernity emerged in the past 100 years, there are significant differences in the communication of war across time – differences that reflect not only shifting conceptions of warfare but also of humanity, of self and of Other, that the communication of war has historically made available to us (Fussell 1975). If I am interested in the in/communicability of war, then, this is for the sake neither of analysing war as a practice of propaganda nor of exploring how war shapes our collective memory – the two major paradigms of war communication studies. Rather, I am interested in it because if, following Hegel, war is not only what it inhumanely does to people (its instrumental dimension) but also what it imagines people to become as human beings (its existential dimension), then studying war has something important to tell us about historical change in the moral order of modernity.[2] Despite its in/communicability, I argue, war does speak; and, in so doing, it tells us not only about what violence and its agents are like but also about what we should be like. To paraphrase Boltanski (1999), in order to universalize, war becomes eloquent, recognising and discovering itself as emotion and feeling. How do the wars of the past 100 years speak? Which emotion do they mobilize in order to imagine who we should be and how we should think and act? What do they tell us about the ways in which our war imaginary has changed and the kinds of people we are invited to become as a result? It is these questions that I now turn to explore.

It is, in particular, the spectacle of the battlefield as a key moment of in/communication about the war that I focus on. From the multiple spaces of war, it is the battlefield, the site where killing takes place on an unimaginable scale, that becomes the most evident and poignant site for the performances of the war imaginary. In this site the ambivalence of liberal modernity, summed up as it is in the incongruous coexistence of inhumane violence with visions of humanity, is most compellingly enacted. The problem of the in/communicability of war is now grasped neither as silence nor as celebration, but as a struggle of representation over how technologies of killing reconfigure human bodies in the spaces of combative action. It is, I argue, in the course of this struggle that the war imaginary attempts to resolve the impossible tension of liberal modernity, by provisionally reconciling the brutality of death with respect for human life.

Drawing upon iconic photojournalism from the first half of the 20th century (both world wars) and the first decade of the 21st (War on Terror, 2001 to the present), I explore how the staging of the battlefield, in attempting 'to convey the picture of that wild agony of peoples', has variously changed in terms of three key dimensions: technologies, bodies and landscapes. Despite the wealth of visual material that exists on these various 'moments' of battlefield action, my choice of, specifically, iconic imagery draws attention to the enduring, ubiquitous and recurring presence of particular photographs that have, in time, acted as 'symbols of cultural and national myth' and so shaped the war imaginary of the West (Griffin 1999: 123).[3]

Staging the battlefield

The term 'staging' suggests that, despite the claim to objective truth which the professional credibility of photojournalism relies on, the spectacle of war always emerges within specific 'spaces of appearance' – institutionalized sites of spectatorship, where the regulation of visual performance plays an important role in the production of moral imagination.[4] In the case of war propaganda, Butler argues, such regulation applies 'not only on content – certain images of dead bodies in Iraq, for instance, are considered unacceptable for public visual consumption – but on what "can" be heard, read, seen, felt and known' (2006: xx). Breaking from conceptions of aesthetics as apolitical, this approach to the battlefield as 'staged' points to war photojournalism as an aesthetic practice of power, through which the spectacle of combative action is institutionally regulated so as to become morally acceptable for visual consumption – that is, as legitimately representing 'what "can" be heard ... seen ... felt' at specific historical moments.

I therefore approach my first analytical category, the aesthetic quality of war photography, as evidence of this visual regulation along the three key representational axes of the battlefield: i) military technology and its organization of ii) human bodies within specific spatial zones of activity, or iii) landscapes. It is this focus on the aesthetic strategies, through which historical configurations of 'combative agency' become intelligible via images, that allows me, in a second move, to reflect upon the moral agency that such images make possible for their public. The analytical category of moral agency, then, opens up to critical scrutiny the role that war photojournalism plays in addressing Hegel's existential question of war – the question, let us recall, of which conception of humanity we adhere to and who we are proposed to become as spectators. It is in this sense that war photojournalism becomes eloquent as a resource of collective moralization and, in so doing, sustains what Hutchings and Frazer call 'the distinction and relation between civic and military virtue' (2011: 58). I begin with the early 20th-century battlefields of the two world wars and proceed to address the contemporary moment, in the battlefields of the War on Terror.

The first half of the 20th century

It was during 1914–1918 that war first became visible to civilians: 'During the First World War,' Carmichael says, 'it was for the first time possible for people to see and read about a major conflict more or less as it happened' (1989: 4). This new visibility of the war was, however, shaped by two factors: the large scale of war operations, which defied 'spectacularization' by the technical apparata of the time, and the strict state regulation of the management of war information (Carruthers 2000: 57–8). As a result, First World War photojournalism was defined, on the one hand, by the photographers' continuous efforts to capture the huge scale of events on the battlefield and, on the other, by a visual production that never challenged official interpretations of the war. The bulk of pictures from this war were consequently 'antiseptic', consisting mostly of 'archaic images of individual suffering and heroism' (Farish 2001: 279).

Despite the enormity of its war operations, far exceeding those of the two world wars, photojournalism became more dynamic and open, both because technical equipment was now more powerful and mobile, and because the information strategy of the Allied Forces changed from rigid control to 'regulated truth telling' (Roeder 1995). Rather than correcting the wrongs of First World War propaganda, however, this turn to the truth was accepted as a pragmatic move in the face of the fact that 'war on this scale couldn't simply be hidden, however much states might seek to obscure their losses' (Carruthers 2000: 93). A more humane and tragic imagery of the battlefield now emerged as a result, though one that shares with the First World War a similar ethics of heroism (Winter 1995). Let me summarize the key aesthetic features of the photography of the two world wars in terms of its use of technologies, bodies and landscapes.

Aesthetic quality in photojournalism of the two world wars

Technologies: The vast majority of First World War photography is about groups of soldiers posing with or using technology in the battlefield – primarily artillery, such as guns and cannons, but also objects and vehicles, such as gas masks (from 1915) and tanks (from 1916). This recurring connection between soldier and technology, always articulated in productive relationships of complementarity (soldiers in control of the operation of machines) or extension (soldiers' activity protected or maximized by machines), operated within a 'prosthetic imagination', characteristic of the early 20th century. This was an imagination celebrating the synergies between man and machine as a guarantee for victory in war: 'War is beautiful', as futurist Marinetti put it, 'because it initiates the dreamt-of metalization of the human body' (1930 in Der Derian 2005: 27). Part of a broader utopian vision of modernity, this technological imagination dominated the military register, seeking to glorify the first large-scale industrialized war as 'total war' (Forster 2000: 4). However, it dominated, the photographic register too, where the professional ambition was to capture the war in its visual plenitude, through the camera's 'total gaze' (Carmichael 1989). The emergence of 'composite photographs', which used multiple negatives to condense large-scale action within one photo frame, further perfected the prosthetic imagination of the First World War in that it facilitated the representation of more inclusive configurations of technologies with human bodies in the battlefield (Hood 2011). Both guns and pictures were, in this way, celebrated as part of a technological fantasy, where machines are put to the service of the body's agentive capacities.

Imagery of the Second World War battlefields are characterized by a similar configuration of soldiers and technology, this time, however, placed within concrete narratives of dramatic action. One such category of iconic images is Robert Capa's 'magnificent eleven' – his D-Day landing photos – which showed Allied soldiers with rifles and equipment, hunkered down, drifting or crawling in shallow water, just before they stepped onto Omaha Beach. New shooting techniques (using a wide-angle lens), which put the viewer in the scene of action, but also a new sensibility characteristic of this war, the 'concerned photographer' (Capa 1968), gave rise to a moral imagination that inserted the body in discourses not only of heroic sacrifice but also of psychological agony and human loss (Griffin 1999). While still operating within the realm of objective representation, Capa's aesthetic, with its bold emphasis on black-and-white and the out-of-focus frame, invites a more intense relationship with combative agency than First World War pictures did – one that, in Friday's words, is mediated by 'an artist who can transfigure human suffering and a spectator who can redeem this suffering, ... by grasping important moral insights' (2000: 375). If the D-Day landing images used snapshot aesthetics to introduce moral insight into war photojournalism, the dropping of atomic bombs in Japan sustained an amoral aesthetic grounded on large-scale depictions of war. Part of a number of aerial shots at long distance, the pictures of the mushroom-shaped cloud rising above Hiroshima are some of the most iconic yet ambivalent 20th-century representations of technology. Despite being now at the heart of combative action, technology and its horrific effects on civilian populations were marginalized in favour of a phantasmagoric spectacle of destruction. This is because war photojournalism offered a sublimated representation of the atomic impact – that is, a representation of 'the feeling of the colossal', which alerts us to the impossible proportions of the catastrophic cloud but leaves out the moral dimension of human death (Derrida 1987: 32). Unable to obliterate this tragedy from subsequent imageries of the event's aftermath, however, photographs of the mushroom cloud ultimately led to a new and complex language for speaking about Second World War technology that mixed 'responses of pride, parochial possessiveness, creative resistance, denial and despair' (Taylor 1997: 580).

In summary, the technological imagination of the First World War, relying heavily on a utopian vision of progress, became in the Second World War more ambivalent in two ways: on the one hand, technology became increasingly integrated into a more humane imagination of combative action, at the heart of which lay the agency of the soldier in battle; on the other, technology became increasingly dystopian – it operated less as an instrument of victory and more as an instrument of evil that threatens humanity.

Bodies: The prosthetic imagination of First World War, which connected technology and the body in relationships of complementarity and extension, inevitably also projected a view of the body as itself a machine – a physiological unit geared towards maximal performance in battle (Bourke 2008). Evident in images of combatants as adept operators of heavy artillery or fearless users of machine-guns in the trenches, this incorporation of the soldier into the utopian technological narrative of war reproduced a discourse of heroic virtue and steely patriotism. It did so, however, at a cost. It ignored the contradictory relationship between body and technology that, in the context of the first industrialized war, span out of control and gave rise to the mass phenomenon of war neurosis or shell-shock. Far from a pure fear of death, Leed argued, the unprecedented rise of war neurosis in the Western Front was a direct consequence of the new relationship of bodies-in-battle stuck in immobilized warfare and the new, long-distance calculations of risk that this warfare entailed. The dominance of long-range artillery, the machine-gun and barbed wire had, in other words, imposed new rules for the conduct of war, making the bodily symptoms of war neurosis 'the direct product of the increasingly alienated relationship of the combatant to the modes of destruction' (Leed 1979: 164).

Just as First World War photojournalism ignored the complex emotionality of combative agency in favour of a romantic celebration of the soldier as a war machine, it also largely ignored the dead body in the battlefield (Carruthers 2000). It is not so much that pictures of the dead were unavailable but rather that such imagery was heavily regulated and carefully crafted to portray the dead enemy rather than the dead friend (Carmichael 1989).[5] Building upon the American Civil War documentary style, the representation of these dead bodies took place through an objectivist aesthetic that emphasized the mass nature of war killing. It did so by portraying the dead as part of 'regularised compositional wholes', such as landscapes of barbed wire or trench lines, often accompanied by captions, such as 'The Dawn of Passchendaele' or 'Death the Reaper', that contextualized the scene in broader narratives of the 'picturesque' (Griffin 1999: 136–137; see also Huppauf 1997).

By the time of Second World War, the status of the body was subject to similar transformations as technology. On the one hand, the body continues to be registered in discourses of technological militarism, particularly in the celebration of new war machinery, such as aircraft carriers and armoured vehicles that made the war more mobile. On the other, the body also began to appear dissociated from such technology and, after President Roosevelt's recommendation to show more 'blood and gore' (1943 in Roeder 1995: 28), a different imagery started to appear – one that, whist coexisting with the heroic, came to acknowledge the traumatic impact of battle upon soldiers, both physical and emotional: 'a grittier perspective now emerged', Carruthers says, one in which 'fear, boredom and courage all found a place' (2000: 94). Even though this new discourse of moral agency did serve the purposes of hardening public morale, it also inevitably introduced a new legitimacy for the wounded body and, with it, a new conception of heroism not as the negation but as the conquest of fear: 'the legend that soldiers don't cry', as war photographer Dickey Chapelle put it, 'robs them of their personal victories over fear and pain' (quoted in Benoit 2004).

In summary, the move from First World War to Second World War marked a shift from discourses of the 'body as machine' to the 'body as fragile', both physically, through the acknowledgement of injury and death, and psychologically, through a recognition of the intense emotionality involved in battle. Despite this 'new frankness', in Fussell's words, however, both world wars were marked by a predominantly romantic discourse of combative agency that celebrated soldierly suffering as heroic and, consequently, sought to sustain a largely cleansed photojournalistic depiction of the battlefield – one that, ultimately, only 'showed intact bodies and revealed little of the agonies of death' (Roeder 1995: 9).

Landscapes: Its multiple theatres of action granted, the most iconic imagery of the First World War photojournalistic landscape is the Western Front's No Mans' Land – a scape characterized by what Huppauf calls a 'total negation of habitual perception', ravaged as this landscape was by an amorphous mass of battlefield waste (1996). Far from simply destroying the topological order of pre-war life, this visual representation of No Man's Land came to replace modernist conceptions of rural landscape as a zone of natural beauty and innocence with a new imagination of nature as a zone of technological destruction – threatening, infertile, directionless: 'the war explodes the landscape back into a state of wilderness,' says Huppauf, 'which is, at the same time, the landscape of modern technology' (1996: 46). Unable to capture action as it happened, these photojournalistic images were rather static, concentrating on the aftermath of war, wherein fusions of mud, crater marks, bomb debris and human bodies construed the battlefield as a liminal space between here and there, us and enemy, life and death (Leed 1981: 14). It was, again, a sublime register that framed this scary liminality in that the battlefield was now grasped through a double move: framed as it was by an aesthetic of the aftermath, the initial horror of death bodies was quickly replaced by a sense of safe distance from the scene and offered itself to spectators as an object of reflexive contemplation (Boltanski 1999).

Out of the multiple landscapes of Second World War photojournalism, the most iconic ones involve city bombings: the Blitz of London and the aftermath of the atomic attacks on Japan. Unlike the pictorial representation of the Western Front, which rests on a strict separation between combative and non-combative landscapes, the photojournalism of the Second World War reflects, thus, a blurring between the two in a new conception of the battlefield, which now included the category of civilians into the sphere of legitimate killing. As acts of expressive violence, prioritizing a symbolics of destruction over material military gains, these bombings operated less as strategic operations and more as horror spectacles that had 'to be seen and to strike fear in the hearts of the observer, the real target of an act of terror' (Bousquet 2006: 744). The key characteristic of such spectacular photojournalism, therefore, is the long-distance shots of cityscapes in flames (London) or in ruins (Hiroshima). Distance, as mentioned earlier, abstracts from the details of human injury and death in order to focus upon the magnitude of the battlefield in a God's-eye view of hyperdestruction. A sublime aesthetic emerges as a result, which locates this battlefield in a hybrid register of 'ecstatic destructiveness' (Bousquet 2006).[6] At the heart of this aesthetic lies, once again, an ambivalent technological imagination that fuses a dystopian vision of inhumanity with a utopia of peace, in a new formulation of liberal ethics, where extreme violence is now explicitly acknowledged as the most effective means to achieve lasting peace. Hiroshima and Nagasaki, the most radical instances of this vision, are the boundary markers of this transformation towards a Cold War morality, where the world order now rests upon the constant threat of nuclear annihilation; or, in Huppauf's words, where 'it is possible to maintain a system driven by a mentality of violence but control its consequences, namely individual acts of violence and war' (1996: 9).

The landscapes of war are perhaps the clearest manifestation of the liberal paradox of war. In different ways, No Man's Land and the city ruins of aerial bombardment throw into relief a predominantly dystopian vision of technology. Either as a liminal zone of waste that defies rationalization or as the apocalyptic horizon of burning hell, the sublime portrayal of landscapes undermines both the romantic optimism of technologies and the heroic celebration of bodies that, in various degrees, dominated the war imaginary of the first half of the 20th century.

Moral agency in photojournalism of the two world wars

The category of moral agency, let us recall, examines the role of photojournalism in addressing Hegel's existential question of war: Which conceptions of humanity, of self and Other, and of moral agency does such photojournalism come to legitimize?

The conception of humanity emerging out of the photojournalism of the battlefield, in the early 20th century, is radically ambivalent. It is, as we saw, a humanity suspended between discourses of technological perfectibility, glorified in the prosthetic imagination of bodies as weapons or the suppression of emotion, and discourses of corporeal fragility, testified in the pictorial acknowledgment of suffering and death as well as in the recognition of fear in combat. While the self gradually opened up to discourses of imperfectibility, however, the enemy is firmly placed in the realm of radical Otherness. It is only enemy soldiers who are shown in a state of absolute fragility, death, while the mass suffering inflicted upon innocent civilians is prohibited from view. Both voyeurism and invisibility operate here as effective strategies of dehumanization that sustained a fantasy of enemy lives as inhuman or simply irrelevant (Fussell 1975).

If the Otherness of the enemy is an eternal theme of war, however, the ambivalence of the self reflects a historical shift in conceptions of humanity during the first half of the 20th century. It marks a departure from early chivalric genres of moral agency as aristocratic valour towards a new discourse of agency as military servitude – one that recognizes heroic virtue not in the artful dexterity of the distinguished warrior but in the disciplined skill of the nationalized soldier, thrown as he is into industrialized battlefields of mass killing. These soldiers of the first half of the 20th century, what Walzer calls 'soldiers as instruments', are not 'members of a fellowship of warriors; they are "poor sods just like me" trapped in a war they did not like' (p. 36). Evident in the dystopian vision of battlefield landscapes as liminal zones of disintegrated matter or apocalyptic bombardment, this humble agency of the soldier does not, however, mark the end of heroism.

Rather, this humanity redefines heroism within a new moral sensibility, informed by, what I earlier called an aesthetics of the sublime – an 'emotionally detached and amoral representation of mass environmental destruction and death' that turns the battlefield into an object of reflexive contemplation (Huppauf 1997: 138–139). Far from a purely stylistic decision, the sublime is no doubt the consequence of institutional restrictions for war correspondents as well as of the technological norm of the 'total gaze' that journalists sought to capture in the battlefield (Farish 2001). Yet, at the same time, the distanced objectivity of the sublime is also a key aesthetic response to a deeper crisis of representation arising in the early 20th century's war, namely the lack of an appropriate language to capture the experience of the battlefield through conventional visual practices – the paradox of in/communicability in the era of photography and film. This is evident, for instance, in First World War photojournalistic techniques of manipulation to portray the vast scale of simultaneous scenes of violence; and in the rhetoric used by X. Lawrence, the only military photographer to fly above Hiroshima, who could only capture the spectacle of the atomic bomb through the use of epic language: 'awe-struck, we watched it shoot upward like a meteor coming from the earth instead of from outer space... it was a living thing, a new species of being, born right before our incredulous eyes' (quoted in Dower 2010 275).

The 'poor sods' in these sublimated battlefields were thus heroes not because they possessed a masterful combative agency but precisely because they were all too aware of themselves as both agents and victims of mass-scale killing: 'however profound the despair of the individual,' as correspondent Philip Gibbs described the advance of the Somme, 'the mass moved as it was directed' (1920: 359–360). And even though other public genres, such as poetry and painting, addressed this crisis of representation through the modernist registers of irony and the surreal – that is, ways of signifying the battlefield that emphasize bitter knowingness or the irrationality of futile sacrifice – photojournalism operated as a gatekeeping genre that sustained more conventional narratives of war. Even Capa's concern with human suffering worked, in fact, to individualize and authenticate, rather than break with, the discourse of heroic sacrifice (Coker 2001). In so doing, early 20th-century photojournalism attempted the impossible task of renewing the promise of humanity under inhumane conditions through a sublimation of the battlefield. In the process, it maintained the traditional conception of the enemy as dehumanized other but did not, ultimately, manage to keep intact the conception of the self – its humanity is increasingly problematized not as a taken-for-granted property of every human being but as a precarious condition, both physical and psychological, that war tragically disintegrates.

Wars of the 21st century

If the first half of the 20th century introduced a new visibility of the battlefield, the 21st century is marked by a thoroughgoing technologization of war – a tight articulation of war with technology that goes beyond simply 'reporting' the battlefield and refers to the very constitution of war through a media logic, as 'mediatised conflict' (Cottle 2006). While this new articulation emerged as early as the Vietnam War, the first 'televised war' ever, mediatization gradually became a military strategy throughout the 1980s and early 1990s, culminating with the first Gulf War in 1991. Despite being celebrated as the first real-time war, offering battlefield access from cameras adjusted on aircraft cockpits, this war's imagery was, however, largely confined to 'night-vision' visuals that 'fictionalized' combative action and thus maximized, rather than diminished, the distance from the sites of combat (Der Derian 2005). Earning thus its name as a 'virtual' war, the Gulf conflict anticipated the digital nature of the War on Terror, in that it used information systems both as propaganda mechanisms and as logistical systems of the battlefield. In this ever-evolving media ecology of war, photojournalism continues to play a key part but, given the recent proliferation of real-time distribution platforms, such as the internet, digital cameras and mobile phones, its scope becomes more differentiated and its status is challenged (Hoskins and O'Loughlin 2010).

Aesthetic Quality in the War on Terror

Technologies: Similar to the prosthetic imagination of the early 20th century, technology continues to be celebrated in 21st-century photojournalism. Now, however, the articulation of the mechanical with the corporeal is radically intensified. State-of-the-art sensory devices, high-tech weapon systems and uniform fabrics or designs are only some of the ways in which the prosthetic imagination of the 20th century has given rise to a new digitalized body – the cyborg soldier. Constituted through technoscientific discourses of military action, which further locate this body in virtual reality-simulated exercises and digitized battlefields, the cyborg soldier is no longer defined by the ways in which the physicality of his body is complemented or extended by weapons but by a whole new 'juncture of... metals, chemicals, and people that makes weapons of computers and computers of weapons and soldiers' (Gray 1997: 8). However, even if this technological imagination renders combative agency 'post-human', in that action in battle is now regulated by technologies that imitate and perfect the biological senses (Lenoir 2000), this agency is simultaneously associated with a new emphasis on humanitarian action. From aid packages to medical equipment and from mechanical tools to children's toys, the representation of combative action, embodied as it is in the figure of the soldier, has less to do with the infliction of suffering and more to do with assisting vulnerable others: 'Smiling and nurturing yet strong; kind and friendly but armed; as well as secure and trustworthy yet militaristic', Koitanen claims, 'are the visual features recurring in the images and determining this figure' (2011: 35). 'Embedded' forms of reporting, which brought together journalists and the military in intimate relationships of collaboration, contributed to this humanitarian visualization of the army and, in so doing, established a new sensibility of benevolence at the heart of the War on Terror. Seeking to legitimize the peacekeeping and nation-building NATO operations in Afghanistan and Iraq, such visual images cannot, however, break free from the constitutive contradiction of liberal morality, namely that military humanitarianism is, in fact, a war operation that, in the name of peace, costs hundreds of lives every year. If anything, as Der Derian argues, the War on Terror has reversed the mortality rates between soldiers, now safer, and civilians, now rendered more vulnerable: 'war-related fatalities have been reversed in modern times, from 100 years ago when one civilian was killed per eight soldiers, to the current ratio of eight civilians per soldier killed' (2005: 26).

Bodies: Historical continuity in photojournalistic representations of the body is established through the persistent invisibility of 'our' dead. Controversies ensuing from the rare depictions of death in the War on Terror, either literally (in Julia Stevenson's 2009 *New York Times* image of a US Marine lethally wounded on the legs) or metonymically (in the 2005 Associated Press imagery of a series of US flag-draped coffins on their way out of Iraq), testify to the deep anxieties that define the figure of the soldier as cyborg. What these contested visualities suggest is that while constructed as a perfected version of the biological body, the cyborg is simultaneously unable to overcome its mortality, and therefore remains radically vulnerable (Masters 2006: 112). This ambivalent humanity, fully technological yet mortally fragile, is also combined with a thorough psychologization of combative agency. Going far beyond the simple recognition of fear, there is today an intense focus on the visualization of the soldier's tortured psyche that replaces earlier masculinist conceptions of military humanity with a new sensibility of agony in battle, now termed post-traumatic stress disorder (PTSD) (Coker 2001). Evident in the proliferation of a subjectivist aesthetic in war images, including Craig Walker's 2012 Pulitzer Prize-winning photography of an Iraq War veteran suffering from acute PTSD, the depiction of soldiers in intense sorrow or panic attacks not only involves a conception of the battlefield as a space of individual trauma but also repositions photojournalism as itself an intimate practice of witnessing personal pain. A century away from First World War pictures of the soldier as machine, these images may project a moral agency of emotional fragility but cannot ultimately resolve earlier tensions of the soldier as a killing machine. Despite their hyperemotionalization of warfare, then, 21st-century imageries of the cyborg approximate the First World War imageries of soldiers in that they are both torn between the push of technological fantasy and the pull of bodily mortality: 'military technologies have been "techno-masculinized" ', as Master says, 'while human soldiers ... have been "feminized" and reconstituted within the realm of those needing "protection" ' (2005: 114).

This emergence of subjectivist photojournalism, as a new visual aesthetic for resolving the liberal paradox of war, further characterizes the imagery of the West's Others. What the trophy snapshots of Abu Graib torture reflect is not only a process of dehumanization, by which the bodies of Iraqi prisoners are subjected to humiliating rituals, but also the uncanny ways in which the all-familiar practices of ordinary witnessing now capture the disturbed emotionality of 'our' soldiers as the 'other within': 'the media publicity by the photos of Abu Graib', Grusin claims, 'lies less in the significance of what they show us than...in the feeling that in looking at the Abu Graib photos we are participating in our ordinary practices of mediality' (2010: 60). Ordinary witnessing may have introduced the theme of atrocity in the subjectivist aesthetics of the snapshot but it did not fully replace the power of earlier, objectivist registers. Reminiscent of Second World War city bombings, the 2003 bombardment of Baghdad, for instance, is cast in the register of 'shock and awe', which celebrates the ecstatic destructiveness of the cityscape while hiding away the responsibility of the bombers and the 'collateral damage' of Iraqi victims (Chouliaraki 2006).[7]

Landscapes: The landscapes of 21st-century war accentuate the blurring of boundaries between battlefield and civilian sites that we encountered in the photojournalism of the Second World War. Rather than aerial warfare, however, it is now terror attacks at the heart of urban life that redefine the battlefield. While, therefore, the fields of Afghanistan and Iraq continue to be the main theatres of combative action, photojournalistic representations of the battlefield have come to include the close-up suffering of civilians in Afghan and Iraqi cities but also in Western cities, such as New York, London and Madrid. Characterized by an aesthetics of the aftermath, these images represent sites of atrocity where emergency services, pools of blood, bodies and scattered personal items come to stand for the horrors of urban killing. Even though the aftermath is a historical trope of atrocity, dominant, as we saw, in First World War battlefields as an objectifying device of the Western Front, this aesthetic now re-emerges invested with a new emotionality. This is evident in professional photojournalistic imagery, such as the 2012 Pulitzer Prize-winning image by Massoud Hosseini of a young girl screaming at the site of a suicide bombing, but also, importantly, in the practice of amateur photojournalism, as reflected in the early 9/11 shaky videos of the World Trade Center plane crashes and the grainy mobile camera pictures from the 7/7 London Underground attacks. What these images share is, again, a register of ordinary testimony, which prioritizes not a plenary view of the landscape after combat but an intimate view of human suffering from the perspective of people who have been subjected to it (2009. A new authenticity of photojournalism emerges as a result – one that rejects the objectivism of the 'total gaze' and embraces the testimonial truth of the person in the street (Chouliaraki 2010). Drawing upon an aesthetic of unreconstructed (non-edited) and embodied (randomly framed and erratically moving) mediations (Pantti

2013), the landscapes of the War of Terror potentially inscribe any territory within ever-expanding violent cartographies and, in so doing, install an emotionality of perpetual threat at the heart of liberal ethics (Furedi 2007).

Moral Agency in the War on Terror

The conception of humanity in 21st-century warfare has redefined the relationship between self and Other in ways that both evoke and surpass older tensions between 'man' and 'machine'. Even though the human body and its relationship to technology still remains the focus of military performance, we can see that this body is now embedded in broader calculations of life and death, where technology is not only a means of killing but also a means of maximizing survival and managing human livelihoods – the lives of both soldiers and local Others. This distinction between an early 'disciplinary' and a contemporary 'biopolitical' form of humanity (Foucault 1987) points, in turn, to a new combative agency that concomitantly moves 'away from exclusive reliance on the extermination of "enemies" towards the targeting of whole populations for political support and a treatment of those populations as the decisive "variables" that determine mission success or failure' – what Bell refers to as the 'civilianisation of warfare' (2011: 310). This new articulation of the liberal paradox away from extreme violence and around the biopolitical imperative of managing lives is visually expressed in an aesthetics of trauma, where war is represented both as an intimate experience of personal pain and as a public act of peacemaking. Let me summarize these in turn.

Reflected in a series of prize-winning images on the intimate emotions of the soldier, the moral agency of civilianized war, I have argued, is imagined through subjectivist registers, which abandon the objectivity of the 'total gaze' or the sublime in favour of an intense affective expressivity – both towards the self, as in imagery of soldiers in distress, and towards Others, as in imagery of smiling soldiers with Afghan or Iraqi children (more on which below). Even though the problematization of the soldier machine had already started as early as the Second World War, the contemporary dominance of an aesthetics of trauma over the sublime challenges the traditional morality of combative agency in important ways. Celebrated as a triumph of the modernist 'culture of sympathy', this 'increasing respect for humanism and human life' is seen to be leading to a thorough 'humanisation' of warfare, where the liberal ideal of avoiding cruelty has now replaced the grand narratives of imperialism or nationalism that drove earlier wars (Coker 2008: 457).

This revaluation of humanity as biological life, however, may simultaneously be seen to reflect an intensification, rather than a relaxation, of the power relations by which 21st-century warfare seeks to regulate its subjects. The biopolitical force of these power relations lies, according to Dillon and Reid (2009), in transforming the battlefield from an antagonistic confrontation with the enemy into a site for the micromanagement of individual lives without, simultaneously, being able to escape the nature of war as a practice of sacrificing lives, of killing and being killed: 'Even though many recent military operations have been characterized as peace-keeping missions or stability operations', an important study, funded by the Iraq Afghanistan Deployment Impact Fund, claims, that 'many of these efforts may share the same risks and stressors inherent in combat – exposure to hostile forces, injured civilians, mass graves, and land mines, for example' (2008: 6). Expressive of the moral and emotional tensions at the heart of this radical ambivalence of humanitarian wars, recent photojournalism depicts multiple US atrocities in Iraq and Afghanistan, thereby further complicating the aesthetics of trauma with insights of the self as perpetrator – what in military euphemism is now called 'combat and operational stress reaction'.[8] At the same time, as civilianized battlefields expand further into Western centres, the biopolitical grip of war on civilian populations is increasingly manifested in the testimonial imageries of new media devices, as they are now used not only by citizens, so as to sentimentalize the new urban battlefields, but also by states, so as to monitor and securitize the public spaces of the West (Grusin 2010).

Beyond conceptions of the self, however, the photojournalistic imagery of humanitarian soldiers also evokes a new conception of the Other. Systematically depicting soldiers in empathetic exchanges with local populations, this is, again, a photojournalism of subjectivism that is firmly inscribed within what Boltanski (1999) calls the 'topic of sentiment' – a mode of representing human suffering that evokes gratitude towards the benefactors and tender-heartedness towards the beneficiaries of the exchange. Part of the military communication strategy to 'win hearts and minds', this sentimentalization of warfare may manage to give voice and visibility to local Others, positioning them as audiences of the West, but it does so at a cost. This is because the systematic visualization of local children, women and elderly as vulnerable recipients of aid construes these Others as subordinate to the humanitarian soldier. If they are not infantilized, when portrayed to gratefully accept what 'we' have to give them, they are either annihilated, in that they are simply not part of the visual economy of the war, or become fully 'Othered', in that they are portrayed as subhuman – in the imageries of the dead Saddam Hussein, Abu Ghraib or murdered Afghani families. Suspended between annihilation and demonization, then, the imagery of local others in 21st-century photojournalism erases the possibility of what Butler calls 'recognition' (2006), of acknowledging their cultural difference or political dissent as legitimate responses to the presence of foreign military forces on their ground, in Iraq and Afghanistan. Rather, what the visual sentimentalization of the humanitarian exchange achieves, according to Holmqvist, is forging encounters of 'non-recognition' that subject local populations to a double violence – symbolic, in that it humanizes 'them' only as subordinate and vulnerable to 'us', and physical, in that it continues to kill 'them' unless they desire the same as 'us': 'the "other" of this present-day war', she argues, 'is not thought of as an Other but rather a different version of the self' (2012: 9).

In summary, the war imaginary in the 21st century has taken a turn towards subjectivist aesthetic, which places a moral agency of expressive sentimentality at the centre of the battlefield. This aesthetic of trauma attempts to resolve the liberal paradox of war by construing combative agency as a primarily humanitarian agency, where the digitalization of warfare goes hand in hand with an equally pervasive psychologization of war relations. Grounded on a photojournalism of embedded reporting and ordinary testimony, both of which, in different ways, favour intimate descriptions of combative exchange, this aesthetic breaks with the register of the sublime and its proposal for an objective contemplation of the war in order to tell more personal, post-heroic stories of benevolent action. Despite its ambition to rescue the humanity of the battlefield, however, affective expressivity seems to accentuate the split between war as protecting and war as killing. It may intend to break from early stereotypical portrayals of soldiers as human machines, yet it inscribes them into a different, but perhaps equally inhumane, matrix of power relations through the tactical regulation of human lives in contexts of deliberate killing. Similarly, it may attempt to acknowledge the humanity of others, yet it ultimately manages to either collapse this humanity to a Western vision of the self or to demonize it as impenetrable Otherness. The photojournalistic aesthetic of trauma, in conclusion, may be celebrated as humanizing war, but it only manages to throw into dramatic relief the injured subjectivities that are positioned within its discourse.

Conclusion: How war speaks

The liberal paradox, a moral discourse that installs war at the heart of modernity's vision for perpetual peace, is reflected and reproduced in the war imaginary of the past 100 years. What my historical trajectory of iconic photojournalism has shown is that humanity emerges as an ambivalent signifier in this imaginary, torn between the utopia of invincibility and the dystopia of destruction. In the wars of the early 20th century, this ambivalence is expressed through objectivist aesthetic registers, notably a sublimation of the battlefield that invites a reflexive engagement with the spectacle of warfare in two of its most important manifestations – as heroic, in imageries of 'our' technological might and dramatic action, or as horrific, in imageries of 'their' dead bodies and the ravaged landscapes of combat. In the wars of the 21st century, the ambivalence of humanity is articulated through increasingly subjectivist aesthetic registers that may still selectively resort to sublime representations (of others) but now focus on war as an intensely psychological experience in two of its most prominent manifestations – the humanitarian battlefield, in imageries of benevolent encounters between troops and locals, and the traumatized individual, in imageries of victims in the expanded, civilized landscapes of war.

Even though, as I have argued, photojournalism remains one of the most conservative genres of the war imaginary, traditionally inclined to echo the values and objectives of the military, this aesthetic variation is indicative of, on the one hand, institutional changes in the technologies and professional styles of reporting, including the emergence of citizen-journalism, and, on the other, a concomitant cultural change in its performative practices through which we are called to imagine humanity. It is through these shifting visions of humanity that despite its lack of 'a code of words', war does speak, communicating something important about the changing moralities of the war imaginary, in its centennial course.

Central to this imaginary is the shift from a combative agency of military servitude, which, in the early 20th century, construed the battlefield as a site of heroic action that invited the sacrifice of human lives in the name of transcendental ideals, towards the agency of the cyborg which, in the 21st century, construes the battlefield as a site of post-heroic action that invites a calculative approach at the service of biological lives (soldiers or local Others). The move from the sublime to the traumatic, then, is the aesthetic trace of a more fundamental transformation in the moral order of modernity. Originally catalysed by the catastrophic

First World War and later by the Cold War, this is a shift from a deontological morality, which grounded war on an antagonistic politics of sovereignty in the name of potent ideologies (Kaldor 2008), towards a utilitarian morality, which grounded war on a humanitarian politics of pity in the name of more modest tasks – of 'alleviating the immediate images of death and suffering' (Coker 2001: 130). While still exercising brutal forms of violence, symbolic and physical, war as a humanitarian endeavour reflects, in this sense, the most radical fusion between the classical liberal ethics of avoiding cruelty as society's ultimate value with late modernity's biopolitical predicament for subtler but more effective forms of violence – a fusion made possible by a neoliberal utilitarian ethics of managing the livelihoods of the battlefield, at minimal cost (Dillon and Reid 2009).

While the historical move towards humanitarian war and its aesthetics of trauma invites further empirical research into the political practices and popular genres through which war becomes eloquent, it is important, in conclusion, to turn from variations in eloquence to the only perpetual silence of war – 'our' dead. As a master signifier of the aesthetics of battlefield, 'our' dead are, let us recall, both neatly absent from and poignantly present in the photojournalism of war. By occupying this borderline position, 'our' dead both gesture towards the inhumanity of war and, at the same time, constantly remind us of the fragility of humanity: 'the dead body', as der Derian puts it, 'is what gives war its special status. This fact can be censored, hidden in a body bag, air-brushed away, but it provides, even in its erasure, the corporeal gravitas of war' (2005: 30). It is precisely this irreducible 'corporeal gravitas' of the dead body that acts as the 'constitutive outside' of the war imaginary, perpetually generating the in/communicability of war in the centennial trajectory of liberal ethics. In all its aesthetic manifestations from the sublime to the traumatic, I have shown that this in/communicability is a crucial part of our collective imagination in that by speaking about the battlefield, it also speaks of us – of who we are and how we should feel as witnesses of its horrors.

Notes

1. See Winter (2010) for the tension between representation and silence in the context of war.
2. See Hassner (1994) and Coker (2001; 2008) for discussions.
3. Due to its temporal proximity, the iconic photojournalism of the War on Terror cannot be claimed to enjoy the universal recognizability and acclaim of earlier visualizations of the battlefield. Instead, the iconic is here primarily

defined as award-winning photojournalism (Pulitzer Wold Press Awards) but also as photojournalism that has generated global controversies (such as the 2004 Abu Graib images).

4. See Chouliaraki (2006) and Silverstone (2007) for an elaboration of this Arendtian position.

5. See Winter (1995) for the exceptional controversy provoked by the news film *The Battle of the Somme*, where images of dead soldiers were shown in cinema theatres across the UK.

6. Anticipated already in 1914 by German Admiral von Tirpitz, who opposed aerial bombs for 'killing old women', the sublime aesthetic of Second World War bombings is nonetheless imagined as a triumph in the admiral's concession that, if, however, 'one could set fire to London in thirty places, then what in a small way is odious would retire before something fine and powerful' (quoted in Dower 2010: 271).

7. Even though outside the scope of this chapter on iconic photojournalism, a key feature of contemporary mediations of war lies in the emergence of non-Western transnational media, such as Al Jazeera. Adhering to a news ethics of atrocity that exposes the hypocrisy of Western, 'antiseptic' broadcasting, these networks render alternative representations of dead bodies available to all so as to confront the West with its own 'Otherness' – the inhumanity within (Silverstone 2007).

8. Available at http://www.huffingtonpost.com/mark-c-russell-phd-abpp/ptsd-veterans_b_1228546.html (downloaded, 19 May 2012).

References

Allan S. (2009) 'Citizen Jounralism and the Rise of "Mass Self-communication": Reporting the London Bombings', *Global Media Journal. Australian Edition* 1(1): 1–20.

Bell, C. (2011) 'Civilianising Warfare: Ways of War and Peace in Modern Counterinsurgency', *Journal of International Relations and Development* 14: 309–332.

Boltanski, L. (1999) *Distant Suffering. Politics, Morality and the Media*. Cambridge: Cambridge University Press.

Bourke, J. (2008) 'Why Does Politics Turn to Violence?', in Edkins, J. and Zehfuss, M. (eds) *Global Politics: A New Introduction*. London: Routledge, 370–398.

Bousquet, A. (2006) 'Time Zero: Hiroshima, September 11 and Apocalyptic Revelations in Historical Consciousness in Millennium', *Journal of International Studies* 34: 739–765.

Butler, J. (2006) *Precarious Life: The Powers of Mourning and Violence*. London: Verso.

Capa, C. (1968) *The Concerned Photographer*. London: Grossman Publishers.

Carmichael, J. (1989) *First World War Photographers*. London: Routledge.

Carruthers, S. (2000) *The Media at War. Communication and Conflict in the 20th Century*. New York: St Martin's Press.

Chouliaraki, L. (2006) *The Spectatorship of Suffering*. London: Sage.

Chouliaraki, L. (2010) 'Ordinary Witnessing in Post-television News', in Chouliaraki L. (ed.) special issue on *Self-Mediation: New Media, Citizenship and the Self in Critical Discourse Studies* 7(4): 305–319.

Chouliaraki, L. (2012) *The Ironic Spectator. Solidarity in the Age of Post-humanitarianism*. Cambridge: Polity.

Coker, C. (2001) *Humane Warfare: The New Ethics of Postmodern War*. London: Routledge.

Coker, C. (2008) *Ethics and War in the 21st Century*. London: Routledge.

Cottle S. (2006) *Mediatized Conflict: Developments in Media and Conflict Studies*. Maidenhead: Oxford University Press.

Der Derian, J. (2005) 'Imaging Terror: Logos, Pathos and Ethos', *Third World Quarterly* 26(1): 23–37.

Derrida, J. (1987) *The Truth in Painting*. Chicago: Chicago University Press.

Dillon, M. (2008) *The Liberal Way of War*. Plenary Lecture at the Pontifica Universidad Catolica de Chile. Available at http://www.biopolitica.cl/docs/Dillon_The_Liberal_Way_of_War.pdf (available 11.05.2012).

Dillon, M. & Reid, J. (2009) *The Liberal Way of War: Killing to Make Life Live*. London: Routledge.

Dower, J. (2010) *Cultures of War. Pearl Harbor, Hiroshima, 9–11, Iraq*. New York: Norton Publications.

Farish, M. (2001) 'Modern Witnesses. Foreign Correspondents, Geopolitical Vision and the First World War', *Transactions of the Institute of British Geographers* 26(3): 273–287.

Forster, S. (2000) 'Introduction', in Chikering R. & Forster S. (eds) *Great War, Total War: Combat and Mobilization on the Western Front, 1914–1918*. Cambridge: Cambridge University Press.

Foucault, M. (1987) 'The Subject and Power', *Critical Inquiry* 8: 777–789.

Frazer, E. and Hutchings, K. (2011) 'Virtuous Violence and the Politics of Statecraft', *Machiavelli, Clausewitz and Weber Political Studies*, 59(1): 56–73.

Friday, J. (2000) 'Demonic Curiosity and the Aesthetics of Documentary Photography', *British Journal of Aesthetics* 40(3): 356–375.

Furedi, F. (2007) Politics of Fear. Beyond left and Right London: Continuum.

Fussell, P. (1975) *The Great War and Modern Memory*. London: Stirling Press.

Gibbs, P. (1920/2009) *Now It Can Be Told*. Maryland: Wildside Press.

Gray, C. H. (1997) *Postmodern War: The New Politics of Conflict*. New York: The Guilford Press.

Griffin, M. (1999) 'The Great War Photographs: Constructing Myths of History and Photojournalism', in Brennen, B. & Hardt, H. (eds) *Picturing the Past. Media, History and Photography*. Chicago: University of Illinois Press.

Grusin, (2010) *Premediation. Affect and Mediality after 9/11*. London: Palgrave.

Hassner, P. (1994) 'Beyond the Three Traditions: The Philosophy of War and Peace', *Historical Perspective in International Affairs* 70(4): 737–756.

Hood, J. (2011) *War Correspondent. Reporting under Fire Since 1850*. London: Anova Books, Imperial War Museum.

Hoskins, A. and McLoughlin B. (2010) *War and Media. The Emergence of Diffused War*. Cambridge: Polity.

Howard, M. (1978/2008) *War and the Liberal Conscience*. New York: Columbia University Press.

Huppauf, B. (1996) 'Walter Benjamin's Imaginary Landscape', in Fischer, G. (ed.) *With the Sharpened Axe of Reason. Approaches to Walter Benjamin*, 33–54. Oxford: Berg.

Huppauf, B. (1997) 'Modernity and Violence. Observations on a Contradictory Relationship', in Huppauf, B. (ed.) *War, Violence and the Modern Condition*. Berlin: de Gruyter.

Kaldor M. (2008) *Old and New Wars*. Cambridge: Polity.

Koitanen, N. (2011) 'Humanitarian Soldiers, Colonised Others and Invisible Enemies', *Visual Strategic Communication Narratives of the Afghan War FIIA Working Paper 72*, 1–115.

Leed, E. (1979) *No Man's Land. Combat and Identity in World War I*. Cambridge: Cambridge University Press.

Lenoir, T. (2000) 'All but War Is Simulation: The Military-Entertainment Complex', *Configurations* 8: 289–335.

Masters, C. (2006) 'Bodies of Technology. Cyborg Soldiers and Militarised Masculinities', *International Feminist Journal of Politics* 7(1):112–132

Pantti, M. (2013) 'Getting Closer? Encounters of the National Media with Global Images', *Journalism Studies* 14(2): 201–218.

Roeder, G. (1995) *The Censored War: Experience during World War II*. New Haven, CT: Yale University Press.

Silverstone, R. (2007) *Media and Morality*. Cambridge: Polity.

Taylor, B. (1997) 'Nuclear Pictures and Meta-pictures', *American Literary History* 9(3): 567–597.

Winter, J. (1995) *Sites of Memory. Sites of Mourning: The Great War in European Memory*. Cambridge: Cambridge University Press.

Winter, J. (2010) 'Thinking about Silence', Ben-Ze'ev E, Ginio R. and Winter J. (eds) *Shadows of War: A Social History of Silence in the Twentieth Century*, 8. Cambridge: Cambridge University Press.

Part III
Mediations

10
On Whose Terms Are You Shown?
(or, at least, following what principles?)

Daniel Dayan

Appearing in public: Can you challenge your own media image? The red thread of Lyotard's 'Differend'

What are the facts that reach the status of 'shared facts'? Through which mechanisms do they become recognized, accepted as facts? 'Reality', writes Lyotard, 'is a status of the referent that results from the effectuation of procedures of fact-establishment' (Lyotard 1988: 32). Such procedures are defined by agreed protocols and their effectuation is entrusted to specific institutions. I would call such institutions the 'reality-pronouncing institutions'.

Attempting to discuss the pronouncements of such institutions is sometimes impossible. Instead of leading to a debate, the discussion may turn into what Lyotard calls a differend. This occurs when the procedure dealing within a given conflict or litigation is addressed in the idiom of one of the parties, so that the claims of the other party cannot be expressed in that idiom and therefore cannot be heard. A differend occurs when the lack of a universal discourse leads to judging a genre via another genre so that one of the genres becomes both judge and party.

Here is an example of a differend. It opposes two discursive genres, each of which constructs the referent 'people'. For the (communist) party, 'the people' is the referent of a 'dialectic' genre. As 'proletariat', 'the people' stands for an emancipated working humanity. But to members of the 'working class', 'the people' can be the referent of positive sentences about actual experiences. Asserting that the working class only exists as a proletariat, and that the party is exclusively entitled to speak in the name of the proletariat, results in depriving actual workers of the possibility of expression. These workers, says Lyotard, are condemned to silence.

Like any litigation, a differend may originate with a given 'damage'. But there exists further damage. The second level of damage typically occurs when a litigator 'is deprived of... the freedom to make his or her ideas or opinions public, or simply of the right to testify to the damage' (Lyotard 1988: 5). A litigation involves a mere plaintiff. In a differend the plaintiff suffers a wrong and becomes a victim: s/he is 'deprived of the... means by which to bring to the knowledge of others in general... the existence of a damage'. This silence may remain enforced even when there is a formal possibility of testifying to the damage. It happens when 'the testifying takes place but is deprived of authority' (Lyotard 1988: 5). Thus certain statements can be made yet cannot be heard. In a differend, says Lyotard, what suffers, what is exposed to threats, is expression or expressivity itself.

The victims of a differend or their advocates may, of course, resist the monopoly granted to the institutions that silence them. They can seek justice in spite of those institutions by moving the litigation to other arenas, by relying on other institutions entitled to pronounce factuality. Yet there are cases in which Lyotard comes to the point of wondering if 'the only "authority" left to the victims who attempt to bear witness to their wrong is... that of vengeance' (Lyotard 1988: 30). Lyotard, however, suggests another possibility: philosophy.

Philosophy's role is one of giving the differend its due, of allowing for the wrong to find an expression and for the victim to turn into an ordinary plaintiff. Attending the differend places philosophy in the centre of the search for justice. Thus the 'usurpation of authority' that Marx denounced in *Capital* (Lyotard 1988: 84) can be seen as a differend: the result of an economic 'monolingualism' which was leaving wage labourers no choice but to negotiate contracts in the language of capital, a language in which 'labour' is a commodity which it is legitimate to sell (Lyotard 1988: 171; cf. Hall 2011). Lyotard sees Marx's work as an attempt to address the differend that arises from the pain of the worker; as an attempt to 'find the idiom in which the suffering due to capital can be expressed'. In other terms, the very existence of differends is the symptom of a democratic deficit.

This deficit has become particularly – and paradoxically – visible in the case of news media. When non-journalists enter into debate with journalists concerning the establishment of current political-historical realities, journalists become both litigators and judges. Laymen make assertions but these assertions cannot be heard.

Take a public statement by a political actor that has been i) provoked; ii) decontextualized; and iii) shortened into a 'sound bite'. This statement is now a 'simulacrum' that can be manipulated at will (Baudrillard 1978). Can such a statement be disowned by its supposed author? Hardly so. Once validated by the media the simulacrum tends to be accepted as fact by all parties involved, including eventually the presumed author of the statement who knows that further protests would only result in attracting more attention. Transformed into a 'victim', the political actor usually gives up to the media discourse.

Here is another situation. Spectators watch a programme destined for the general public, and in which a group or community they identify with is submitted to specific accusations. They know that certain of these accusations are not justified and that certain 'facts' are incorrect or doubtful. As members of the general public they routinely trust the media to express their own views. Yet their direct knowledge challenges the media account. Can they discuss such facts? Is a debate possible? Or are they doomed to become the victims of a differend?[1]

Those who become media victims may seek a validation of their claims in court. Or they can appeal to history. Yet courts may align their language on that of the media and the sanction of history may take centuries. But even in the case of the courts validating their claims, the differend may remain.

Here is a ruling concluding a trial during which vocal critics of a French channel (FR II) were sued for libel by that channel.[2] The court ruling dismissed the accusation of libel, stating that those who expressed doubts about the facts presented by the French channel were 'exerting their right to a free critique' and had not trespassed the limits of 'freedom of expression'.

But this court ruling triggered a wave of indignation among media personnel. A petition signed by more than 1000 journalists stated that the court ruling was creating a 'right of defaming journalists', and that 'it allowed anyone to revile the honour and reputation of information professionals under the pretext of "good faith", the "right to free criticism", and "freedom of expression" '.[3]

This petition was caricatural by the ease with which it decided who should be entitled to 'free criticism'. The numerous journalists who signed it seemed unaware that the freedom of the press is nothing but an extension of the individual freedoms that they wished to curb (O'Neill 2008). But the petition went further: it haughtily dismissed the possibility of a debate between 'information professionals' and simple spectators. It asserted that lay spectators 'know nothing of journalistic fieldwork, especially, in a zone of conflict'. They were therefore not entitled to discuss the 'facts' offered to them.

Note that an interesting language game was taking place. Members of the public were challenging the account of given realities. Journalists answered by commending the professionalism of media procedures. A 'dialogue of the deaf' substituted for a debate between litigators. Challenging the media performance was impossible for lay citizens who were de facto reduced to silence. Lyotard would say that the point of this language game was precisely one disqualifying lay citizens, of silencing them. Following a principle often used by military establishments to curb civilian enquiries, 'professionalism' was used as a shield against discussion. Journalists were to be trusted 'a priori'.[4] Their opponents became victims. Once more, the casualty was expressivity.

*   *   *

Media used to be instruments of a democratic conquest. Many examples show them changed into a fortress, imposing transparency on other institutions, refusing it for themselves. In line with Lyotard's view of the differend as an indicator of issues to be addressed by politics, I believe that one of the most promising approaches to media theory consists in starting from differends in which media are involved; in listening to the grievances of silenced litigators. If one cares about democracy, these grievances must be taken seriously. 'The victims of a differend once understood language as an instrument of communication but...through the feeling of pain that accompanies their enforced silence...they learn to recognize that what remains to be phrased exceeds what can presently be phrased' (Lyotard1988: 13). Differends can serve as our teachers. They point to what remains to be phrased.

The differends I have stressed here concern a key issue: the issue of 'appearing in public' as opposed to being shown, forced into visibility, 'outed', defamed. Hannah Arendt says that politics consists in 'appearing in public'. But on whose terms do we appear? Do we control our appearance? And, if we have no control over it whatsoever, isn't there a risk for each of us to be pronounced a windmill or a giant, for political reality to turn into a quixotic exercise?

This chapter will show that this issue, the numerous differends that it triggers and the pain that such differends generate all call for a new paradigm for the study of news media. This paradigm challenges the usual formulations of the professional ethics of journalism. It speaks no longer of information but of 'monstration'. It speaks no longer the language of 'objectivity' but that of performance. It finally shows that, far from leading to an amorphous relativism, insisting on the performative dimension of media, facilitates a new critical discourse. But before introducing this paradigm, a second exploration is necessary. It follows the steps of Roger Silverstone (2006) whose book *Media and Morality* anticipates many of my points.

Appearing on whose terms? And why media ethics is not merely a matter of 'hospitality': Silverstone, Derrida

Roger Silverstone's model of the journalist as 'host' appears in the context of the 'mediapolis': the 'mediated public space where contemporary political life increasingly finds its place, both at national and global levels'. The mediapolis is largely inspired by Hannah Arendt's 'Polis'. It is not the city-state in its physical location but 'the organization of the people as it arises out of acting and speaking together' (Arendt 1958: 198). Offering a characteristic combination of moral and dramaturgic concerns, the polis is a space of appearance: 'the space where I appear to others as others appear to me' (*ibid.*).

This space of appearance is ruled by distance, which, for Silverstone, is not 'just a material, a geographical or even a social category'; it is a moral category. Moral distance is the distance that the media as representatives of a 'we' assign to others. Silverstone conceptualizes 'moral distance' in terms of an 'ethics of hospitality' inspired by the work of Derrida. The media are referred to the role of the host.

*   *   *

There is, for Derrida, a linguistic and philosophical affinity between ethics and home, between ethics and ethos. 'Insofar as it has to do with the ethos, that is the residence, one's home, the familiar place of dwelling … ethics is thoroughly coextensive with the experience of hospitality' (2001: 16–17). For Derrida, 'hospitality goes to the heart of our relationships with others. Indeed it is constitutive of such relations.' Silverstone stresses that Derridean hospitality is an obligation with no corresponding right. Hospitality means 'welcoming the other in one's space, with or without any expectation of reciprocity'. The law, of course, sets limits on who will be welcome and under what terms; 'in some sense the law is by definition inhospitable'. But Derrida 'distinguishes between unconditional and conditional hospitality, the first beyond, the second within, the law'. Derrida's true hospitality, concludes Silverstone, is 'unconditional...breaking all bounds, unconstrained by the forces of law and urban and national self-interest'.

* * *

Silverstone's ambition is to translate Derrida's philosophy of hospitality into guidelines for media practice. He sees media hospitality as 'a willingness to ensure that...the bodies and voices of those who might...be otherwise marginalized will be seen and heard on their own term' (Silverstone 2006: 143). This hospitable publicizing relies on imagination. For him, the virtue of 'imagination' allows us 'to put that which is too close at a certain distance and to bridge abysses of remoteness until we can see and understand everything that is too far away from us as though it were our own affair' (Arendt quoted in Silverstone 2006: 46).

Thus, for Silverstone, 'imagination' is that which serves the purpose of distancing oneself from oneself, and 'proper distance' is that which permits sharing the position of the Other. In regard to the Other, 'proper distance' therefore means no distance at all. What is 'proper' is the erasure of any distance. Instead of a 'proper distance', he could speak here of a 'required proximity'. In fact this is exactly what he does when he stresses 'the degree of proximity required in our mediated inter-relationships...for a duty of care, obligation and responsibility' (Silverstone 2006: 47).

Silverstone knows that the type of unconditional media hospitality that he advocates is almost impossible. Even when it is not flatly denied, media hospitality remains parsimonious, cautiously granted. Terrorism is a case at hand.

Let us imagine, Silverstone asks, 'the disinterested, or fair, reporting of terrorism in a society recently terrorized...What kinds of distance are appropriate in such representation? Do we really see the face of terrorists? Do we listen to the terrorists on their own terms? Can we hear what they may have to say?'[5] (Silverstone 2006: 141)

In order to justify the granting of hospitality to face and the voice of the terrorist, Silverstone turns again towards Derrida: 'Hospitality, in its pure and unconditional form does not involve, nor is it dependent on, an invitation. It is only when someone enters our lives, and is welcomed, without having been invited, that we can truly accept the otherness of the other.' (Silverstone 2006: 140) In media terms, as well as in material terms, he concludes, there is a difference between the hospitality of invitation and what Derrida calls the hospitality of visitation. It is the latter which is increasingly required in a truly cosmopolitan society:

'there has to be space for the unbidden and the uninvited, both in the material as well as the mediated world' (Silverstone 2006: 142).

One may doubt that terrorism offers the best opportunity for exercising 'hospitality by visitation'. Visitation may affect many forms. For example, knocking on my door is not the same as exploding it.[6] But I would like to take issue with some of Silverstone's more basic assumptions. Directly entailed by his stand on the Other, his 'proper distance' is equated by him with proximity. Is 'proximity' the only (moral) definition of what a 'proper' distance should be?

Silverstone writes: 'No presumptions should be made about an unreflecting, universal, generalisable, uncomplicated "we". The "we" both is, but crucially is also not, the plural of the "I". I would answer that no presumptions should be made either about an unreflecting, universal, generalizable uncomplicated "other"' (Silverstone 2006: 3). Yet Silverstone's book speaks of the Other as if the use of capitals subsumed every possible alterity. He makes it very clear that the Other is not the one I have invited, but whoever comes to me, invited or uninvited. Maybe so. But why is this visitor alone? Why the singular? What about the claims of many others to be recognized? What about the faces of many others to be seen and the voices of many others to be listened to? What about the fact that there are simultaneously many ways of being not me? The Turk may be my Other. But the Armenian is not me. The Janjawid is my Other. But the Darfour civilians are not me. The Balkan Moslems might be my Other. But the Serbs are not me. This entails a simple consequence. In most situations involving news reporting, focusing on the dual pair of 'me' and the 'Other' is a misleading utopia.

Instead of pairs, there are at least triangles. Obvious in Boltanski's (1999) description of distant suffering (where one finds at least a triad: perpetrator, victim, spectator) triangles are not to be found in Silverstone's book. In fact, his moral approach tends to do exactly what he insisted the media should avoid: either incorporating or demonizing the other. He notes that this Other was sometimes pushed 'to a point beyond strangeness, beyond humanity'; and he was sometimes drawn 'so close as to become indistinguishable from ourselves'. This Other was pulled 'too close' or pushed 'too far'. In both cases the resulting distance was morally unacceptable and the media performance was torn between symmetrical immoralities: the 'immorality of distance' and the 'immorality of sameness or identity'.

This being said, Silverstone divides Others into big Others (targeted for hospitality) and smaller Others (dissolved altogether, or treated as if they were undistinguishable from ourselves). Once this is done, he stages a big Lévinasian face to face, a theatre of alterity, a sublime encounter of I and thou.

I enjoy the sublimity of the encounter. I object to its dualistic character. 'Mediapolis' is not a 'pas de deux', nor is it the culminating duet of an opera. I do not like the idea of gesturing over the heads of those who have been absorbed into 'sameness' while respectfully addressing a succession of majestic Others (sooner or later to be dethroned). Abolishing some of the Others in our moral world certainly simplifies it. Do we need this simplicity?

*   *   *

The status conferred to Silverstone's Other strictly determines his view of distance. His proper distance is the distance which encourages responsibility. Faced to otherness, proper distance means in fact no distance at all, except from myself. But what is the sort of distance that would be deemed 'proper' if one acknowledges the multiplicity of others?

If instead of being confronted to some major, monumental, generalized Others I acknowledge that there are many others awaiting my response at any given moment, the calculation of a proper distance radically changes. Proper distance can no longer be offered as a synonym for proximity. It now defines the point from which I am capable of hearing the respective claims of many others. Proper distance involves the reintroduction of some actual distance. It is the amount of distance that one needs if one seeks to go beyond a fusional relationship with some privileged category of others.

Put differently, proper distance needs to be equitable distance. This equitable distance – or 'equidistance' – introduces an ethical dimension that Silverstone tends to downgrade. Media morality is not merely a matter of hospitality; it is also a matter of justice. The multiplicity of others, is, after all, what mediapolis is about. As to hospitality, it should never consist in shutting someone out.

*   *   *

I disagree with Silverstone. Yet I know it is he who warns journalists against making the Other into a version of self. Obviously he is not advocating such a confusion. The same is true of 'proper distance'. When Silverstone sees 'too far' and 'too close' as instruments of 'symmetrical immoralities', he clearly means that proper distance is not just the absence of any distance. Proper distance is the moral distance one should adopt when it comes to depicting humans. Through the metaphor of 'distance', Silverstone raises a larger ethical question. Do the media acknowledge the humanity of those they portray? Do the providers of visibility express regard for those they show?

I believe this question is crucial even though Silverstone answers it by conflating reporting and hospitality. I believe the conflation is inaccurate, largely because what is shown in the news is not merely a matter of 'being' (either similar or different) but a matter of 'doing' and accountability for one's deeds.[7]

I suggest that Silverstone proposes not an ethics of hospitality (except at the most general, abstract level) but an ethics of visibility. Visuality is a technical matter. Visibility is a moral, social, political category. Reporting practices are not only a matter of visuality, but a matter of visibility.

*   *   *

I believe that another model is relevant to the ethics of visibility. This is 'the model of the witness', a model that has been studied in all sorts of contexts, from the judiciary to the theological to the journalistic. The model of the witness comes equipped with its own set of ethical dimensions. It has to do with truth. It has to do with truthfulness. It has to do with the connection between truth and justice. It also has to do with personal commitment (witnessing is a risky matter). It finally involves a sociology of media organizations, seen as 'witnessing architectures' (Ashuri and Pinchevski 2009) or, to use Lyotard's phrase, 'factuality pronouncing institutions'.

Yet the model of the witness is not sufficient to deal with the task at hand. A witness – the type of witness that John Durham Peters defines as an 'active witness' – is not merely someone who has attended some situation or event. A witness is someone called upon to provide a depiction, a narrative, a set of images of what took place. In other terms an active witness is a performer. His/her performance calls for yet another model (Peters 2001). This new model is concerned with the process whereby actions, interactions or reactions are identified or interpreted in order to be shown or told. Some of the dimensions of the portrayed situation will survive the exercise; some will be 'lost in translation'. Like ethnographers, repertory theatre directors or piano players, journalists can be defined as cultural translators. They can be compared to this wonderful fictional character that the novelist Jhumpa Lahiri invented as a go-between for foreign doctors and vernacular-speaking patients. Lahiri's go-between was neither a doctor nor a nurse; he was the ambassador of inchoate pains, 'the interpreter of maladies' (Lahiri 1999).

Journalists are not 'interpreters of maladies'. They are providers of templates for inchoate, unfinished events (Kitzinger 2000; Hoskins 2010). They are providers of interpretants for disputed interactions. They are providers of selective visibility. They record fragments of behaviours and use them as building blocks for the construction of acceptable simulacra. Obviously, the word 'acceptable' is no less essential here than the word 'simulacra'.

* * *

I would finally like to suggest that both the model of the witness and the model of the translator can be incorporated into a last and more general model. Implied by Silverstone in every other sentence, this model stresses those actions which consist in pointing, showing and calling attention. This model needs now to be spelt out. I call it the 'model of monstration' (Dayan 2006; 2012; in press).

Monstration, performance and the ethics of regard: Austin, Ricoeur, Honneth

Media have long enjoyed a privilege earned in the 18th century, with the emergence of a public sphere aimed at allowing rational and informed citizens to discuss state decisions. Yet, in regard to actual media practices, democratic theory often serves as an alibi.

If the role of news media merely consisted in providing information, too many exceptions and deviant practices would transform media theory into a casuistry.

Rather than starting from what practitioners claim – or wish – to do, let us therefore observe what they actually do. Let us suspend the self-definition of news institutions; put this self-definition between brackets; note that, in many instances, what we call 'information media' are mostly concerned with modelling public behaviour.

Media are institutions that confer visibility on events, persons, groups, debates, controversies and narratives. They are in charge of managing collective attention. Information may or may not be available on 'information media'. Visibility is unavoidable.

In crude terms, journalists are people who get paid to show stuff. Sometimes this 'stuff' deserves to be defined as 'information'. Sometimes not. Media are calling attention to something by showing it. How and why do they show it? Why are they showing it in this way? What is it? Where is the rest of it? What have they chosen not to show? These are naïve questions. These are key questions. I propose to replace the notion of 'information' with a less problematic one: 'monstration'.

'Monstration' comes from the French verb *montrer* ('to show'). So does the English word 'monster'. (A 'monster' is someone on display, as in a circus or fairground.) There are countless forms of monstration ranging from the organization of spectacles to what psychoanalysts call 'interpretation' (the fact of highlighting unconscious motives in the discourse of an analysand). Art historian Hans Belting says that behind any image one must imagine a body that gestures, calling for your attention (Belting 2004). Monstration is typically performed by individuals. But it also involves groups, 'moral' persons, institutions such as museums, festivals, monuments, movie theatres, galleries, zoos, fairs, installations and fashion shows. Venice film festival calls itself La Mostra ('the monstration').

Certain institutions are exclusively devoted to monstration. Others provide monstrations while serving other purposes. This is the case for scientific experiments, court trials, presentations of medical patients, line-ups of suspects and demonstrations of new technologies. All societies assign boundaries to the activities of monstration. These limits can be individual, as in Goffman's 'back region' (Goffman 1959, but they can also be professional (rules of confidentiality), political (classified documents) or religious. (Australian aboriginal rituals put the monstration of sacred objects off limits to the uninitiated; Michaels 1982.)

There is a catholic liturgy called 'monstration' of which the following is an example. In 1228 the relics of Quintinus (martyred in AD 300) and of two other saints were set in reliquaries. Occurring every year in the Saint Quentin basilica in Northern France, a monstration offers a ceremonial display of the holy relics (Shortell 1999). This is informative since the relics bear witness to a given sequence of events. Yet this informative dimension is just one element within a larger performance. It is literally anecdotal. Veneration is the reason why the relics are displayed. Is the situation really different when it comes to media?

*   *   *

Media monstrations create faits-accomplis. They do so i) by asserting or denying the existence of given interactions; ii) by imposing judgement on their protagonists; and iii) by displaying respect or disrespect towards them. 'There is', says Radcliffe-Brown, 'a ritual relationship whenever a society imposes its members a given attitude towards a given object' (Radcliffe-Brown 1952). In that sense, media constantly perform monstration rituals.

Most news items are about actions or interactions. In reference to Austinian pragmatics, I am proposing here that the fact of showing such interactions is in itself a form of symbolic action (Austin 1962). As a form of action, monstration lends itself to ethical evaluation. For Judith Butler (2006), interpreting a photograph amounts to interpreting what is already an interpretation. An image provides an attitude, together with the situation that motivated it. This is certainly the case for news media. The constative dimension of media images always reaches us wrapped up in gestures.[8]

With a few notable exceptions there is always a point to showing something. Acts of monstration can be performed by verbal means, by visual means or by a combination of both. And, of course, the media are eminently concerned since they are society's major institution of monstration. In reference to Austin's vocabulary of 'speech acts', I would describe the news media as performers of three major 'monstrative acts'.

The first monstrative act is an 'exercitive'. It consists of showing or not showing, and of all the shades in between. Showing an interaction salutes it as meaningful. Refusing to show it dismisses it. The second monstrative act is a 'verdictive'. It consists of judging the protagonists of an interaction, in displaying them as good or bad, as perpetrators or victims, as admirable or despicable. The third monstrative act is what Austin calls a 'behabitive'. It consists of responding to those involved in an interaction and takes the form of regard/disregard; respect/contempt; deference/challenge; sympathy/distance. This response is either directly that of the media themselves or that of third parties whom the media often use as proxies.

Austin was quite aware that the limits between different sorts of speech acts are porous. In the case of the news media, this porousness means that all monstrative acts are behabitives of one form or the other; that all monstrative acts call for an ethics of regard.

Take the case of media exercitives. They consist in acknowledging situations, in pronouncing them as facts and in deciding how important such facts are. But acknowledging facts means taking account of those whom these facts concern. By stating the existence and importance of a given situation, exercitives of monstration are performances through which individuals or groups are regarded or disregarded. Ignoring certain facts, negating someone's claims, amounts to disregarding the claimant. When a claimant's 'facts' are expelled from the realm of shared realities (from what Olivier Voirol calls 'interobjectivity'), their expulsion becomes that of the claimant as well (Voirol 2007; Lyotard 1988).

There are two novels called *The Invisible Man*: one by H G Wells (1952) and one by Ralph Ellison (1952). Invisibility in the first is a matter of perception. Wells's hero manages to disappear. Invisibility in the second novel is a matter of ethics. Ellison's invisible man is indeed a man of flesh and bones but one does not wish to see him. He is invisible, says Axel Honneth, not because he is transparent or because people are blind but because an 'inner disposition' compels those in front of him to refuse acknowledging his existence. The same inner disposition is bitterly resented by Primo Levi and triggers the famous nightmare in which, returning from the death camps, the Italian writer attempts to tell what he has been through. While he speaks, listeners stand up one by one and leave.

Recognition, says Axel Honneth, depends on expressive gestures through which human beings confirm to each other their social value. Invisibility can amount to being expelled from the circuit of recognition (Honneth 1996). In this case, invisibility is a performance which negatively combines the original meaning of the French word *regard* ('gaze') with its usual English meaning ('respect'). Invisibility performs a moral death, commits a social assassination. This is perhaps why 'negationism' matters so much. Ignoring certain facts (and, in our case, refusing to show them) allows the disregarding of those who went through the suffering inflicted by these facts. Ignoring certain facts amounts to making persons invisible. In other terms, beyond their multiplicity, beyond their diversity, all of the illocutionary acts involved in news as monstration involve an ethical dimension. Monstration is always a matter of regard. This is where I concur with Silverstone.

* * *

What is at stake in monstration directly concerns democracy. Far from eliciting viewer responses based on the contents of received information and on subsequent deliberation, media monstrations tend to provide such responses within the new items themselves. The fact of showing or not showing, and the decision of 'how much to show', are often arbitrary decisions, taken outside a space of discussion, and unaddressed by deontologies. Media that ostensibly call for debate tend actually to pre-empt it.[9]

Protests are too easily rebuked in the name of 'professional expertise', leading to those communicative pathologies denounced by Jean-François Lyotard.

Differends prosper in the absence of a language in which the role of 'factuality pronouncing institutions' could be precisely discussed. This chapter has been attempting to discuss such a language. Speaking of 'information media' was premised on a normative myth; on a form of wishful thinking that assumed that media consist in providing information.[10] I argued that any discussion of journalism should address what journalism verifiably does: monstration. And, since journalism is a public performance, I also argued that the deontology of journalism should be based on a performative model.

Can a performative model serve as a basis for evaluation? Can we formulate a normative discourse in the vocabulary of performance? Let me answer by returning to one of the models I evoked earlier. The model of the journalist as interpreter; the model of the journalist as cultural translator. As Ricoeur (2007) puts it, no translation is perfect. This is why the same texts may not only be translated and translated again, but also be rephrased within the same language. A perfect translation is nowhere to be found. There are only translations that are better or worse, richer or poorer, more relevant or less relevant, more comprehensive or less comprehensive. Turning towards another sort of interpretive performance, I could similarly argue that there is no perfect way of playing Beethoven but that this unattainable perfection has never prevented anyone from evaluating pianists, conductors and orchestras. Some interpreters are great. Some are lousy. Some performances are better, some performances are pathetic. What about the performances of news media?

Like other interpreters, journalists are condemned to finding the right balance between comprehensivity and relevance. In their case, such balance can be defined in reference to the second model I evoked: that of the journalist as witness. As shown by John Peters, any active witness offers a performance (Peters 2001).

As to the myth of a perfect objectivity, it is mostly brandished as an excuse for sloppy journalism or invoked as a scarecrow by those who wish to escape any normative evaluation.[11] Listen, by contrast, to the following statement by a brilliant 'performer': someone who knows that evaluation starts once we acknowledge that there is no perfect way of doing ethnography. Clifford Geertz writes: 'I have never been impressed by the argument that, as complete objectivity is impossible (as of course it is)...one might as well let one's sentiments run loose...That is like saying that, as a perfectly aseptic environment is impossible, one might as well conduct surgery in a sewer' (Geertz 1973).

Thanks

Nick Couldry directed me to Ricoeur's work on translation and Amit Pinchevski insisted that I should read Lyotard's differend. Thanks to both.

Notes

1. As members of the stigmatized group they feel they are no longer 'ratified' recipients of the media discourse, but rather 'eavesdroppers' of a conversation from which media pronouncements have expelled them (Goffman).
2. The ruling by the Paris Court of Appeals (21 May 2008) reversed a first decision pronounced on 19 October 2006 in the libel suit opposing France-Television (France II) to M. Philippe Karsenty.
3. 'Appel pour Charles Enderlin' in *Nouvel Obs.com*, 10 June 2008; *Le Monde*, 8–9 June 2008. The petition was also made available in the daily newspaper *Marianne*.
4. This probably explains why it took more than seven years and a court order for France II to show the rushes from which images of the debated facts had been excerpted.
5. Silverstone's prescription relied on a misapprehension of the words of terrorists. He assumed that these were essentially expressive words – that they fulfilled a need for communication. He urged us to treat these words as if they were based on a dialogic quest for common grounds. Yet, since its inception, terrorism was conceived as 'propaganda by the act'. Why should it suddenly change nature? Why should holy warriors embrace Habermasian ethics? Why should suicide bombers morph into shepherds of Arcadia?
6. Silverstone's programme was in fact applied in the case of a young French terrorist who executed two soldiers and a group of children in the South of France. 'Media Hospitality' was a recipe for catastrophe. Mohamed Merah's 'face' and 'words' were abundantly circulated on French media. Smiling to the camera in a posed photograph, the slim, rather handsome youth became an overnight celebrity. His words were extensively quoted. The daily *Liberation* devoted a whole issue (18 July 2012) to reproducing verbatim extracts of a 173-page transcript of Merah's last conversation, including his justification for killing Jewish toddlers. Reproducing the terrorist's discourse 'on his own terms', the media became a recruitment agency. Following the extensive showing of Merah's face and words, anti-Semitic violence throughout France rose by 50 per cent (BFM TV news, 9 October 2012).
7. Hospitality seems to me almost as irrelevant as another notion that Silverstone brings into the discussion: forgiveness. He writes: 'hospitality is dangerous. It is not without risk.' But 'hospitality has much in common with true forgiveness'. 'To give hospitality to the terrorist' and 'to forgive the unforgivable' are the true expressions of the primary ethic. I agree that forgiving, like hospitality, is ethically crucial. But why should it be relevant to media ethics? Why should the media forgive? Forgiving is the privilege of victims. Are witnesses entitled to forgive in the name of victims?

8. In a process that closely resembles Barthes's famous 'rhetorics of the image' (Barthes 1964), the content of news pieces is only the first layer of a discourse whose second layer is always 'performative'.

9. Does this means that the attitudes displayed in the news irresistibly become those of the spectators and that the media perform the perceptions of publics? Does it mean that media users have no other option but that of adopting the assessments, judgements and attitudes pronounced by the media? No. Stressing the performative dimension of monstration is not the same as crediting the media with an irresistible power. As pointed to by Austin in his discussion of 'infelicities', performatives can fail. A speech act may be ill-suited to the situation it addresses. The author of a pronouncement may have no authority to issue it and so on. See Dayan (in press).

10. Of course, I am not stating that information is always absent. I believe, more empirically, that it should be treated as a variable rather than as a definition. The question is: Is there information?

11. The powerful binary opposition objectivity/subjectivity also served a much healthier function but it was a colossus with clay feet. All it took to tripping it was for the militant journalist to declare it undesirable: it was hegemony by another name; for the postmodern journalist to proclaim it impossible: it was a misapplied construct, an intellectual fallacy; for the less sophisticated journalist to embrace 'subjectivity': it was a birthright. All this involved, of course, some overkilling. Something that is impossible does not need to be undesirable as well. As to the vocabulary of 'rights', it seems unconvincing on the part of those whose immense power consists in deciding what is 'factual'. Like a screen formation in psychoanalysis, the notion of 'objectivity' was the symptom of a lack. It pointed to the need for a normative discourse. It was not up to the job but served as reminder.

References

Arendt, H. (1958) 'The Human Condition', *Between Past and Future*. New York: Penguin, 227–264

Ashuri, T. and Pinchevski, A. (2009) 'Witnessing as a Field', in P. Frosh and A. Pinchevski (eds) *Media Witnessing*. Palgrave Macmillan.

Austin A. J. (1962) *How To Do Things with Words*. Cambridge: Harvard University Press.

Barthes, Roland (1964) 'Rhétorique de l'Image', *Communications* 4, Paris: Seuil.

Baudrillard, Jean (1978) 'La Précession des simulacres', *Traverses* Paris: Centre Pompidou.

Belting, Hans (2004) 'Anthropologie de l'image', *Cahiers du collège Iconique* XV–I Paris, 2004.

Boltanski, L. (1999) *Distant Suffering*. Cambridge: Cambridge University Press.

Butler, Judith (2006) *Precarious Life: The Powers of Mourning and Violence*. London: Verso.

Dayan, D. (ed.) (2006) 'Quand montrer c'est faire', in *La Terreur Spectacle*. Paris-INA & Bruxelles: De Boeck.

Dayan, D. (2012) 'Mentir par les médias', *Ecrire L'Histoire*. No special 'le Mensonge', T 1–9, 3.

Dayan, D. (in press) 'Dealing in Attitudes. Television and Monstration', *Divinatio*. Special issue *Is Democracy Sick of Its Own Media?* Sofia.

Derrida, Jacques (2001) *On Cosmopolitanism and Forgiveness*. Trans. Mark Dooley and Michael Hughes. Preface by Simon Critchley and Richard Kearney. London and New York: Routledge: 16–I7.

Ellison, Ralph (1952) *The Invisible Man*. New York: Random House.

Geertz, Clifford. (1973) 'Thick Description', in *The Interpretation of Cultures*. New York: Basic Books.

Goffman, Ervin (1959) The Presentation of Self in Everyday Life. New York: Anchor Books.

Goldfarb, Jeffrey (2006) *The Politics of Small Things*. Chicago: the University of Chicago Press, 17.

Hall, Meredith (2011) 'On Infringement: Intellectual Property and the Incommensurable Discourses of Liberalism's', NSSR Seminar Paper. Media & Visibility.

Honneth, Axel (1996) *The Struggle for Recognition: The Moral Grammar of Social Conflicts*. Cambridge: MIT Press.

Honneth, Axel (2005) 'Invisibilité: sur l'épistémologie de la "reconnaissance"', *Réseaux* in Voirol, O. (ed.), *Visibilité/Invisibilité. Réseaux*, 23(129–130): 41–57.

Hoskins, Andrew and O'Loughlin, B. (2010) *War and Media: The Emergence of Diffused War*. Cambridge: Polity Press.

Kitzinger, J. (2000) Media Templates: Key Events and the (Re)construction of Meaning. *Media, Culture and Society* 22(1): 61–84.

Lahiri, Jhumpa (1999) *The Interpreter of Maladies*. New York: Houghton and Mifflin.

Libération (18 July 2012) Special issue: *Le Flic et le Terroriste*. Transcripts of the tapes of Mohamed Merah's exchanges with the French Police, introduced by Nicolas Demorand and Patricia Tourancheau.

Lyotard, Jean-François (1988) *Le Différend*. Paris: Minuit.

Michaels, Eric (1982) *TV Tribes*, PhD dissertation. University of Texas, Austin.

Nouvel, obs (2008) 'Pour Charles Enderlin', Nouvel Obs. 4 June, 2008; also *Le Monde*, 8–9 June 2008.

O'Neill, Onora (2008) 'Does Freedom Trump All Other Media Norms?', *The Ethics of Media: Philosophical Foundations and Ethical Imperatives*. Conference convened by Nick Couldry and Mirca Madianou. Cambridge University CRASSH. Ap 4, 5.

Peters, John Durham (2001) 'Witnessing', *Media Culture & Society*, 23(6): 707–723.

Radcliffe Brown, W. (1952) *Structure and Function in Primitive Society*. London: Routledge and Kegan Paul.

Ricoeur, Paul (2006) 'Translation as Challenge and Source of Happiness,' in *On Translation*. Trans. Eileen Brennan. New York: Routledge, 3: 31.

Shortell, E. M. (1999) Le démembrement de saint Quentin: architecture gothique et monstration des reliques. Saint-Quentin: Bibliothéque municipale.

Silverstone, Roger (2006) *Media and Morality: On the rise of the Mediapolis*. Cambridge, Polity. 46: 48 & 141: 42.

Voirol, Olivier (2005) 'Visibilité, Invisibilité' *Réseaux*, 23(129–130): 9, 31.

Voirol, Olivier (2007) Presentation to Daniel Dayan and Dominique Pasquier's seminar. Ecole des Hautes Etudes en Sciences Sociales. Spring term.

Wells, H.G. (1952) [o.p. 1897] *Invisible Man*. London: Collins.

11

Ethics of Mediation and the Voice of the Injured Subject

Mirca Madianou

One of the topics to emerge from the Leveson Inquiry on the 'culture, practice and ethics of the press'[1] in the UK concerns the experiences of those who had been unwillingly exposed or mistreated by the tabloid press. The constant theme in these often poignant accounts is the feeling of violation and vulnerability that individuals – both celebrities and ordinary members of the public – experienced, not only in the context of the phone-hacking scandal but also in several other instances of tabloid journalism. This was a rather rare moment when the voice of the injured subject was granted visibility.

Why does it matter to understand the voice of the injured subject? First, there are democratic and ethical reasons. If the ability to give an account of oneself is an essential feature of what it is to be human, voice is understood not just as a process but also as a human value (Couldry 2010: 1) which matters for democracy, justice and development. In this chapter I argue that listening to the voice of the wronged subject also matters in social science research because it gives us insight into the workings of mediation, still profoundly asymmetrical despite digital developments. Understanding the symbolic power of mediation is an important starting-point for any discussion of media ethics. This is because mediated communication, whether it involves traditional media institutions or individuals using digital platforms, is fundamentally different from face-to-face communication. Yet approaches to liberal media ethics often presuppose a model of communication as co-presence. Understanding the workings of mediation is important for arguing why freedom of expression – an individual right – cannot be applied to media institutions, a point eloquently made by Onora O'Neill (see Chapter 2 this volume). Here I argue that this argument is justified not only because media institutions – unlike individual subjects – are powerful organizations which need to be accountable (see O'Neill, Chapter 2 this volume) but also because communication through media, whether traditional mass media or new digital platforms, is structurally different from communication in a situation of co-presence. The media are not neutral conveyors of meaning; mediated communication is asymmetrically structured and its structuring inevitably shapes the experience of communication. As our lives are increasingly connected by – even lived in – media (Deuze 2012), we need to understand the structural transformation of mediated communication and its consequences when thinking through the ethics of media.

In order to illustrate the asymmetrical structure of mediation, this chapter will draw on the narrative accounts of people who found themselves inadvertently exposed by the media. The perspective of the wronged subject juxtaposed with the symbolic power of media institutions reveals the asymmetries of mediation in a very powerful way. Listening to the voice of the injured subject, although revealing, is not common practice. Such accounts are not readily available – wronged subjects are often silent – and when they do exist their voices are often drowned amongst the louder ones of more powerful institutions, such as the media themselves. This chapter draws on a rare occasion when the voices of those who had negative direct experiences with the media were publicly recorded. I analyse here the witness statements at the Leveson Inquiry, which was set up in July 2011 in order to investigate 'the relationship of the press with the public, police and politicians' following the phone-hacking scandal.[2] I focus in particular on the evidence provided to the inquiry during Module 1: 'the relationship between the press and the public' focusing on 'phone hacking and other potentially illegal behaviour' and its consequences for the people affected.[3] The witness statements and inquiry proceedings – all publicly available on the inquiry's website – provide a rich account of the experiences of those who found themselves inadvertently exposed in the news. Although several of the witnesses in the Leveson Inquiry were celebrities, who are already used to media exposure and who presumably possess the cultural, social and economic capital to respond to the media, many of the witnesses were people who found themselves in the public spotlight because of circumstances that were not of their own making. Such cases included members of the public who suffered the loss of a family member (the Bowles, Dowler, McCann and Watson families); who were wrongly accused of a crime (Christopher Jefferies); or worked for someone famous (Mary Ellen Field). My analysis has examined these accounts as well as the accounts of some celebrities, such as

Max Mosley, who reported mistreatments in the hands of the tabloid press.[4]

More difficult to identify are the cases when wronged subjects do not seek, or are not given the opportunity, to reply to the media. Given that these accounts and narratives are not publicly articulated they are harder to find and to assess. Social research has a bias for studying voice, for it is hard – if not impossible – to study silence. In my past research on news consumption I came across examples of participants who privately (in the interview context) expressed their disaffection or disenfranchisement with the news media and mediated public life in general (Madianou 2005a; 2012). To complement the analysis of the publicly articulated voices in the Leveson witness transcripts I will refer to this earlier work, which concerns the members of a minority group in Athens, Greece, and the narrative of a working-class English woman from East London. In both of these examples the disaffection expressed towards the media was largely due to people's negative personal experiences with the news media and journalists. In neither of these cases did participants reply to the news media in an attempt to correct their distorted representation. In this sense, both cases represent examples of 'silenced' voices. Understanding silenced voices matters particularly because it contributes to understanding the reasons which caused this silence – what Butler calls the materialization process (Butler 2005; see also Couldry 2010: 3).

The final example which I will consider here acknowledges that it is not just media institutions that can inflict harm. Individuals use digital platforms to produce their own content and this communication is a form of mediation. The case discussed here is one of unwanted mediated exposure through social media and the equally mediated response by the exposed subject. This is the 2012 'sex-tape' scandal involving the British popstar and television presenter Tulisa Contostavlos, who responded to her ex-partner's secretly filmed intimate *YouTube* video with a recorded reply (again on *YouTube*) in which she 'set the record straight' (Wiseman 2012). That case reminds us that mediated harm can be the result of personal use of social media, although in this example there was, comparatively, more symmetry in the media used for exposure and reparation.

Although these three types of accounts are taken from very different empirical contexts they are representative enough to illustrate the argument that our ethics of media discussion has to take into account an understanding of the workings of mediation and its symbolic power. Even though it is not the intention of this chapter to balance the tensions between generic notions of freedom of expression and privacy (for a discussion, see Gies 2007),[5] some conceptual clarity is necessary. Freedom of expression has become the generic term to refer to the freedom of speech both of individuals and of media institutions (for a discussion, see O'Neill, Chapter 2 this volume),[6] and collapsing individual self-expression and press freedom leads to confusion. In Mill's classic text (1989), self-expression was a means to protect individuality, so it is clear that the idea of self-expression cannot be applied to institutions such as the press or the media. Apart from arguing that freedom of expression becomes an altogether different category in conditions of mediation, I also observe that the individual right of freedom of expression cannot be straightforwardly applied to individuals acting through digital platforms because mediated communication engenders new forms of harm which would not have been possible otherwise. Listening to the voices – or lack thereof – of exposed subjects will reveal that mediation has the potential to amplify the emotional consequences of negative media exposure with serious practical and symbolic consequences for the individuals concerned. One of the consequences is the potential silencing of individuals, which also has implications for the normative project of voice as value (Couldry 2010).

Theoretically, this chapter draws on theories of mediation (Livingstone 2009; Madianou 2012; Silverstone 2005; Thompson 1995) and mediatization (Couldry 2012; Hepp 2012; Lundby 2009). By focusing on the perspective of the injured subject it contributes a 'bottom-up' perspective to this volume and the media ethics literature more broadly, which only recently has started to address the question of audiences.[7] The following paragraphs focus on the key for this chapter concepts of mediation, voice and harm.

Voice, harm and the architectures of mediation

This chapter is concerned with how voice and harm are transformed in the context of mediated communication. Being able to express an opinion and give an account of oneself is a fundamentally human need (Butler 2005; see also Couldry 2010: 7). Having a voice is also integral to the struggle for recognition (Honneth 1996; 2007) and visibility in the increasingly media-saturated social and political life. The sociological study of voice is distinct but interconnected to the normative dimension of voice as value (Couldry 2010), and the imperative to support a 'moral culture' that can counter the negative consequences of harm, disrespect and social exclusion by empowering those individuals who feel disrespected to articulate their experiences in the democratic public sphere (Honneth 2007: 78). It is only by understanding the harmful processes which obstruct voice – what Butler (2005) calls materialization – that we can develop a normative framework of ethics of media. Here I will argue that mediation may be an important factor that can potentially contribute to, or accentuate, the silencing of voices in situations of unwanted exposure. Understanding the workings of mediation is fundamental to any discussion of media ethics and for the support of moral cultures of recognition (Honneth 1996).

Mediation refers to the structural transformation which occurs with the introduction of media in the context of communication.[8] At a first level this means that mediated communication is not the same as face-to-face communication. Mediation introduces technological, institutional and economic parameters to the communication context while it also affords certain interactions but not others. Writing in 1995 and therefore before the proliferation of digital interactive communication technologies, Thompson developed a typology between face-to – face, mediated and quasi-interactive mediated communication (Thompson 1995). His argument is that face-to-face communication is fundamentally different from mediated communication (e.g. the communication between two individuals through phone calls) and mediated quasi-interactive communication, which is the communication through traditional media, such as the press and television, which are largely monological. The fact that mediated quasi-interactive communication can reach large audiences which are despatialized gives rise to 'a new visibility': a new mediated social relationship between the audience and the broadcast individual which is no longer reciprocal in character (Thompson 2005): 'Individuals can be seen by many viewers without themselves being able to see these viewers' (Thompson 2005: 35). Although the new visibility has been discussed in terms of its consequences for the political sphere (Thompson 2000; 2005), in my earlier work I became interested in the consequences of mediated visibility for ordinary members of the public in situations of unwanted exposure when individuals cannot interject their own account as they will never know all the readers who read their private story (Madianou 2012).

The recent technological convergence has a number of implications for mediation. The proliferation of communication technologies and platforms which continually intersect means that both mediated communication and communication through traditional media are no longer sustained by one medium or technology, but through an integrated assembly of media that form an environment of polymedia (Madianou and Miller 2013). In the case of interpersonal communication, individuals can choose from an environment of communicative opportunities and affordances in order to suit the relationships and purposes in question (Madianou and Miller 2013). Convergence is also evident in journalistic practices (Deuze 2004), while the proliferation of news platforms can even lead to the decentralization of news narratives, as is evident in the discussion of 'polymedia events' when news stories unfold across a range of platforms as part of the polymedia environment (Madianou 2013). Moreover, convergence unsettles typologies such as Thompson's (1995) discussed in the previous paragraphs as the boundaries between mediated and mediated quasi-interactive communication become blurred. With interactive technologies enabled within traditional one-to-many media and vice versa, the potential for audiences to publicly articulate their voice is stronger than ever before.

These observations, however, should not be interpreted as evidence that the symbolic power of mediation is weakened. In the case of news, the affordances of new communication technologies can even heighten the effects of mediation. For example, the fact that online news content is no longer ephemeral but permanent and retrievable potentially increases the size of audiences attending to the message exponentially. In this case the affordances of an internet-mediated platform have implications for the temporality and reach of the message without fundamentally transforming the structure of mediated communication. Even in the case of citizen journalism, which is inevitably centred on the promise of voice, there are evident asymmetries when it comes to whose voice is articulated and, ultimately, listened to (Chouliaraki 2013). Finally, the fact that personal communication is increasingly conducted via digital platforms means that it can acquire features of 'quasi-interactive', or mass mediated communication. The collapse of private and public boundaries on social media such as *Facebook* and *Twitter* can lead to personal views being broadcast to infinite audiences (Marwick and boyd 2011). As the widely reported UK case of Paul Chambers highlighted, what would have been an innocuous joke about blowing up an airport, had it been mentioned in the course of a personal conversation, led to his arrest for inciting terrorism when it appeared on *Twitter*. Mentioning terrorism on *Twitter*[9] seems to be the equivalent of 'shouting "fire!" in a crowded theatre'. The media, broadly defined, can create new forms of harm; in order to address the ethical implications of mediated harm, we first need to comprehend the architectures of mediation.

Apart from referring to the transformation that occurs with the introduction of media in social communication, the concept of mediation can also capture deeper, cumulative social consequences that extend beyond a specific communicative context. Described by Silverstone as a fundamentally 'dialectical process' (2005), mediation also refers to the ways in which media technologies transform social processes whilst being socially shaped themselves. Here mediation converges with the parallel term 'mediatization' (Couldry 2012; Hepp 2012). Mediation does not just alter the relationship between the particular exposed subject and its audience; it introduces a new mode of relating at a distance which has implications for a number of processes, including the broader conduct of politics (see Langer 2011 on the personalization of politics and Thompson 2000 on mediated political scandal). The following empirical discussion will reveal the emergence of a new form of mediated harm, which is qualitatively different from the harm that occurs in non-mediated environments. Unpacking this mediated harm is an essential first task for the conversation on ethics of media.

Listening to the voices of the injured subjects[10]

Violation and loss of control

The most prominent theme when reading the witness statements of the Leveson Inquiry is the profound feeling of violation and loss of control that members of the public experienced when they found themselves in the public spotlight. This applies most poignantly to those individuals and families who attracted the attention of the media under the tragic circumstances of losing a family member or being wrongly accused of a crime. Their invasion of privacy heightened what was already a dramatic situation of dealing with death, loss or false accusations. Given such harsh circumstances it is not surprising that some witnesses used very powerful terms to describe their experiences. For Kate McCann, the mother of the missing toddler Madeleine who vanished in Portugal in 2007, the publication of her private diaries by a Portuguese and British tabloid amounted to 'mental rape'. Sally and Bob Dowler, parents of the murdered schoolgirl Milly, expressed their situation very clearly:

> What we did not appreciate was the extent to which newspapers would intrude on our private turmoil and how little control we would have over where the lines were drawn in that respect.
> (Sally and Bob Dowler, joint witness statement, paragraph 6)

In their joint statement, the Dowlers describe their distress when they saw the publication of a private moment during which the mother, Sally, was photographed breaking down as she touched a poster of her then missing daughter. This image, which appeared in a tabloid newspaper, was taken during a private walk to retrace Milly's steps before her disappearance. It later emerged that the details of this private walk had become known to the reporters illegally through the hacking of the Dowlers' mobile phones. 'It was distressing to think that someone had been secretly photographing us during this intensely private moment' (Sally and Bob Dowler, joint witness statement, paragraph 7). Other families, such as the McCanns, reported direct confrontations with journalists who camped outside their home, tapped on their car windows and chased the family as they exited their house in order to take pictures that could then be used in the news.

Infinite audiences

One of the great transformations of mediation is the size of the audience which attends to the message. Even though face-to-face exposure might still have been distressing or unpleasant, it would involve a finite audience, largely known to the subject, who could in turn approach the audience and try to set the record straight. In a mediated context this is simply not possible. The publication of a story introduces a different scale to the experience: the audience is potentially infinite and at the same time unknown to the exposed subject. Moreover, it is dispersed spatially as the exposed individual and his/her audiences do not have to share the same location. This can be understood as an example of the 'new visibility' (Thompson 2005) to refer to the new social relationship between the broadcast individual and his/her audiences. Listen to Max Mosley, former president of Federation Internationale d'Automobile, who found himself involved in a widely reported sex scandal: 'Everytime I visit a restaurant or shop anywhere in the world, I have to prepare myself that the individuals working there or other customers know' (Witness statement by Max Mosley, paragraph 68).

This theme is echoed in the statement by Giles Crown on behalf of Edward Bowles, father of Sebastian, the 11-year-old boy killed in a bus accident in a Swiss motorway tunnel during a school ski trip in 2012. One of the most poignant moments in that statement concerns the publication of a photograph of the nine-year-old daughter of the family grieving over the death of her brother (Giles Crown witness statement, paragraph 10). The 'Helena photograph' (as it became known) also appeared in the Belgian media, including the cover or a popular magazine: 'Edward saw the magazine in a supermarket whist with Helena as it was prominently displayed beside the narrow entrance to the main body of the shop and they were both very upset by it. As they passed it, another member of the public pointed to them both' (Giles Crown witness statement, paragraph 22).

The consequences of this exposure to a deterritorialized and potentially infinite audience can be devastating. Christopher Jefferies, who had been wrongly accused for the murder of a young Bristol architect in 2011, found himself in what can be described as a public witch-hunt. Even though another man was eventually arrested and convicted of the murder, the press coverage about him was so intense and so negative that

> after being released on bail I spent almost 3 months confined to my friends' houses. Even after I returned home and tried to return to some form of normality, I remember being very apprehensive about going into cafes or shops because I did not know how people would react to me.
>
> (Christopher Jefferies witness statement, paragraph 53)

The McCanns describe how they encountered their audience through the hate mail they received during the first year after their daughters' disappearance: 'During this time we also received a large volume of hate mail including a death threat which I believe was largely attributable to these articles and their reporting of the investigation.' (Witness statement Gerry McCann, paragraph 45). What emerges from these statements is that the effects of the sheer size and abstract nature of the audience have tangible consequences for the exposed individuals, illustrated by their unwanted recognition by people they don't know. None of the witnesses wanted to be recognized for the circumstances for which they attracted publicity. Yet it is precisely for those circumstances that they were fingerpointed in public. This is a case of mediated quasi-interaction in the sense that the exposed subjects found themselves in largely non-reciprocal communication with members of the audience. People whom they would never know became aware of some very private moments and details, with harmful consequences for the exposed individuals.

Commodification and economics

A significant dimension of the publication of these private stories is the feeling that these private lives and tragic circumstances are effectively sold for advertising revenue. This is expressed most clearly by Gerry McCann and Max Mosley, and it is worth quoting them at length:

> This suggested that the newspapers were demanding stories as they were commercially valuable to them and/or because they had to keep up with their competitors. This was confirmed by Peter Hill, the then editor of the *Daily Express*, who admitted to the Culture, Media and Sport Committee in 2009 that '[these stories] certainly increased the circulation of the *Daily Express* by many thousands on those days without a doubt'... [The editors] considered their ability to make money from the additional sales of the newspapers carrying the stories to be more important than taking into account our legitimate concerns as to the accuracy of the reporting and the effect it would have on our family – most significantly the search for, and well-being of our missing daughter.
>
> (Gerry McCann witness statement, paragraphs 39 and 61)
>
> Later that year the *News of the World* would boast of the unprecedented 600% growth in traffic to its website driven by exclusives such as the Max Mosley video. The boast can only have been made to attract greater number of sponsors and advertisers and their revenue.
>
> (Max Mosley witness statement, paragraph 64)

Such views are not even contested by the media representatives themselves. Richard Desmond, owner of The Express newspapers, admitted at the inquiry that the McCann stories increased the papers circulation (Transcript of Afternoon Hearing). Trevor Kavanagh (associate editor of *The Sun*, one of the Murdoch-owned newspapers implicated in the hacking scandal that sparked the inquiry) stated in his own evidence: 'news is as saleable a commodity as any other; newspapers are commercial, competitive businesses, not a public service' (Trevor Kavanagh, witness statement). Such statements, including Richard Desmond's provocative 'I don't understand the meaning of the word ethics' and 'if you agree that newspapers are important they should be allowed to report on opinions' suggest that in certain quarters the notion of press freedom is synonymous with the freedom of the market to do as it pleases (Fenton 2013). Collapsing freedom of expression, democracy and free market in one category is not only conceptually flawed but also practically dangerous.

The power asymmetry between individuals and media institutions is also felt at an economic level. Witnesses said that dealing with the press was extraordinarily all-consuming as well as extremely expensive. Those affected often had to hire professionals to deal with the situation (e.g. the McCann family), as well as with lengthy and costly lawsuits. Max Mosley provides clear evidence for this: To date I estimate that I have spent well over five hundred thousand pounds attempting to deal with the consequences of the publication of the Article on the Internet (Max Mosley witness statement).

Given these conditions and the fact that a lawsuit will almost certainly intensify media coverage, it is not surprising that many witnesses to the inquiry decided not to take action.

Technological convergence

The effects of mediation through traditional news media outlets are heightened in a converged media environment. For example, the publication of news stories online makes their content more permanent, in the sense of permanently retrievable. This has implications for the temporality of the news story which can potentially be viewed by an ever-proliferating audience as stories can be forwarded and reposted while videos and photographs can be embedded in other platforms, such as social media. News stories can go 'viral' in a converged media environment as they spread through a range of platforms which elsewhere I have theorized as 'polymedia storytelling' (Madianou 2013), drawing on the theory of polymedia developed in the context of interpersonal communication (Madianou and Miller 2013). Audiences for online news are further deterritorialized and not confined to the traditional boundaries of national publics. Additionally, audiences are temporally diffused as the message is permanently available and can be accessed long after the initial publication or broadcast. In sum, the permanence of content, and its storage capacity, retrievability and reach, are features of online news mediation which accentuate traditional news mediation. The following extract from Max Mosley's witness statement (paragraph 62) clearly illustrates the above points: 'the article was viewed 435,000 times (during its two days online) while the video footage available on the website was viewed 1,424,959 times'.

In a digital media environment it is possible to know the number of times a video or a picture has been viewed but, far from personalizing the exposed individual's relationship to their audience, the number of views highlights the abstract nature of the audience and the message's potentially infinite reach. The permanence of content is evident in Mosley's experience. Although he was successful in legally getting the newspaper to remove the defamatory content from its own website, it was impossible to fully remove all relevant content from the web:

> Although the amount of material available on the internet has been greatly reduced, it is still available. Despite this ongoing investment, I have to live with the knowledge that it will probably never be fully removed... In effect the information I wished to keep private and which the *News of the World* was held to have published unlawfully will forever be known and accessible to the world at large.
>
> (Mosley witness statement, paragraph 67)

Digital media operate in synergy with traditional news media. Despite their interactive nature, digital platforms when exploited by mainstream media appear to heighten the effects of traditional news mediation. The affordances of internet-mediated platforms (e.g. the permanence of content, storage capacity, retrievability and reach) can accentuate the effects of mediation and its asymmetrical power structure. Note that this observation applies to the use of digital media by mainstream media organizations and is not meant as an inherent feature of all new media platforms, some of which can potentially offer opportunities for voice – a point to which we shall return later in the chapter.

Voiceless

The Leveson Inquiry witness statements provide highly articulate accounts of the consequences of invasion of privacy and even defamation.[11] What makes them particularly poignant apart from the individual circumstances is the fact that more often than not wronged subjects do not have the opportunity to express their negative direct experiences with the media. In an attempt to cast some light on this apparent lack of data, I here return to my earlier work on news consumption where I encountered two such cases of media injury. The first example is the story of Laura, a young working-class woman from Dagenham, East London, who had found her experiences as an underage mother reported in the local newspaper (Madianou 2012).

I met Laura as part of my study on news in everyday life. For her, news was not relevant in her everyday life and it quickly emerged that her early direct experience with the news media prevented her from trusting journalists. The publication of her story to a potentially infinite audience introduced a structural transformation: the others through whom she defined herself were multiplied and at the same time generalized as an abstract category of individuals whom she could never meet to articulate her own version of events. Laura never even thought of writing a letter to the editor as an attempt to set the record straight, which suggests that the asymmetries of mediation converge with other social inequalities. A working-class teenage woman, she remained voiceless in contrast with the celebrity witnesses of the Leveson Inquiry, such as Max Mosley and Hugh Grant, who were prepared to take a stand. The publication of Laura's story to a potentially infinite audience, the indifference with which her private life was publically judged[12] and her own inability to respond accentuated feelings of shame and pointed to the symbolic power of mediation. This experience left its indelible marks as it framed Laura's wider attitude towards journalists, the news and public life more generally.

The symbolic power of mediation can affect social groups and not just individuals. In my work with members of the Turkish-speaking minority in Athens as part of a wider study of media, nationalism and identities in Greece (Madianou 2005a), I encountered anger, disaffection and withdrawal among members of the community who felt that their neighbourhood was systematically misrepresented by the national press. Participants brought up several examples of personal contact with journalists when 'their words' had been twisted or taken out of context (Madianou 2005b: 532–536). This negative experience with journalists echoed wider social inequalities and exclusions, such as discrimination in the job market and housing. When I asked members of the neighbourhood if they had ever considered setting up a local radio station, they 'hadn't even thought about it'. 'They wouldn't even let us', said one of my participants, revealing the extent of deep disempowerment and lack of confidence (Madianou 2005b: 535). Elsewhere I argued that this can be understood as an example of mediation as different media-related experiences converge: the negative experiences with the media frame (Couldry 2000) affected the participants' trust in media, which in turn shaped their interpretation of the news and their wider sense of public disconnection, while the combination of all of these factors contributed to the degree of disempowerment revealed in the lack of any enthusiasm to establish community media that could potentially make their voices heard (Madianou 2005b: 535). This example, which is typical of the struggle – and failure – for recognition (Honneth 1996), shows how mediation can converge with other social processes and ultimately accentuate a cycle of disrespect (Honneth 2007), social exclusion and boundary-making (Madianou 2005b) which can potentially have wider consequences for public life and democracy.

Mediated harm and reparation through digital platforms

As a counterpoint to the above examples we finally consider a case of individual use of social media and its harmful consequences, as well as the opportunities for reparation afforded by digital platforms. This is the sex-tape scandal involving the British popstar and television presenter Tulisa Contostavlos, an intimate tape of whom was uploaded on the social platform *YouTube* on 17 March 2012 by her ex-boyfriend (as he later admitted in court). In this example, a personal (rather than institutional) act of communication, which clearly intended to harm, was amplified through its mediation as the offensive video was viewed by millions of viewers globally. At one level the dissemination of a scandalous video via social media, even if initiated by a private individual, shares some of the features of traditional mediation. Social media like *YouTube* (owned by the internet giant Google) are largely centralized institutions and dominant online players. Still this case is interesting in that Contostavlos used precisely the same platform to record her own version of events. Days after the offensive video appeared online and as various media platforms, old and new, were quick to brand her a 'slut' (Wiseman 2012), Contostavlos uploaded her own video in which, in her own voice, she gives her account:

> When you share an intimate moment with someone you love, that you care about and trust you never imagine that at any point it will be shared with people around the world ... It's a pretty tough time for me, but I don't feel I should be the one to take the heat for it. This is something he took upon himself, to put the footage online ... I'm not going to sit here and be violated or taken advantage of.[13]

The Contostavlos case ended with her winning a court apology by her ex-boyfriend in July 2012. As a result of the litigation, 60 websites were forced to remove the offensive content.[14] To some extent this example suggests that interactive platforms overcome the largely monological nature of quasi-interactive mediated communication (Thompson 1995) in the sense that the injured subject can directly address his/her audience in a way that the exposed subjects of traditional media would never have been able to. But before celebrating the democratic potential of social media we need to recall that Contostavlos was a celebrity, a known artist and television personality who could attract attention on *YouTube*. Even in this case the number of hits that the sex video received dwarfed those of her response.[15] It is hard imagining the home-made video of an unknown girl attracting much attention. It is hard imagining any teenage girl having the courage to make such a video in the first place. Contostavlos had the confidence and social capital to make her voice heard.

Conclusion

This chapter exposed the workings of mediation by looking at their consequences for individuals who have been exposed by the media. I argued that examining people's direct experiences with the media reveals the structural changes introduced by mediation and also its symbolic power. Understanding these processes is paramount in making the argument that face-to-face communication is fundamentally different from mediated communication and thus individual rights, such as freedom of expression, cannot apply to both. The chapter mainly considered the witness statements at the Leveson Inquiry into the culture, practice and ethics of the press (Module 1) but, in order to balance the argument with evidence of silent voices – voices of injured subjects which were not publicly articulated – I referred to earlier work that investigated two such cases. The story of Tulisa Contostavlos who contested a situation of intimate exposure through social media completed the range of examples discussed by highlighting the similarities and differences of mass-mediated and digitally mediated personal communication. These are, of course, very different cases but the advantage of bringing together such diverse empirical contexts is that they can cast light on different dimensions of mediation. The witness statements of the Leveson Inquiry – a rare occasion when injured subjects were invited to voice their experiences – suggest that the injuries of defamation, privacy invasion and lack of power to control one's representation are profound and long lasting. Listening to people's accounts, one realizes quickly that the negative experience with the media is not just a matter of inconvenience but a far more deeply unsettling and violent experience. This makes the cases of silent voices even more poignant. The discussion of the narratives of the voiceless subjects suggests that the symbolic power of mediation extends beyond the communicative context and can potentially contribute to larger processes of social exclusion, disrespect (Honneth 2007) or boundary-making (Madianou 2005b; 2012).

In this context, mediation becomes part of the problem of materialization (Butler 2005) rather than just the vehicle for its reporting. Mediated harm is qualitatively different from harm caused by individual speech in a face-to-face setting. The fact that offensive messages can be broadcast to infinite audiences can amplify the harmful effects for the exposed individual. Social media may provide a platform for wronged subjects to speak back and address their audiences in a more direct way, but social media without social and symbolic capital are not likely to provide a platform for voice. The Contostavlos example is as much evidence of the power of social and cultural capital as it is of the power of social media. Moreover, our discussion showed that personal communication through digital platforms can acquire features of quasi-interactive mediation as the collapse of private and public boundaries in social media can potentially broadcast personal views to infinite audiences.

A theme that emerged from the Leveson Inquiry witness transcripts is that technological convergence can heighten the effects of news mediation. The affordances of online news platforms (permanence of content, storage capacity, retrievability and reach) can turn an ephemeral story into a permanent feature and thus increase exponentially the size of audiences attending to the message. This observation confirms that despite digital developments, mediation remains a profoundly asymmetrical process where the exposed subject is dwarfed by an infinite and abstract audience that is hard to address. The symbolic power of mediation is underlined by the marketization of news stories sustained by an ideology that erroneously collapses freedom of expression with freedom of the market and democracy.

The aim of this chapter is to uncover the workings of mediation as this understanding is a prerequisite to the development of a normative framework of voice as value and ethics of media. Recognizing the structural difference of mediation compared with face-to-face communication provides an additional reason why freedom of expression cannot be applied to mediated communication (see also O'Neill, Chapter 2 this volume). Although the aim here is not to identify a moral framework that can support the articulation of voices in the mediated public domain, the previous discussion directs us to a couple of points. Arguing that individual freedom of expression cannot be applied to news organizations does not, of course, mean that the media should be censored. But an ethics of media needs to recognize the symbolic power of mediation and provide audiences with the platform to articulate their voices, especially in cases of defamation or injury. Policies such as the right to reply (Phillips, Chapter 15 this volume) are important first steps in encouraging voices to be heard, but such policies will only be meaningful if these voices are given prominence and listened to. Tucking a public apology in the 'Letters to the editor' page will not counter the damage of frontline news. The structural asymmetry of mediation cannot be entirely corrected but there are ways to ensure that it is balanced with an ethics of care and responsibility. Developed by Gilligan (1993 [1982]) in the 1980s in order to capture the gendered differences of moral development, and since reworked into a more coherent normative theory by other feminist scholars (Held 2005), the ethics of care approach rests on the premise of non-violence, that no one should be hurt (Gilligan 1993 [1983]: 174). It is this principle that can protect from injurious speech and can support our 'living well through media' (see Couldry, Chapter 3 this volume). Although identifying normative frameworks will inevitably always be a highly contested process, recognizing the power of mediation and the responsibility that comes with it can provide us with a starting-point around which some consensus might emerge.

Acknowledgements

I would like to thank Nick Couldry and Lieve Gies for comments on an earlier draft.

Notes

1. http://www.levesoninquiry.org.uk/. Last accessed 27 April 2012.
2. The phone-hacking scandal is an ongoing (at the time of writing) issue involving allegations that employees in the now-defunct *News of the World* and other UK newspapers published by News International had been involved in unlawful interception of private communications, police bribery and other illegal activities as part of their news-gathering practices. It is alleged that more than 5000 individuals may have been affected by these practices. The inquiry, established under the 2005 Inquiries Act, is chaired by Justice Leveson. http://www.levesoninquiry.org.uk/. Last accessed 7 May 2012.
3. The other modules are on the relationship between the press and the policy (Module 2), the relationship between the press and politicians (Module 3) and the recommendations for a more effective policy and regulation that supports the integrity and freedom of the press while encouraging the highest ethical standards (Module 4). http://www.levesoninquiry.org.uk/about. Last accessed 1 May 2012.
4. Although the chapter largely draws on inquiry-related documents, the purpose was not to develop a full study of the whole inquiry (for such academic

work, see e.g. Fenton 2013; Petley 2012) but to use the statements of the mistreated individuals in order to gauge the symbolic power of mediation.
5. The complexity of the issues is evident in the discussions surrounding privacy injunctions (informally called 'superinjunctions' or 'gagging orders') in the UK where courts prevent the publication of information which is deemed private or confidential. As feminist critics remind us, cases of sexual disclosure are gendered and asymmetrically structured, with women often in the most vulnerable position (Richardson 2012: 158), suggesting that the balancing of freedom of reporting and privacy will often vary according to the case in question.
6. Both the Universal Declaration of Human Rights and the European Convention on Human Rights use the term 'freedom of expression'.
7. See the emerging literature on the ethics of audiences in relation to distant suffering and action at a distance (Hoijer 2004; Ong 2011; Kyriakidou 2012).
8. The concept of mediatization is related to mediation as used here and, despite increasing convergence between the two terms (see Couldry 2012), there are some significant differences between the terms, as well as among authors who use the terms. I cannot provide a comprehensive review of the term here (see Hepp 2012; Livingstone 2009; and chapters in Lundby 2009 for excellent overviews).
9. http://www.guardian.co.uk/law/2012/jul/27/twitter-joke-trial-high-court
10. This section draws on the witness statements and transcripts of hearings at the Leveson Inquiry, all of which are publicly available in alphabetical order at http://www.levesoninquiry.org.uk/evidence/.
11. The inquiry witness statements differ from discourses obtained in an interview context as they are prepared and written statements rather than spoken discourse. Methodologically, this chapter compares different types of data but that is a necessary compromise in order to cover as broad a range of examples as possible.
12. See Sennett (1980) on the connection between indifference as symbolic power leading to shame.
13. http://www.youtube.com/watch?v = Nvq2bdn_SKw. Last accessed 13 September 2012.
14. http://www.guardian.co.uk/culture/2012/jul/12/tulisa-contostavlos-apology-sex-tape?intcmp=239.
15. At the time of writing (September 2012) the Tulisa response has been viewed more than 8 million times.

References

Butler, J. (2005) *Giving an Account of Oneself*. New York: Fordham University Press.

Chouliaraki, L. (2013) 'Re-mediation, Inter-mediation and Trans-medation: The Cosmopolitan Trajectories of Convergent Journalism', *Journalism Studies*, vol. 14 (2): 249–266.

Couldry, N. (2000) *The Place of Media Power*. London: Routledge

Couldry, N. (2010) *Why Voice Matters: Culture and Politics after Neoliberalism*. London: Sage.

Couldry, N. (2012) *Media, Society, World*. Cambridge: Polity.

Deuze, M. (2004) 'What is Multimedia Journalism?', *Journalism Studies* 5(2): 139–152.

Deuze, M. (2012) *Media Life*. Cambridge: Polity.

Fenton, N. (2013) 'Cosmopolitanism as Conformity and Contestation', *Journalism Studies*, 14(2): 172 – 186.

Gies, L. (2007) *Law and the Media*. London and New York: Routledge

Gilligan, C. (1993) [o.p. 1982] *In a Different Voice*. Cambridge, MA: Harvard University Press.

Held, V. (2005) *The Ethics of Care. Personal, Political, Global*. Oxford and New York: Oxford University Press.

Hepp, A. (2012) 'Mediatization and the Molding Force of the Media', *Communications* 37(1): 1–28.

Hoijer, B. (2004) 'The Discourse of Global Compassion: the Audience and Media Reporting of Human Suffering', *Media, Culture and Society* 26(4): 513–531.

Honneth, A. (1996) *The Struggle for Recognition. The Moral Grammar of Social Conflicts*. Cambridge, MA: MIT Press.

Honneth, A. (2007) *Disrespect*. Cambridge: Polity.

Kyriakidou, M. (2012) Watching the Pain of Others: Audience Discourses of Suffering in Greece, unpublished PhD Thesis, London School of Economics.

Langer, A. (2011) *The Personalisation of Politics in the UK: Mediated Leadership from Attlee to Cameron*. Manchester: Manchester University Press.

Livingstone, S. (2009) 'On the Mediation of Everything', *Journal of Communication* 59(1): 1–18.

Lundby, K. (ed) (2009) *Mediatization: Concept, Changes, Consequences*. New York: Peter Lang.

Madianou, M. (2005a) *Mediating the Nation: News, Audiences and the Politics of Identity*. London: UCL Press/Routledge.

Madianou, M. (2005b) 'Contested Communicative Spaces: Rethinking Identities, Boundaries and the Role of the Media Among Turkish Speakers in Greece', *Journal of Ethnic and Migration Studies* 31(3): 521–541.

Madianou, M. (2012) 'News as a Looking Glass: Shame and the Symbolic Power of Mediation', *International Journal of Cultural Studies* 15(1): 1–14.

Madianou, M. (2013) 'Humanitarian Campaigns and Social Media: Network Architectures and Polymedia Events', *Journalism Studies* 14(2): 249–266.

Madianou, M. and Miller, D. (2013) 'Polymedia: Towards a New Theory of Digital Media in Interpersonal Communication', *International Journal of Cultural Studies* 16(2): 169–187.

Marwick, A. and boyd, d. (2011) 'I Tweet Honestly, I Tweet Passionately: Twitter users, context collapse and the imagined audience', *New Media and Society* 13(1): 114–133.

Mill, J. S. (1989) *On Liberty and Other Writings*. Cambridge: Cambridge University Press.

O'Neill, O. (2013) 'Media Freedoms and Media Standards', in Couldry, N., Madianou, M., Pinchevski, A. (eds) *Ethics of Media*, London: Palgrave.

Ong, J. (2011) The Mediation of Suffering, unpublished PhD thesis, University of Cambridge.

Petley, J. (2012) 'The Leveson Inquiry: Journalism Ethics and Press Freedom', *Journalism*13(4): 529–538.

Phillips, A. (2013) 'Journalism, Ethics and the Impact of Competition', in Couldry, N., Madianou, M., Pinchevski, A. (eds) *Ethics of Media*, London: Palgrave.

Richardson, J. (2012) ' "If I Cannot Have Her Everybody Can". Sexual Disclosure and Privacy Law', in Richardson, J. and Rackley, E. (eds) *Feminist Perspectives on Tort Law*, 145–162. London and New York: Routledge.

Sennett, R. (1980) *Authority.* New York: Knopf.

Silverstone, R. (2005) 'Mediation and Communication', in Calhoun, C., Rojek, C. and Turner, B. (eds), 188–207. *Handbook of Sociology*, London: Sage.

Thompson, J. B. (1995) *The Media and Modernity*. Cambridge: Polity.

Thompson, J. B. (2000) *Political Scandal*. Cambridge: Polity.

Thompson, J. B. (2005) 'The New Visibility', *Theory, Culture and Critique* 22(6): 31–51.

Wiseman, E. (2012) 'Tulisa Is Feminism's New Hero', *Guardian* 24 March 2012, http://www.guardian.co.uk/lifeandstyle/2012/mar/24/tulisa-contostavlos-feminisms-new-hero, last accessed 26 April 2012.

12
A Meta-ethical Analysis of Moral Discourse on the *Jeremy Kyle Show*

Peter Lunt and Joseph Livingstone

Introduction

Television talk shows have become a staple of broadcast schedules around the world, providing members of the public with the opportunity to express their views and concerns, and to participate in mediated public discussion and debate (Livingstone and Lunt 1994). Some talk shows, particularly those that are sensationalist or appear to promote conflict, have attracted a variety of ethical concerns. These include the potential for exploitation of vulnerable participants who are unaware of the hazards of displaying their problems in public, the potential dangers of public exposure of emotions in the programmes and the dumbing down of public discourse and debate. These new forms of broadcasting are often compared unfavourably with the public service broadcasting values of objectivity, neutrality and quality that are presumed to apply to established factual genres, notably the documentary and current affairs (Gamson 1998; Shattuc 1997).

The *Jeremy Kyle Show* is a prime example of a programme that has attracted ethical criticism. A UK daytime talk show (although recently with a US version) broadcast on the main independent television channel (ITV), it shares with other sensationalist talk shows (e.g. *The Jerry Springer Show*, Lunt and Stenner 2005) its often confrontational focus on conflicts among participants from white, lower working-class backgrounds (Skeggs and Wood 2012). It centres on the discussion of unresolved conflicts and hidden secrets between couples and within families or friendship groups, under the direction of the host, Jeremy

Acknowledgements: Many thanks to the editors and Sonia Livingstone for constructive feedback.

Kyle. Characteristically, he directly and robustly confronts, even accuses, his participants, in contrast with those talk show hosts who favour a supportive, therapeutic or forensic interrogative style (see Shattuc 1997; Livingstone and Lunt 1994; Lunt and Lewis 2008), and a variety of devices are used to bring out and intensify the underlying conflicts.

Having interviewed show participants, Williams (2011) reports that each 'side' has their own green room, enters and exits the stage from a different direction, and is clearly prompted by the researchers and producers to take a confrontational line. Challenging the producer's claims that the show responds to genuine needs (see http://www.itv.com/lifestyle/jeremykyle/), Williams articulates four ethical concerns about the *Jeremy Kyle Show*:

- that it draws people into public confrontation where they might otherwise have found a peaceable way to resolve their differences;
- that it contributes to a representation of a feral underclass and the idea of 'broken Britain';
- that its claims to support upset or vulnerable participants are overstated;
- that it overstates its claim to address and resolve families' problems and thereby promote openness and honesty in society.

How should academic analysis of the ethics of this programme position itself, given the opposed views expressed by the programme's producers and critics? One approach would be to take sides in the debate directly, either regarding the *Jeremy Kyle Show* as affording resolution of personal and social problems, or critiquing it as an unethical exploitation of participants and audiences. Instead, we suggest that what matters about these programmes is the way in which they conduct the ethical disputes themselves. In particular, we argue that ethical disputes on the programme combine the expression of different stances or normative positions with meta-ethical arguments about the grounds or basis for ethical positions or judgements, reflecting broader social dilemmas (Billig et al. 1988). Thus we propose that it is worth analysing the ethical disputes on the programme because of the value in understanding the meta-ethical assumptions made by participants in asserting their arguments.

To the extent that morality is a social phenomenon, any particular ethical dispute takes place in a given social context and may be significant for social life more widely (Boltansky and Thévenot 2006). Talk shows, such as the *Jeremy Kyle Show*, can be interpreted as enabling the public expression of voices that might otherwise not be heard, thereby affording recognition of diverse views and perspectives on issues of personal or social importance (Honneth 1995). At its most positive, this could offer an account of the media as providing public value by representing and reflecting upon the diversity of values, identities and conduct typical of complex, late modern society. Since the main trope of the programme is ethical dispute, we follow Boltanski and Thévenot (2006) in interpreting public disputes as expressing the contradictions, tensions and indignities of living in late modernity. This leads us to examine the relation between moral questions and social order so as to identify a mode of analysis that grants disputes a legitimate place in public life. We therefore analyse the meta-ethics of the portrayed disputes while also locating these disputes within a broader sociological context.

Moral theory and meta-ethics

Normative moral theories typically involve concepts related to truth claims, metaphysics and moral psychology, thereby implicating themselves in broader philosophical debates and traditions about truth, metaphysics and psychology. Meta-ethics is the study of these assumptions themselves, thereby focusing attention on how we understand moral psychology or agency (e.g. as virtue, as an attempt to persuade or as an expression of interests or common humanity) as well as how we understand metaphysical and factual claims. Some moral theories assert that moral statements are either true or false, but there are disagreements about whether moral statements refer to a realm of moral facts or to facts that are given a moral interpretation.

Meta-ethics is not so much a unified theory as a way of analysing the characteristics of normative moral theories – their view of the world, their methods and their assumptions about the nature of moral agency. By contrast, normative moral theory aims to establish general principles that can distinguish between right and wrong, good and evil. Within this there are three main approaches to moral philosophy, each with a different way of establishing moral principles: deontological, consequentialist and virtue ethics (Baron et al. 1997). First, deontological approaches, which in modern philosophy derive from Kant's writings, contend that universal responsibilities or duties are those which any reasonable person would support, once detached from their personal interests and motivations. Faced with ethical dilemmas, the deontological approach suggests that principles of disinterest and respect for others should guide judgements and conduct. Second, consequentialism argues that it is the consequences of actions that render them good or bad. In response to a moral dilemma, this approach enquires into the consequences of different actions and urges that the right action is the one that brings the most positive and the fewest negative consequences. Third, virtue ethics seeks to establish general moral principles based on the ethical stance of an ideal agent of virtuous character and motives. This approach asks: How would a truly virtuous person act in the face of a moral dilemma?

The coexistence of three different approaches to moral theory and the varied positions adopted within each approach have contributed to widespread acceptance of moral relativism. The apparent incommensurability of different moral theories has led some to argue that the aim of resolving moral disputes or conflicting interpretations is not achievable as a rational project (MacIntyre 1981). Take the well-known case of emotivism (Ayer 1936), in which the meaning of moral statements is understood as combining the expression of moral feeling (as disapproval or approval) with the attempt to persuade others of one's stance. Emotivism took an explicitly meta-ethical position, asserting that all moral theories, statements and judgements must be understood in this way; that ethical judgements are not statements of fact nor do they reference a particular domain of moral facts; and that moral psychology consists only of disapproval and the attempt to persuade others.

Meta-ethics changes the focus of moral philosophy from the question of which actions are right or wrong (whether this is understood as asking whether they conform to universal principles of fairness, whether they should be judged by their consequences or whether they match what a good person would do) to the question of what we mean by saying that something is good or bad, whether it is justified to base our actions on such claims or what it is for something to be 'morally true'. Within meta-ethics, different questions are asked (Miller 2003: 2). For example: Are moral or ethical statements based on beliefs or do they express moral attitudes (i.e. what is the meaning of moral discourse)? Do moral facts or properties exist (metaphysical questions)? Can moral judgements or claims be true or false (epistemological questions)? And, last, are there psychological dimensions to moral and ethical statements (phenomenological questions)?

In our analysis of ethical disputes on the *Jeremy Kyle Show*, below, we suggest that an important part of any ethical dispute instantiates meta-ethical considerations over and above the expression of different normative positions. Using the analytic categories of meta-ethics to analyse these disputes, we challenge the view that the statement of a moral position exhausts what there is to know about that position. Meta-ethics is neutral with respect to particular normative moral positions and therefore can be used to understand the differences between normative positions as these are conditioned by particular mediated contexts.

In addition to bringing meta-ethics to the attention of media scholars and demonstrating its potential value as a framework for the analysis of mediated moral discourse, we consider that meta-ethics represents an alternative to recent calls for media academics to take a normative stance on media ethics (e.g. Christians et al. 2009; Couldry 2006; Pinchevski 2005; Silverstone 2007). Christians (2000) expressed concern that academic analysis of media ethics tends to be uncritical, replacing substantive moral questions with technical questions. By contrast, we argue that meta-ethics indeed involves substantial moral questions that potentially provide a fruitful perspectives on media ethics (Kiernan 1997).

Within philosophy, meta-ethics affords the analysis of moral discourse in terms of its constituent presuppositions and commitments. So too, in this chapter, we draw on meta-ethics to analyse a moral dispute in a television talk show in terms of its presuppositions and commitments. Just as meta-ethics is distinct from normative moral theory, so our analysis examines moral discourse without making judgements, instead revealing the diversity of positions and perspectives articulated in the mediated ethical dispute, including how these reflect an engagement with meta-ethical questions. So, by analysing the meta-ethical assumptions and disagreements in the televized dispute, we can reflect also on the underlying sociological dilemmas (e.g. in the case examined below, the responsibility of family members). Although our focus is not on the normative positions espoused by the participants, we inevitably refer to their positions since these are grounded in particular meta-ethical assumptions about the relationship between facts, values, moral psychology and metaphysics.

An ethical dispute on the *Jeremy Kyle Show*

In this chapter we analyse an episode of the Jeremy Kyle Show that was broadcast in 2008 and was entitled 'Refusing a DNA Test for 4 Years – What are You Hiding?' The programme opens with the host giving a brief outline of the protagonists and the background to the story. He introduces a family drama in which a grandmother (Joan) and aunt (Sharon) are concerned about their son/brother's (Andy) relationship with the woman (Leanne) he lives with. The couple in question have two children; one is a baby and the other four years old. The grandmother and the aunt are convinced that their son/brother is not the father of the first child, although they accept that he is the father of the baby. The women accept the roles of grandmother and aunt to the baby but not to the couple's older child. They want a DNA test for the older child to establish paternity, which the child's mother has refused, resulting in considerable family tensions.

Our focus is on the interaction between host and participants on the *Jeremy Kyle Show*, examining how the discussion that emerges is, to a large degree, a discussion of the ethical dilemmas arising from the everyday lives of the participants. We are particularly interested in the argumentation strategies that the host uses to elicit, interrogate and confront the views of participants. In this way we reveal the meta-ethical positions adopted by the participants, locating their ethical disputes in relation to contemporary sociological questions regarding the nature of relationships and families.

It is common practice in talk shows to begin with an elicitation phase in which the initial guests, often representing one side of an argument or dispute, are questioned by the host to get the background to the story and their perspective (Livingstone and Lunt 1994; Lunt and Stenner 2005; Shattuc 1997; Gamson 1998). This show is no exception. It first introduces the grandmother and aunt, who enter from stage right:

> Kyle: Let's get to the bottom of this story. Let's get the facts down. This centres on her oldest child, a boy called Callum?
> Grandmother: Yes.

The first question from Kyle suggests the possibility of finding common ground by determining 'the facts' which form the basis of the family's problem. It also establishes an argument context in which the starting-point is an initial stage of building consensus based on facts (Walton 1989). However, from a meta-ethical perspective, this focus on facts has a particular resonance. The host's choice of starting-point indicates his own view about the importance of facts in justifying ethical positions. Naturalism is an influential approach to meta-ethics in which moral judgements or beliefs are held to be 'truth apt', meaning that a judgement or belief can be true or false, justified/unjustified; for naturalists, this is achieved by reference to facts about the world. Naturalism also suggests that everyone has ethical intuitions that constitute a natural moral theory, and that there is a strong connection between facts and values such that agreement on facts leads inevitably to certain value positions. In this context the mother's agreement to Kyle's early statement is significant. He continues:

> Kyle: ... who is four. *You* and *you* refuse to accept this child?
> Aunt: Yes.

This second question rapidly takes us beyond agreement on facts, for the host now frames Joan and Sharon's refusal to accept the child as a member of their family as an ethical problem on which he (and we) are bound to disagree with them. In meta-ethical terms, framing the actions of the mother and daughter as a 'refusal' sets up a particular account of their moral psychology which rules out alternatives (e.g. explanations based on 'inability', as in being 'unable to accept' the child). It is thereby implied that there exists a 'natural' response of empathy and affection for the child, but that the women, for reasons not yet presented, are not acting as one might normally expect. Therefore they are positioned as having to account for their counter normative conduct. In this context it is interesting to note how ready both women are to accept Kyle's articulation of their position at this stage, as if at some level they do not contest the naturalistic account of the links between facts, feelings, values and conduct that might lead to their accepting the child. Having thus established a frame that calls for an account from the women, the host begins to explore their reasons for acting in the way they have:

> Kyle: Why?
> Grandmother: Because we think he's not my grandson.

By introducing a new fact – that there may be no genetic link between the women and the child – the reason why the women appear to have accepted Kyle's naturalistic theory while maintaining their position becomes clear. They do not dispute the naturalistic connection between facts (of genetics) and values (loving a child). Instead they assert a different account of the facts (lack of a genetic link and, therefore, non-acceptance of the child). Kyle follows up by asking for the grounds for their assertion:

> Kyle: Why?
> Grandmother: Because he doesn't favour anybody... you know, he has no resemblance to anybody.

This is surely an unexpected response which raises the question of what is an adequate test of genetic connection (compared with the certainty of a DNA test). Possibly, too, it raises a more fundamental doubt about how a grandmother can ever know she has a genetic connection with a grandchild. Although the significance of this doubt is not yet clear, at a meta-ethical level it contrasts with the assurance granted by traditional marriage relations (of legitimacy if not genetic certainty) and DNA testing. On the one hand, one might doubt the adequacy of the grandmother's test, but on the other, one is drawn into the genuine doubt about the parentage of a child that a grandparent must face. However, the host does not pick up on these questions and instead continues his line of questioning into the motivations and actions of the grandmother and her daughter:

Kyle: When did you decide that?
Grandmother: Oh, when...first time he was born. I went in, I checked him and he didn't look anything like my son.
Kyle: But you had suspicions before he was born...
Grandmother: Yes.
Kyle: This isn't just about you two having doubts about the child's paternity, you two have refused to bond with this kid.
Grandmother: Yes.

Kyle continues to bypass the implications of what the grandmother has implied, above, instead seeking to bring her and her daughter to account for not acting in the normal and expected way towards a four-year-old child. From a meta-ethical perspective, this interaction is interesting because the host challenges the direction of the link between the women's suspicions and the evidence that brings the genetic link into question. He suggests that a pre-existing prejudice influenced the perception of the child rather than their suspicions being a natural reaction to the visual evidence. This reading of the position adopted by the women reinforces the idea that they are not acting naturally but are driven by prejudice. Kyle now begins to explore the broader background to the story and invites the studio audience to express its reactions to the moral judgements and reported actions of the two women, while simultaneously finessing the description of their conduct:

Kyle: Just slow down a minute. They have another child who is ten months old, but Callum gets nothing. He gets no presents [gasps

of disapproval from studio audience], he gets no cuddles and you
haven't even put him in your will.
Grandmother: No. [broader gasps from audience]
Kyle: Do you think that's altogether fair on a four-year-old?

Kyle's description of the grandmother and her daughter's conduct brings
out their apparent lack of empathy towards the child, and he successfully enlists the studio audience to reinforce the idea that their refusal
to recognize, love or give presents to the child is unnatural, especially
since they treat the couple's second child so differently. Implicit in this
line of questioning is a normative account of 'natural' bonding, which
should lead any reasonable person to treat a four-year-old child who is
part of their family in a certain way. Any doubt in family relationships,
it is further implied, should be resolved in the best interests of the child.
The grandmother attempts to explain her position:

> Grandmother: Well, like I said, I can't bond with him because the
> simple reason is if I bond with him for four years then I find out
> that he's not my [grand]son I'm really going to be upset and I can't
> afford to be upset, I don't want to be upset.

We now begin to see the position adopted by the women. In an
important sense they do not disagree with Kyle: if the child were genet-
ically related to them they would act in the|way that he suggests.
The grandmother effectively asserts that a genetic link is defining of
a grandparental relationship ('he's not my [grand]son') and that her
commitment (moral psychology), emotions and responsibilities depend
upon the genetic link with the child. From a meta-ethical perspective, she implies an emotional normativity in which feelings provide
a justification for conduct rather than being seen as a response to circumstances or events. Although we are not told the reasons, the claim
is that accepting a child that is not genetically 'yours' would lead to significant emotional consequences of even greater importance than any
consequences for the child. We see also that the grandmother and aunt
have been able to agree to many of Kyle's arguments during the programme because they accept his normative conception of 'family'. The
difference is that the grandmother insists on a genetic basis for the family whereas Kyle, it is now clear, proposes that family affiliation and the
emotional needs of a child should override genetics.

We can now also understand the grandmother's claim that she can't
bond with the child. This directly contradicts Kyle's appraisal of her

which was that she 'refused' to bond. This is a meta-ethical disagreement because it references a broader debate about moral psychology.
Whether the grandmother does not bond because she chooses not to
(refuses) or whether there is some sense in which she is unable to bond
is a question to be answered, or at least debated, within the area of moral
psychology. Since Kyle and the women are unaware of this, however,
they ultimately misunderstand each other on this point and, worse, they
think that they understand each other when they don't. Kyle thinks
that the women are choosing not to bond because it enables him to
make them accountable. The women simply regard Kyle as failing to
realize that they are unable to bond, not realizing that it is not that he
fails to realize this fact but that he is unable to realize it because of the
structure of the normative system he articulates. Of course, whether the
women are able to bond or not is not important here; what matters is to
recognize that this aspect of their disagreement is meta-ethical.

The grandmother's response is also interesting because she does not
take up Kyle's invitation to discuss (or contest) whether her treatment of
the child is fair, instead focusing on the reasons for her actions. Indeed,
she appears to agree in principle with the arguments proposed by Kyle
and the sentiments expressed by the audience. However, where for Kyle
the right course of action appears to be obvious even in the face of uncertainty about paternity, the grandmother takes a different position. She
has weighed the consequences to her of mistakenly loving a child not
genetically hers against the consequences to the child of not being loved
by his 'grandmother'; and she judges in her own favour. Although she
says that her motive is that she would be too upset if a mistake were later
to be realized, she does not specify this in any more detail. This is a critical turning-point in the show. We might speculate that she has religious
beliefs or otherwise strongly held traditional conceptions of family such
that she would be compromising these beliefs by bonding with such a
child. Kyle attempts to provide a summary of the position of the two
women:

> Kyle: But isn't the point as parents or siblings or whatever that even if
> we disagree with what our loved ones are doing, aren't we supposed
> to keep our traps shut, stand three feet backwards and wait to pick
> up the pieces if it all goes wrong?

Here, Kyle offers a moral rule of thumb to the effect that members
of extended families should adopt a pragmatic approach to the paternity of children and act 'as if' such children are equal to those born

within marriage and with guaranteed paternity. This suggests a complex arrangement between autonomy, family membership, and the rights and duties of family members, although here it is presented as common sense.

In the second part of the programme, Kyle sets up the expectation that the show's aim will be to persuade the child's mother to have a paternity test done for the child. Kyle wants to know what the grandmother and aunt will do if the test demonstrates a positive match between the child and the son. He implies that the 'right' answer is to apologize and seek to bond with the child. Along with lie detector tests, DNA tests play a special role in the *Jeremy Kyle Show*. Both raise important questions about the relationship between facts and norms within the moral arguments that unfold on the show. They reinforce the idea that the complex ethical disputes in a family hinge on either trust (Is someone telling the truth?) or paternity (What are the facts of the genetic relationship?).

Indeed, by the end of the show the child's mother has agreed to have a DNA test. This is a planned exit for the programme and reinforces the naturalistic frame by suggesting that the facts as revealed by DNA testing will settle matters. However, as the analysis above indicates, although evidence of the paternity of the child will have an important bearing on future relations in the family, there are many other issues and questions that surround the case and distinguish the positions of the protagonists. In the arguments about what the key facts are, what the appropriate psychological reactions are and what the responsibilities of the extended family are, there is a mixture of normative positions and meta-ethical debates.

The sociological background

Throughout the show the grandmother holds on to her position that she cannot, in the circumstances, show affection and bond with the child since his paternity is in doubt. Her moral attitude is grounded in her emotional reaction to the child's mother, though this has barely been explored. She has been the butt of Kyle's questioning and angry accusations as well as open disapproval from the studio audience. How could she remain so steadfast in her moral argument? A possible interpretation is that her position makes sense against the background of broader debates about family values. The emergence of the 'plastic' family (Giddens 1991), in response to trends in divorce, cohabitation and diverse patterns of parenting, means that traditional conjugal role relationships are no longer taken for granted, and guidelines for responsibility and commitment in family life have become unclear and open to negotiation. For Giddens (1991), the plastic family is an example of release from tradition that affords the opportunity for individuals to work out their own position with others in a reflexive manner.

Given these transformations in the notion of family, we can now understand the debate between Kyle and the grandmother as offering two accounts. Although the deeper reasons for not accepting the child do not emerge in the discussion, we may speculate that if a person has religious beliefs, or a strong sense of duty and commitment to traditional family values, it might be asking too much to expect them to play the role of grandparent where there are doubts about marriage or parentage. Under such circumstances the grandmother appears to question the responsibilities of the extended family, and one may imagine many in the audience facing similar dilemmas. Given the uncertainties associated with changing family structures, we can raise ethical questions about the certainty and confidence of the host in managing the dispute. Kyle could, one imagines, just as easily have turned the programme on its head and put the onus of accountability on the young parents, asking why they do not get married or how they can expect the extended family to accept a child whose parentage is doubtful.

We can interpret both Kyle's and the grandmother's positions as responses to these broader questions about the role and responsibilities of grandparents in the context of transformations in family life. On this reading, Kyle's position becomes contradictory, as he appears to stand for family values yet urges the mother and sister to set aside these values and embrace more liberal, post-traditional values. However, as Giddens (1991) suggests, in post-traditional relationships the focus is on the quality and potential for self-actualization through relationships, not the mere fulfilling of social obligations. Since these ideas of reflexive modernity put the focus on relationships being provisional, open to question and made by the participants, they provide a possible justification for grandmother and aunt in our show to base their actions on their feelings about their relationship with Andy and Leanne rather than on their duty towards the child. What Kyle takes to be a problematic prejudicial attitude turns out to reflect legitimate uncertainty over responsibilities in family relationships given the doubts that arise from cohabitation and doubts about paternity.

Conclusion

This analysis of the moral discourse on the *Jeremy Kyle Show* demonstrates the complexity of conversations about family life when traditional forms of family relations, commitments and responsibilities are in flux. The programme explores how the shifting boundaries of the family impact on traditional role relationships (grandmother and aunt) in the context of plastic family ties. The moral discourse is confrontational, led by the host but with considerable resistance from the participants. The analysis raises questions about the ethics of the programme itself, given professional codes of impartiality and balance when reporting the sensitive circumstances of people's personal lives. However, our analysis also reveals the robust way in which the participants defended their position, suggesting a commitment among the participants to articulation and the pursuit of recognition even in the face of public opposition.

A novel feature of our analysis is our exploration of the meta-ethical aspects of the engagement between the host and the guests on the programme. Our analysis is not based on a particular normative position (e.g. concerning the limits of responsibility in contemporary family life) or by a particular approach to media ethics. Instead, we have analysed the moral judgements expressed in the programme in terms of the relation between fact and value, and the assumptions that arguments make about moral facts, beliefs and the psychological dimensions of ethical positions. Meta-ethics enables us to make sense of the interaction between Kyle and the two women in terms of their different positions – not so much on what is right or right or wrong but on what constitutes 'rightness' or 'wrongness'. These differences are not merely normative but also meta-ethical, and so it requires recourse to a meta-ethical analysis to account for certain aspects of their disagreement.

The analysis also demonstrates the complexities of justification and arguments for recognition in mediated contexts. Kyle attempts to determine the rights or wrongs of the women's actions based on the consequences for the child, which he relates to an implicit understanding of social responsibilities. However, the way in which the women account for themselves suggests a different approach, grounded in an emotion-based system for determining what is right or wrong. Because of their different meta-ethical positions, Kyle and the women diverge on what counts as evidence or justification for their normative positions. Our point is that without a meta-ethical analysis, their disagreement would appear purely normative, a reflection of the incommensurability of normative stances.

The conventions of genre and production of the *Jeremy Kyle Show* influenced how the discussion of ethical issues unfolded. In particular, the speed at which the argument progresses under the direction of the host contributes to a lack of care and reflection in some of the arguments. A confusion in normative standards on the part of the host is revealed as tactical insofar as he deploys several rules of thumb that articulate contrary normative positions (traditional and liberal family values, the rights of children, the role of facts about genetic inheritance) in support of the parents and against the grandmother and her daughter. The participants are put on the defensive by the interrogative style of the host. Even though they resist this strongly, the programme does not enable exploration of the reasons for their own stance nor of the broader social implications of the ethical dilemmas that they face.

Kyle's stance positions him as both asking the questions and expressing the opinions that any normal (reasonable) person might ask or want to ask in the circumstances. What results is a particular formulation of the relation between facts and values that reflects the host's assumption that the problems experienced by the family can be resolved by establishing the facts (here, the child's parentage), although he also assumes that normative family commitments offer obvious solutions to domestic problems. The consequence is a tactical exchange in which those accused have to work hard to justify themselves in a context that offers little room for the kind of reflexive discourse in which the grounds and criteria underlying the different positions in play might be fairly heard.

As we noted in the introduction, the programme's producers claim to provide a model of dialogue that affords the resolution of particular problems and a more general illustration of how family disputes can be resolved through open and honest dialogue. Our analysis supports a critical response to such claims, but, against the criticisms presented by Williams, we have demonstrated that a set of arguments and positions on the moral responsibilities of the extended family in the context of transformations in family structures and commitments does emerge from the show. Whatever one thinks about the quality of argument and the nature of ethical debate in the show, it does manage to confront a major issue facing families in contemporary society. In this sense, it does offer a practical illustration of how people are managing their feelings and developing their ethical positions in the context of changing social relationships. Thus the producers may indeed claim to provide some opportunity for public dialogue and interrogation of moral dilemmas of contemporary significance. However, we are more sceptical about their providing a resolution of particular problems or, further, that they offer a model of moral discussion based on honesty and openness.

References

Ayer, A. (1936) *Language, Truth and Logic*. London: Gollanz.

Baron, M. W., P. Pettit and M. Slote (1997) *Three Methods of Ethics*. Oxford: Blackwell Publishing.

Billig, M., S. Condor, D. Edwards, M. Gane, D. Middleton and A. R. Radley (1988). *Ideological Dilemmas*. London: Sage.

Boltansky, L. and L. Thévenot (2006) *On Justification: Economies of Worth*. Princeton, NJ: Princeton University Press.

Christians, G. C. (2000) 'An Intellectual History of Media Ethics', in B. Pattyn (ed.) *Media Ethics: Opening Social Dialogue*. Leuven: Peeters.

Christians, C, T. L. Glaser, D. McQuail, K. Nordenstreng and R. A. White (2009) *Normative Theories of the Media: Journaliusm in Democratic Societies*. Champaign, IL: University of Illinois Press.

Couldry, N. (2006) *Listening Beyond the Echoes: Media, Ethics, and Agency in an Uncertain World*. London: Paradigm Publishers.

Gamson, J. (1998) *Freaks Talk Back: Tabloid Talk Shows and Sexual Nonconformity*. Chicago: University of Chicago Press.

Giddens, A. (1991) *Modernity and Self Identity*. Cambridge: Polity Press.

Honneth, A. (1995) *The Struggle for Recognition: The Moral Grammar of Social Conflicts*. Cambridge, MA: MIT Press.

Kiernan, M. (1997) *Media Ethics: A Philosophical Approach*. Wesport, CT: Praeger.

Livingstone, S. and P. Lunt (1994) *Talk on Television: Audience Participation and Public Debate*. London: Routledge.

Lunt, P. and T. Lewis (2008) 'OPRAH.COM: Lifestyle Expertise and the Politics of Recognition', *Women & Performance: A Journal of Feminist Theory* 18(1): 9–24.

Lunt, P. and P. Stenner (2005) 'The Jerry Springer Show as an Emotional Public Sphere', *Media, Culture & Society* 1: 59–81.

MacIntyre, A. (1981) *After Virtue: A Study in Moral Theory*. London: Duckworth.

Miller, A. (2003) *An Introduction to Contemporary Metaethics*. Cambridge: Polity Press.

Pinchevski, A. (2005) *By Way of Interruption: Levinas and the Ethics of Communication*. Pittsburgh, PA: Duquesne University Press.

Shattuc, J. M. (1997) *The Talking Cure: TV Talk Shows and Women*. London: Routledge.

Silverstone, R. (2007) *Media and Morality: On the Rise of the Mediapolis*. Cambridge: Polity Press.

Skeggs, B. and H. Wood (2012) *Reacting to Reality Television: Performance, Audience and Value*. London: Routledge.

Walton, D. N. (1989) *Informal Logic: A Handbook for Critical Argumentation*. Cambridge: Cambridge University Press.

Williams, Z. (2011) 'Fight Club: Life After the Jeremy Kyle Treatment', *Guardian*, Friday 22 April 2011, http://www.guardian.co.uk/media/2011/apr/22/life-after-jeremy-kyle-treatment?INTCMP=SRCH.

Part IV
Practices

13
'Ethical Living' in the Media and in Philosophy

Sabina Lovibond

1. This chapter originates partly in academic ethical theory, and partly in a more concrete mode of reflection that is likely nowadays to feature in the 'media' experience of any concerned citizen. The term 'ethical living' can serve to mark the point where these discourses connect. My discussion, then, will relate not so much to the 'ethics of media' *qua* code of values or conduct for media professionals but rather to ethics as a subject matter falling within the self-defined sphere of interest of that group. Our (mass) media undoubtedly provide a channel for cutting-edge, first-order ethical debate – and one that, for obvious reasons, favours the fast response and the personal appeal over professorial caution and reserve.

But first I need to be more precise about the kind of ethical debate I have in mind. Ethical living, as traditionally understood, is simply the topic of one of the central branches of philosophy – the topic proposed by Plato when he makes Socrates say in Book I of the *Republic* (352d) that 'our discussion is not about just any old subject matter, but about how one ought to live'. In recent years, however, the term has acquired a more specialized sense and is now quite a well-established category for journalism and general-purpose moral discussion. The *Rough Guide to Ethical Living* takes it to mean

> adapting our lifestyles and shopping habits with the aim of reducing our negative impact (and increasing our positive impact) on the world's environments, people and animals.[1]

In the same vein, the 'Teach Yourself' book entitled *Live Ethically* states that

An ethical person is one who has concern for the well being of others, and who is aware of the impact of their actions on others ... On a global level, the ethical person would want to promote international peace, justice and fair trade, and would accept a responsibility to care for the environment. For the ethical consumer this could translate to boycotting companies and countries that abuse human rights, supporting fair trade initiatives and minimizing use of non-renewable resources.[2]

The idea is that it is open to each of us as citizens (or 'consumers') to work towards a less damaging individual mode of life – especially by reducing our personal 'carbon footprint' and hence our contribution to global warming, but also by trying to become less complicit in the nasty side of commerce and industry, ranging from the use of child labour in clothing sweatshops to the mountain of plastic packaging encasing the food in our supermarkets.

My procedure in the remarks to follow will be, first, to review some intellectual tensions within the media discourse of ethical living, and then to point to some philosophical resources which could be put to use in the internal critique of that discourse, thereby (I hope) contributing something to its overall lucidity and self-confidence. These resources will ultimately be supplied by the familiar ideas of *duty* and *need*.

2. We can begin by noting that the same liberal-minded publications which have pioneered the coverage of ethical living have also provided an outlet for criticism of that coverage from within the environmentalist camp. As the Rough Guide points out, 'Arguments against the "moralization" of consumerism come from both the reactionary right and the radical left':[3] not only from free marketeers who object in principle to the regulation of trade but also from people who regard the whole approach as flawed by an underlying acquiescence in the greed of the developed world. According to this latter group, it is unhelpful to suggest that we can find a way out of our present ecological predicament by purchasing different and worthier (rather than fewer) products – the proverbial low-energy light-bulbs or (for the rich) solar panels or wind turbines. The summer and autumn of 2007 – in effect, the dying days of the last economic boom – seem to have been a key moment for this line of argument, at any rate in the *Guardian*.[4] Thus we were admonished by the following writers:

- *George Monbiot*: 'Two parallel markets are developing – one for unethical products and one for ethical products, and the expansion of the second does little to hinder the growth of the first...No political challenge can be met by shopping' (24 July 2007).
- *Julian Glover*: 'We have a government that wants people to drive less, but builds roads and raises rail fares; to fly less, but expands airports...The state exists to achieve the tasks that individuals cannot manage alone', such as limiting climate change (8 September 2007).[5]
- *George Marshall*: 'Forty per cent of people [according to the latest Mori poll data] now believe that recycling domestic waste, which is a relatively small contributor to emissions, is the most important thing they can do to prevent climate change. Only 10% mention the far more important goals of using public transport or reducing foreign holidays' (13 September 2007, G2).
- *Mark Lynas*: 'The point is to consume less – and no one's going to make any money from that' (17 September 2007, G2).

Meanwhile, affluent 'consumers' continued to party, as reported elsewhere in the same paper. American *Vogue* for September 2007 contained a record 840 pages – seven out of eight of these consisting of advertising – and weighed more than 2kg (1 September 2007: 'The insatiable consumer appetite for opulent cars, ostrich leather handbags, bespoke glad rags and designer sunglasses keeps fashion magazines plump on a diet of full-page adverts', as a *Guardian* standfirst put it). A think tank called the New Economics Foundation calculated that 'if everyone in the world wanted to live like people in the UK, three more planets [i.e. three *planets*?] like Earth would be needed to sustain the current population' (compared to 5.3 for the US, 0.9 for China and 0.4 for India. This made the UK equal-second with France in the world rankings for level of consumption) (6 October 2007).[6] And there was insight, too, into what exactly people were buying (apart from the fashion items already mentioned):

The world has gone mobile mad and gadget crazy as prices fall

...The growth of the [global consumer electronics] market – forecast to be 12.5% this year – is being driven by sales of flat-screen TVs, laptop computers and mobile phones.

(27 October 2007)[7]

But all this comes at a price. The background problem – once again according to Monbiot, citing Professor Rod Smith of Imperial College – is as follows:

> A growth rate of 3% means economic activity doubles in 23 years. At 10% it takes seven years. But... 'each successive doubling period consumes as much resource as all previous doubling periods combined'. In other words, if our economy grows at 3% between now and 2040, we will consume in that period resources equal to all those we have consumed since humans first stood on two legs.
>
> (4 December 2007)[8]

And, of course, much of the stuff produced by our growing economic activity does not just sit around once manufactured. Lynas, in the article already cited, notes that

> The sheer proliferation of electronic household gadgets means that electricity use and carbon emissions are still increasing every year. Energy use in the home has doubled in the past 30 years... The Energy Saving Trust has calculated that all the new entertainment and consumer electronics products in British households by 2020 will need another 14 average-sized power stations just to keep them running.

This theme is developed further in a more recent news item: another report from the Energy Saving Trust (an independent organization that advises on energy economy) has stated that 'despite householders' efforts to switch to energy-efficient products, we are actually consuming more energy than five years ago... The proliferation of new gadgets such as laptops, tablets and powerful desktops shows no sign of abating... Between 2000 and 2009, electricity use from home computing more than doubled.' (3 October 2011)

Our *Guardian* standfirst of 1 September 2007 included the words: 'plump on a diet of full-page adverts'. This is a key point, since it reminds us of the reason why the proposal to *consume less* can occupy no more than a niche in mainstream media. For a contrast that should help to bring out what I mean by 'mainstream', we can turn to an issue of the radical monthly magazine *The Leveller* for April 1980 (an old favourite from my personal archive), which uses its front cover to promote a feature on make-up. The content of this article is actually quite nuanced and manages, I think, to avoid sounding too didactic, but the conclusion is that dependence on cosmetics is an aspect or symptom of female subordination:

> The use of cosmetics is supposed to mean feminine vanity, but in reality it means precisely the opposite – the belief that your face is unattractive and ugly, and money and time has to be spent in compensating for its inherent unpleasantness... I still don't know what will happen when I'm older... But for the time being at least, I know of no face that is actually improved by make-up.
>
> (The writer's name is unfortunately illegible, as is the last paragraph of text, owing to samizdat-style production values.)

So this publication is entertaining the idea of make-up per se as a problem in women's lives (despite the admitted fact that 'putting one's face on' can offer a sense of security or of being in control); it is giving space to the view that in our own enlightened interest, we might consume less (of a certain kind of product), and trying to facilitate the process of reflection that would make this possible. The writer quoted is, I dare say unwittingly, making a move in that last audacious statement – 'I know of no face that is actually improved by make-up' – which echoes another Platonist thought, touching as it happens on the question of female participation in government, namely: 'It's foolish to take seriously any standard of what is beautiful other than the good.'[9] Be that as it may, I think we will wait in vain to see a cover feature of this kind in the *Guardian Weekend* magazine (which runs a 'beauty', meaning 'cosmetics', column in every issue). But then again, the *Leveller* never weighed in at 2kg (like that epoch-making US *Vogue* for September 2007), and – I believe – folded some time in the 1980s.

3. In terms of the kind of ethics discussed by philosophers, we might say that information about environmental damage and abusive economic practices is presented in mainstream ethical living journalism as an appeal to the personal virtue of the reader – that is, to the moral dispositions that govern people's responses to the news, and the day-to-day choices they make in buying goods and services. For example, if we learn that a certain high-street chain is selling children's clothes with decoration sewn on by child workers, this new knowledge offers us a cue for reflection on how we might need to change our behaviour in order to maintain our self-image as conscientious individuals. Specifically, should we now make a point of avoiding shop X, and should we take the time to seek out its website and send a message explaining our reasons?

As 'ethical consumers' we find ourselves at the sharp end of a distinctive array of moral claims, for which our respect (or otherwise) will have a contribution to make to the wider process of moral score-keeping – that is, to determining how we are doing at one moment or another under the heading of this or that virtue of character. The virtues can be understood in this context, in a tradition inherited from Aristotle, as qualities which our parents have tried to establish in us in our early years and which we have to do our best to maintain and improve – typically by resisting certain anti-moral or anti-social impulses which are natural to human beings and need to be kept under control. (Such qualities can therefore be thought of as 'corrective': selfishness, laziness, insensitivity and so forth come naturally to us, and a more or less standard array of virtues, the exact formula to be determined by one's individual constitution, is needed in order to counteract these bad tendencies.)

A point worth noting about the ethics of virtue is that it is open-ended or idealistic. 'Nobody's perfect', and failing to rise to a particular occasion for good action does not automatically make you a *bad* person; but on the other hand, there is no clear limit to the general demands of virtue – no moment when you can say that you have done enough, or are now definitely a *good* person. Some terminology from another canonical ethical theorist may help to bring greater precision to this thought. Kant distinguishes between two main types of duty – 'duties of virtue' and 'duties of justice'. The latter are concerned with other people's rights, and hence with the constraints placed on our actions by the requirement of compatibility with other people's (legitimate) actions. The former are concerned with the ends that every rational agent ought, as such, to adopt: these ends are *our own perfection* and the *happiness of others*.[10] (Not the other way round, because the pursuit of our own happiness is a natural, not a moral, imperative; and the perfection of others – meaning, in this case, other adults – is their business, not ours: something to be achieved by the exercise of their own free will.) Kant also distinguishes between 'perfect' and 'imperfect' duties: a perfect duty requires some definite action (or omission), whereas an imperfect duty leaves us some discretion in deciding how to show respect for it in practice.[11] So, 'loving your neighbour' – in the practical sense of helping your neighbour – would be an example of an imperfect duty (since it is up to us, from moment to moment, to find an appropriate mode of expression of this 'love'), whereas paying your debts is not a matter for the exercise of discretion – you simply have to produce the amount owed: like all duties of justice, this is an example of a perfect duty.[12]

Drawing now upon the terminology just introduced, I want to suggest that the typical subject matter of ethical living in its journalistic context has to do with a species of 'imperfect duties of virtue' – that is, with certain values or ends which it is a duty to adopt as our own, but which allow for an element of 'inclination' as regards the precise way we act in pursuit of them. That there are some duties of this kind seems to be a familiar fact of moral experience. Thus we can recognize, in general terms, a duty to be helpful (to try to conform to the ideal of the helpful person) without thereby committing ourselves to the belief that we have necessarily violated a duty every time we let slip an opportunity for helpful action. And to present ethical living as an ideal to be pursued, or a worthy end to be promoted, by each of us as best we can is a neat ideological move. It licenses us, as readers, to think of ourselves as sharing the relevant ideal (the avoidance of exploitative or environmentally destructive behaviour) but at the same time to exercise discretion in the practical interpretation of it, thereby maintaining a friendly milieu for the usual consumerist messages about fashion, cars, gizmos, foreign holidays and so forth.

4. But what I also want to suggest – and what I think is prompting the discontent of the more austere columnists quoted earlier – is that practices of consumption need to be examined from the point of view of the other division of ethics that comes down to us from Kant, namely the doctrine of right or justice (two terms which I shall treat in this context as interchangeable). In academic philosophy this division is in fact the more famous of the two, being the domain of the well-known 'principle of universalizability' – the version of the categorical imperative which says: 'Act only on that maxim [that is, principle] of which you can will that it should be a universal law.' From Hegel onwards, readers of Kant have tended to worry that reliance on this test makes his ethics too purely formal, so that, with sufficient fanaticism or perversity, one 'could' will the universalization of all sorts of maxims with no discernible basis in ethics as normally understood. (For example, if one didn't care about the survival of an institution such as promise-keeping or private property, one could consent with equanimity to a world in which everyone made false promises or helped themselves at will.) If, however, we allow Kant to defend himself by reminding us of other aspects of his account of moral rationality, the picture begins to change: he can then point to the substantive consequences of a 'respect for rational nature' in ourselves and others, and also to the significance of the 'anthropological' setting of morality – the fact that the beings to whom morality applies are members of a certain natural species.[13]

For present purposes I will limit myself to the 'anthropological' considerations, which seem to bear particularly strongly on environmental ethics. Let's assume that my 'maxims', in this context, are expressed in my present material mode of life – treating the fact that I actually do live in this way as de facto evidence that I believe it to be morally legitimate to do so. (This is, of course, problematic in view of such well-known phenomena as weakness of will, moral ambivalence, hypocrisy and so on – but there is at any rate a respectable tradition, reaching from Plato's Socratic dialogues down to R. M. Hare's prescriptivism, which posits an a priori connection between moral conviction and action.) Then the test which the principle of universalizability invites me to apply ('Do you consent to a state of affairs in which everyone, meaning the whole of humanity, adopts the same maxims as yourself?') is one whose results will be, or ought rationally to be, highly sensitive to empirical information of various kinds – that is, to information about what it would be like if everyone behaved in this or that way. Such information will be, so to speak, 'anthropologically' relevant. So, for example, if there is roughly one car on the planet for every ten human beings (which I believe was the case around the turn of the century, though this figure will now be seriously out of date),[14] then a reply to the question Do I consent to a state of affairs in which every adult human being has their own car? will be, or ought to be, sensitive to various kinds of speculation about what such a state of affairs would be like, extrapolating from what we know about the present state of affairs in which there is a much lower level of car ownership. (When I use the word 'ought' as I have done in this paragraph – as in 'ought to be sensitive' – I don't mean to be saying anything controversial, but simply appealing to everyday ideas about what a sensible person will take into account in practical reasoning. I am leaving on one side the sort of Humian scepticism which might lead one to say that it is not contrary to reason to prefer the destruction of the world to the scratching of one's finger.) In other words, what I 'can' will with regard to this point will be conditioned by my natural needs and susceptibilities as a member of the human species, just as Kant maintains in the *Groundwork* that I *cannot* universalize a maxim of not helping others in need:

> for a will which decided in this way would be in conflict with itself, since many a situation might arise in which the man needed love and sympathy from others, and in which, by such a law of nature sprung from his own will, he would rob himself of all hope of the help he wants for himself.[15]

5. A straightforward and, I think, quite instructive way of applying the principle of universalizability to 'lifestyle' in general is by reference to the global distribution of wealth.[16] Here as elsewhere, what the principle tells us is presumably that we are not to claim for ourselves (individually or collectively – for instance, at the level of the nation-state) benefits which we are not prepared to extend to everyone else, or which we have reason to believe cannot be extended to everyone, given available resources and environmental constraints. So if we assume that no part of the world's population is inherently more 'deserving' than any other, and that being a citizen of a rich country is a matter of luck, a good question to ask seems to be: What standard of living, or what 'lifestyle', could we as a nation have without incurring the charge that we are illicitly claiming special privileges relative to the rest of the world?

In a book published 30 years ago, economist Bob Sutcliffe calculated that if the world's wealth were evenly distributed, everyone could have the average standard of living enjoyed at that time by the population of Argentina, Portugal or Yugoslavia.[17] Bringing the idea up to date in a recent personal communication, Sutcliffe notes that according to World Bank figures for 2010, reduced to US dollars by a process called 'purchasing power parity', the world average income per head in that year was $11,151; countries that closely approximated this figure were Serbia ($11,488), Costa Rica ($11,351), Brazil ($11,127) and Macedonia ($11,072). So, roughly speaking, all countries with a standard of living below these four would currently be beneficiaries in a sharing-out of global wealth, while all those above would find themselves making sacrifices. (I am passing over the huge differences of wealth that may exist within individual countries, since we are already hypothesizing a process of redistribution more radical than the one that would be needed to annul those differences.) As a first step, then, towards ethical living in the sense suggested by the Kantian requirement of universality, we might apply the 'Macedonia test' – not that the relevant figures are likely to remain stable for very long, or that most people reading these words are likely to have any detailed idea of the nature of material life in the countries just mentioned,[18] but the point is that this gives us a concrete and readily intelligible method by which to determine what would have counted in 2010 as *living like a human being* (as opposed to a 'master of the universe', to recall Tom Wolfe's *Bonfire of the Vanities* of 1987). Of course, this can only be a first step towards a universalist characterization of ethical living, because we don't yet know whether a country that passes the Macedonia test at any given moment (say, Macedonia in 2010) is living at a standard that is sustainable in the long term by the criterion given in the *Guardian* of 6 October 2007 – that is, how many planet Earths would be needed to support that standard of living if universalized: if the figure for China is somewhere in the region of 1, it seems likely that even relatively poor European countries like Macedonia and Serbia will already be above 1, in which case passing the Macedonia test will not be enough to certify a mode of life as 'ethical' in the perspective of the future.[19]

I think it is clear enough that this line of thought takes us outside the frame of reference of the ethical consumer *qua* media construct. It suggests, at any rate, that if we are to assent to propositions like that of Peter MacBride that 'Ethical living rarely costs anything other than effort, and will improve the quality of your life',[20] then we must be willing to undertake a fairly drastic overhaul of our understanding of 'cost', 'quality of life' and suchlike concepts – a revision inspired by the same kind of 'alternative' (or rationalist) ideals as the writer quoted earlier who knew of no face that was improved by make-up. Could it really improve the quality of our lives to give up our arbitrarily privileged position within the global economy? Is MacBride's bold claim (which appears on an introductory page of his book, for those who 'have only got a minute') intended as a kind of intellectual stealth weapon – a subtle reminder, perhaps, of the difficulties encountered by a camel in getting through the eye of a needle? On the whole, this seems unlikely. Yet it is hard to escape the sense of something radical lurking just off-stage. For the putative ethical consumer, gradually learning to set aside a few minutes to ponder the responsible use of his/her disposable income, will be a citizen of a country whose relations with the rest of the world are not in fact governed by 'ethics' in anything like the Kantian sense. Noam Chomsky sums up the situation in his book *Failed States*:

> Among the most elementary of moral truisms is the principle of universality: we must apply to ourselves the same standards we do to others, if not more stringent ones. It is a remarkable comment on Western intellectual culture that this principle is so often ignored and, if occasionally mentioned, condemned as outrageous.[21]

Chomsky's immediate target of criticism is the G.W. Bush administration and its media spokespeople (notably in connection with the Iraq War) but, looking a little further back, he also cites 'the officially announced Clinton doctrine that the United States is entitled to resort to "unilateral use of military power" to ensure "uninhibited access to key markets, energy supplies, and strategic resources" '[22] – in other words, to secure its perceived 'key' economic interests. To labour the obvious, this is not a principle of action on the international scene which the US (or the UK) would view as permissible for any arbitrary nation.

6. As stated at the outset, my aim in this chapter is to show how certain lines of self-criticism on the part of the ethical living movement can be clarified by reference to academic ethics, and the specific philosophical item to which I have appealed so far is the distinction between 'duties of right' and 'duties of virtue', the suggestion being that if the demands of consumer-friendly ethical living strike us at times as failing to take the full measure of the abuses they are meant to confront, this can be attributed to the questionable portrayal of what is really a *debt* as being merely a noble *ideal* or 'counsel of perfection'. (Interestingly, Kant anticipates this criticism by maintaining in his *Lectures on Ethics* that 'When we show beneficence to a needy person, we do not give him anything gratuitously, but only give him some of what we have previously helped to take from him through the general injustice.')[23] However, I would like to draw attention in the space remaining to a further bit of philosophical theory which has occupied a somewhat recessive position in recent years, but which may well be – or at any rate arguably ought to be – on the brink of renewal. This is the distinction between 'use value' and 'exchange value'; or better, to avoid any potentially distracting reliance on Marxist terminology, we can revisit Aristotle and say that it is the distinction drawn by him in the *Politics* (Book I, chapters 8–9) between two subdivisions of *chrêmatistikê*, 'the art of acquisition'; or as we might prefer to put it, two senses that can be given to this term. In acknowledging the relevant distinction we may find that the conceptual revisions envisaged just now (around 'quality of life' and so forth) come to seem more feasible, or at any rate less preposterous. We may also begin to see our way forward from the rough-and-ready considerations of distributive justice involved in the Macedonia test – §5 above – to a (somewhat) less historically contingent view of the human economic condition.[24]

In one sense, then, *chrêmatistikê* denotes skill in ensuring a supply of the things 'necessary for life, and useful for the community of the city or household' (I, 8; 1256b29–30). This kind of acquisition is 'natural' (I, 9; 1257a4) and contains its own inbuilt limit, since human beings – like other natural species – have certain objective needs for food, shelter and so forth: thus there is a quantity of food that is enough for a given individual, and eating three times that quantity is not three times as good. In its other sense, by contrast, namely as skill in accumulating wealth for its own sake, the 'art of acquisition' has no inbuilt limit

(I, 9; 1257b19–24), since the kind of value at issue here is non-natural: £3000 in the bank is indeed three times as good as £1000, insofar as wealth (rather than the 'good life' with its more or less determinate requirements) is our aim. Phenomena such as trade and the institution of money are to be understood ethically against the background of the distinction just drawn, or, as Scott Meikle explains,

> The position Aristotle arrives at is that the use made of a thing in exchanging it is good or bad depending on the end served by the exchange... [Thus] whether the use of a shoe in exchange is good or bad depends on the end; on the part the transaction plays in human life. In [one kind of exchange] the end is need or having enough, so the use of the shoe here is good, 'necessary and laudable'... But using a shoe in [the kind of exchange whose purpose is to make money] is not a means to the good life, so the use made of a shoe [here] is not good.[25]

It should be clear from this account that, in stark contrast with the familiar frame of reference within which economic 'growth' is treated as an unqualified good, anyone minded to adopt an Aristotelian approach to the ethics (or politics) of consumption will eventually find themselves committed to assessing their consumer behaviour by the standard of the 'good life' – a problematic notion, no doubt, but still one endowed with some kind of naturally determinate (and hence critical) content. In other words, they will be led to raise questions of the form Do I need this? (where this general form embraces subforms such as Do I need another one? Do I need the latest model? and so on).

Of course, this is all extremely schematic and, at a certain level of detail, bafflingly hard to apply. Should I be asking myself more earnestly whether I *need*, say, a certain paperback novel which tempts me at the station bookshop? Admittedly it will entertain me on the train, but shouldn't I have planned ahead and brought with me one of the numerous books lying unread at home? In which case, even if I can legitimately claim to 'need' it here and now, perhaps I am at fault for having put myself in that position...

I imagine no one, no real-life 'ethical consumer' however stern, actually reasons like this. And they would be within their rights not to do so, for one can certainly acknowledge the critical potential of the concept of need without thereby subscribing to any normative principle to the effect that a person ought to have *nothing* superfluous, nothing idiosyncratic or 'just for fun'.[26] That hardly sounds like a recipe for even the more modest sort of 'good life'. All the same, there is something not entirely satisfactory about advice that, while steering us away from some particularly grievous shopping outrage, seems nevertheless to fly in the face of any consideration of need. For example, 'between the 90s and the mid-2000s, the herd [of cashmere goats in the Gobi Desert of Mongolia] increased...from 2.4 million to 24 million', responding to the global demand for cashmere as an increasingly routine and inexpensive purchase, but causing serious environmental damage through the resulting stress on vegetation and water supplies. The alternative proposed: 'Go higher up the chain to producers who know their suppliers, such as [X, Y and Z]. [Website N] promotes ethical cashmere and gives a fair price to herdsmen committed to sustainable strategies'.[27] Well, all right. But there was a time not so long ago when we were content with sheep's wool. We might even have contemplated darning a hole rather than buying a new jumper.

It can undeniably be argued that if the 'buy nothing' ideal came to command sufficient support, it would put a lot of producers out of business and a lot of individuals out of work – an 'ethical' counterpart, so to speak, of the process that occurs spontaneously in times of economic recession when people buy less stuff, not on principle, but because of a decline in collective spending power. This is the negative route to the prevailing view that growth is in everyone's interest and must be maintained or restored at all costs; and it is hardly surprising to find the discourse of ethical living sometimes deferring to that view. Still, it can do no harm to recall the Aristotelian distinction between good and bad variants of the 'art of acquisition' – the kind that recognizes a natural limit fixed by the requirements of a good human life, and the kind that does not – and to reflect that when King Lear early on in the play of that name says 'Reason not the need!', he is about to learn some hard lessons.[28] (Or, returning to the issue of the 'just for fun' purchase: even if the question Do I need this? is apt to strike us on any particular occasion as annoyingly puritanical, there is surely a time and a place for the closely related Do I need *all this*?)

So, I have attempted to bring out the rather limited nature of the conception of ethics to which ethical living journalism typically appeals; to make some suggestions about how this limitation works, invoking certain tools of mainstream moral philosophy, the distinctions between different species of duty and between different species of value; and to offer these distinctions as a substructure for the more challenging approach (exemplified by writers like Monbiot) which inspired the present discussion. No doubt a willingness on the part of individuals in the rich world to cultivate more frugal and thoughtful shopping habits would be an excellent thing, and it would be quite wrong to belittle such efforts, or to claim exemption from them. However, as will no doubt be apparent by now, I think the malcontents have an incontrovertible case. Personal virtue is as important in matters of 'lifestyle' as anywhere else, but here too it is best viewed as issuing in a succession of autonomous acts of witness or commitment, not as a means to objectives which demand a more traditionally political approach – that is, to ends such as social justice or sane economic order.[29] If the media proponents of 'ethical living' succeed over time (directly or indirectly) in raising this insight to full consciousness, they will have made a solid contribution to the advancement of public discussion.[30]

Notes

1. D. Clark (2006) *The Rough Guide to Ethical Living*. London: Penguin, p. 3.
2. P. MacBride (2010) *Live Ethically*, 2nd edn. London: Hodder Education, pp. 1–2.
3. *The Rough Guide to Ethical Living*, p. 19.
4. Unless otherwise stated, all references to newspaper articles in this chapter are to the *Guardian*.
5. Glover, incidentally, is no leftist – at any rate, he has since accepted a job as chief speechwriter to David Cameron (8 October 2011). Also noteworthy is the subsequent evolution of Lynas (quoted below) into an advocate of, among other things, 'growth-based capitalism' (as reported by Duncan Clark, 1 November 2011, G2).
6. The word 'more' appears to be a slip – an accompanying diagram indicates that it is a question of the absolute number of planets needed.
7. This was a Saturday: in its *Weekend* magazine on the same day, the *Guardian* carried an article by Stephen Fry explaining that he is 'dippy about all things digital' and promoting his forthcoming weekly feature about them.
8. It looks as if '2040' should read '2030' – that is, $2007 + 23$.
9. Plato, *Republic* V, 452e. The translation is taken from G.M.A. Grube and C.D.C. Reeve (1992) Indianapolis/Cambridge, Mass.: Hackett, except that this translation has 'fine and beautiful' for the single Greek word *kalon* – I have omitted the 'fine', which is superfluous in this context.
10. I. Kant (1996) *The Metaphysics of Morals*, translated and edited by Mary Gregor. Cambridge: Cambridge University Press, p. 150.
11. Ibid., p. 153.
12. Christine M. Korsgaard (1996) (to whose painstaking exposition I am indebted here) notes that we might be tempted simply to identify duties of justice with perfect duties, and duties of virtue with imperfect duties – but 'this would be an oversimplification: Kant's categorizations are more intricate than that' (*Creating the Kingdom of Ends*. Cambridge: Cambridge University Press, p. 83). In particular, we should avoid confusing the perfect/imperfect distinction with another distinction between 'strict' and

'broad' duties, even if 'Kant himself does not use the four terms in a perspicuous way' (ibid., p. 20). 'Strictness', says Korsgaard, is a matter of being fully dischargeable. So duties of virtue are all broad rather than strict, because one can never definitely say that one has done enough under the relevant heading; but they are not all imperfect: 'Perfect duties of virtue arise because we must refrain from particular actions against humanity in our own person or that of another' (ibid., p. 21). This might suggest that the strict/broad terminology is what we really need in the discussion to follow. I have nevertheless preferred that of perfect/imperfect, partly because it is more familiar (it is used, for example, by Mill in Chapter 5 of *Utilitarianism*), but also in order to invoke the idea of a mediating role for inclination in negotiating the claims of duty.

13. On this aspect of Kant's ethics, see N. Sherman (1997) *Making a Necessity of Virtue: Aristotle and Kant on Virtue*. Cambridge: Cambridge University Press, Chapter 4, §2. For Kant, as Sherman explains, 'the generation of our specific duties from the fact of our rational nature requires contingent premises that tailor rational agency to human vulnerabilities and powers...to direct the moral project toward the human condition is not necessarily to jeopardize its *a priori* grounding' (p. 129).

14. Since drafting this chapter, I have come across an estimate that 'the total vehicle stock will increase from about 800 million in 2002 to more than two billion units in 2030. By this time, 56% of the world's vehicles will be owned by non-OECD countries, compared with 24% in 2002' (Dargay et al. (2007) 'Vehicle Ownership and Income Growth, Worldwide: 1960–2030', *The Energy Journal*, 28(4) 163–90, at p. 163).

15. I. Kant (1948) *Groundwork of the Metaphysic of Morals*, translated by H.J. Paton as *The Moral Law*. London: Hutchinson, p. 423 (Prussian Academy page numbering).

16. I owe to Pierre Bourdieu ((1991) *The Political Ontology of Martin Heidegger*, translated by P. Collier. Cambridge: Polity Press, p. 44) the information that a 'socialist interpretation of Kant' was offered by Hermann Cohen of the Marburg school, 'a favourite butt of the ideologues of the Third Reich'.

17. B. Sutcliffe (1983) *Hard Times: The World Economy in Turmoil*. London: Pluto Press, p. 10; and compare p. 13, which refers to 'the earth's average income of $2,222 per head (in 1980)'.

18. It is for reasons of 'closeness to home' (and hence imaginative closeness) that I have referred in the text to Macedonia rather than Brazil, the country for which the figure is nearest to the exact mean.

19. This is supported by the statement of Andrew Rawnsley (*Observer*, 6 November 2011) that the average income for China is about $5000 per year.

20. *Live Ethically*, p. x.

21. N. Chomsky (2007) *Failed States: The Abuse of Power and the Assault on Democracy*. London: Penguin, p. 3.

22. Ibid., p. 10; and for more on the de facto repudiation of the principle of universality by the US and its allies dating back to the Second World War, see pp. 82–85.

23. I owe this reference to A.W. Wood (1999) *Kant's Ethical Thought*. Cambridge: Cambridge University Press, p. 273.

24. In the light of live discussion of this chapter, it may be worth stating explicitly that I am enough of a hedonic rationalist (see §§2 and 5 above) not to find the proposed rethink particularly 'preposterous' on my own account, or to regard the giving-up of unearned privileges as mere, unqualified 'sacrifice' (§3). Still, for general dialectical purposes, it would be unwise to assert that international economic justice could be achieved without serious inconvenience to the rich world.

25. S. Meikle (1995) *Aristotle's Economic Thought*. Oxford: Oxford University Press, pp. 55, 56–57. The quoted words 'necessary and laudable' translate Aristotle's *anankaias kai epainoumenês* at *Politics* I, 10; 1258a40. Some square brackets have been used to avoid introducing technical terms from Meikle's discussion.

26. See D. Wiggins (1998) 'Postscript' to *Needs, Values, Truth: Essays in the Philosophy of Value*, 3rd edn. Oxford: Clarendon Press, p. 321. Wiggins is here reprising his essay 'Claims of Need' in the same volume, which affirms the legitimacy of an 'absolute' (not purely instrumental) conception of need, and investigates in detail how this can properly interact with the ideas of justice, rights, interests, equality, and other constituents of practical (political) reasoning.

27. Lucy Siegle, *Guardian Weekend*, 15 October 2011. In citing this article I intend no disrespect to the author, a journalist specializing in consumer ethics who has done more to serve that cause than I am ever likely to. The article in fact contains a variety of practical suggestions, not excluding the advice to make the item you have last longer (with reference to flat-screen TVs, which are apparently implicated in the mining of rare minerals from the seabed).

28. Evidence of an implicit renewal of interest in the naturalistic approach to consumption can be found in some recent 'general interest' texts. John Lanchester (2010) comments on the aftermath of the 2007–2008 crash: 'In a world running out of resources, the most important ethical and political and ecological idea can be summed up in one simple word: "Enough"' (*Whoops! Why Everyone Owes Everyone and No One Can Pay*. London: Penguin, p. 200). In the same vein, Richard Wilkinson and Kate Pickett (2010) argue that

> we have got close to the end of what economic growth can do for us... In poor countries, economic development continues to be very important for human wellbeing... But as nations join the ranks of the affluent developed countries, further rises in income count for less and less.
>
> (*The Spirit Level: Why Equality is Better for Everyone*.
> London: Penguin, pp. 5, 8)

For further development of the Shakespearian theme, see T. Eagleton (2010) 'Communism: Lear or Gonzalo?', in S. Žižek and C. Douzinas (eds) *The Idea of Communism*. London: Verso.

29. Not that the rewards of virtue, in this area at any rate, should be pictured as unproblematically available to all persons of good will. As Adorno puts it, 'Wrong life cannot be lived rightly' (T. Adorno (1974) *Minima Moralia: Reflections from Damaged Life*, translated by E.F.N. Jephcott. London: New Left Books, p. 39).

30. I am grateful to the editors of the present collection for helpful critical comments, and to others who have responded to the chapter at various stages:

participants in the 2008 conference at Cambridge, a seminar audience at the University of Essex, and members of the philosophers' work-in-progress group at Worcester College, Oxford.

References

Adorno, T. (1974) *Minima Moralia: Reflections from Damaged Life*, translated by E. F. N. Jephcott. London: New Left Books.

Aristotle (1957) *Politics*, ed. W. D. Ross. Oxford: Clarendon Press (various translations available).

Bourdieu, P. (1991) *The Political Ontology of Martin Heidegger*, translated by P. Collier. Cambridge: Polity Press.

Chomsky, N. (2007) *Failed States: The Abuse of Power and the Assault on Democracy*. London: Penguin.

Clark, D. (2006) *The Rough Guide to Ethical Living*. London: Penguin.

Dargay, J., D. Gately, and M. Sommer (2007) 'Vehicle Ownership and Income Growth, Worldwide: 1960–2030', *The Energy Journal* 28(4): 163–90.

Eagleton, T. (2010) 'Communism: Lear or Gonzalo?', in S. Žižek and C. Douzinas (eds) *The Idea of Communism*. London: Verso.

Kant, I. (1948) *Groundwork of the Metaphysic of Morals*, translated by H. J. Paton as *The Moral Law*. London: Hutchinson.

Kant, I. (1996) *The Metaphysics of Morals*, translated and edited by Mary Gregor. Cambridge: Cambridge University Press.

Korsgaard, C. M. (1996) *Creating the Kingdom of Ends*. Cambridge: Cambridge University Press.

Lanchester, J. (2010) *Whoops! Why Everyone Owes Everyone and No One Can Pay*. London: Penguin.

MacBride, P. (2010) *Live Ethically*, 2nd edn. London: Hodder Education.

Meikle, S. (1995) *Aristotle's Economic Thought*. Oxford: Oxford University Press.

Plato (1992) *Republic*, translated by G. M. A. Grube and C. D. C. Reeve. Indianapolis/Cambridge: Cambridge University Press, MA: Hackett.

Sherman, N. (1997) *Making a Necessity of Virtue: Aristotle and Kant on Virtue*. Cambridge: Cambridge University Press.

Sutcliffe, B. (1983) *Hard Times: The World Economy in Turmoil*. London: Pluto Press.

Wiggins, D. (1998) *Needs, Values, Truth: Essays in the Philosophy of Value*, 3rd edn. Oxford: Clarendon Press.

Wilkinson, R. and K. Pickett (2010) *The Spirit Level: Why Equality Is Better for Everyone*. London: Penguin.

Wood, A. W. (1999) *Kant's Ethical Thought*. Cambridge: Cambridge University Press.

14
WikiLeaks, National Security and Cosmopolitan Ethics

Damian Tambini

Introduction: Was *WikiLeaks* Pro US?

On Tuesday 22 November 2010, *New York Times* editor Bill Keller attended a tense meeting with national security advisors in Washington. (Keller 2011: 5). During the same week, his counterpart at the *Guardian* newspaper in London, Alan Rusbridger, met with UK government officials and representatives of the US government. The discussions focused on the security implications of plans to publish news stories selected from a cache of more than 250,000 secret cables that whistle-blower website *WikiLeaks* had received from an anonymous source. Would publication lead to persecution of US informants and activists operating in authoritarian countries? Would frontline troops be placed in immediate danger by the release of their position, equipment or plans? Both journalists and government representatives were concerned that making the information public could compromise the security of diplomatic sources, agents and interests.

The meetings in Washington and London were part of the sensitive process of determining which of the cables would be made public and which would – for the time being at least – not be published; which stories of US intelligence activity would be met with public outrage, amusement and debate, and which would, for the time being at least, remain secret. And for those cables that were published, this was part of the process that would decide which details, such as names and places, were to be erased prior to publication. According to Keller, the government officials he met wanted to protect the identities of any individuals who had spoken to US diplomats in oppressive countries, and wanted to remove references to secret US intelligence programmes (Keller 2011: 5). The journalists, not wanting blood on their hands, agreed with much of what was suggested to them. But when officials requested that the *New York Times* should remove remarks by heads of state and other top officials where publication would cause embarrassment or strain relations, Keller was more sceptical and the meeting abruptly came to an end (Leigh and Harding 2011: 191; Keller 2011: 5–6). Whilst journalism ethics generally permit a degree of self-censorship where life and limb are at stake, neither the *New York Times* nor the *Guardian* were prepared to restrict material purely to avoid diplomatic embarrassment.

Two things are worth noting here. First, the approach to potential harms caused by the publication of the cables focused on US and UK national security. Pakistani, Afghan and Chinese officials, for example, were not involved. Second, whilst neither *WikiLeaks* nor its founder Julian Assange conducted detailed negotiations with government officials about what they should and should not publish,[1] they did accept the redactions by the *Guardian* and the *New York Times*. When the first batch of documents was published on the *WikiLeaks* site, they were those selected by the *Guardian* and the *New York Times*, with sensitive details that could compromise operational security removed by the newspapers. Thus the whistle-blower site had delegated to its media partners the task of redacting security-sensitive information from the leaked cables.

This process of apparent self-censorship raises fundamental questions relating to current debates about globalization and cosmopolitanism. Was *WikiLeaks* a genuinely global organization or did it operate within national systems of regulation and military censorship? Did the publication of the US cables represent part of a process of 'taming' *WikiLeaks* to serve the interests of the UK and the US? If *WikiLeaks* or sites like it are able to evade the ethical and legal framework of a single country, might it perhaps develop a more cosmopolitan, global approach to ethical journalism?

Referring to the Pentagon Papers case,[2] which defined the legal immunities of publishers of military secrets in the US, Jay Rosen (2012) and Clay Shirky (2010) see the 'stateless', global nature of *WikiLeaks* as its defining feature:

> Let me propose, for the sake of argument, two labels for action that spans more than one country: international, and global. International actors are actors rooted in a nation, even when they are able to participate in activities all over the world, while global actors are unrooted; global actors have, as their home environment, the globe.... The most dramatic of *WikiLeaks*'s breaks with previous

journalism is the global nature Rosen identified. The biggest differ-ence between the Pentagon Papers case and *WikiLeaks* is not the legal precedent, but the fact that the Pentagon Papers case was an entirely national affair.

(Shirky 2010)

In this chapter I first outline the evolving features of the Wikileaks model of encrypted whistleblowing. Then I examine the background to the current settlement on media ethics outlining the historical develop-ment of what I describe as a 'social compact' – a legal and self-regulatory framework – outlining the responsibilities of free media within a nation-state. I go on to discuss the experience of *WikiLeaks* in relation to that national ethical compact. Then, based on an analysis of published accounts, blogs and online discussions, I examine *WikiLeaks's* approach to its responsibilities, in particular the process of redaction and selec-tion that it applied to the US cables. I also look at the legal framework drawing on case law and comparative research on media ethics and regulation in Europe. Finally, I return to the central question of global media ethics. If media can operate in a global, unregulatable space, what ethical rules might they seek voluntarily to adhere to and how would these norms differ from the settlement within national legal and ethical systems?

In studying *WikiLeaks* I use a 'practical' approach to ethics, build-ing upon Onora O'Neill's *modus operandi* (O'Neil 2000). This does not start from abstract principles but asks 'what assumptions we are already building into our action, habits, practices and institutions'. This more empirical take on global media ethics[3] directs us to examine the ethi-cal experimentation being carried out by *WikiLeaks* – and others on the frontier of structural change. Nick Couldry (2012) raises the question, after Ricoeur, of whether the current juncture of global media consti-tutes a 'limit situation' necessitating a new domain of ethical thinking, and this chapter examines whether *WikiLeaks* can help us to understand this empirically.

What had changed, what had created this potential limit situation, necessitating a groping for a new global ethics? The key feature of *WikiLeaks* during this period was indeed its global, stateless nature or, more precisely, its ability to operate beyond the reach of the law. Because of the problem of jurisdiction (sites mirrored abroad) and iden-tity (use of encryption masks), internet communication is difficult to censor. Whilst China and other authoritarian governments have illus-trated that points of control can be exploited (Deibert et al. 2010), internet communication within and between free-speech jurisdictions is more difficult to control. In its short history, *WikiLeaks's* approach to legal liability has principally been to avoid it wherever possible, by moving around the globe and hiding assets. In 2008, when a California court successfully used an injunction to shut down a *WikiLeaks* site, there were still hundreds of mirror sites available in other jurisdictions around the world. It was, according to Daniel Domscheit-Berg 'virtually impossible' to take *WikiLeaks* offline (Domscheit-Berg 2011: 20–21). With no physical assets, such as offices and printing presses, and with limited financial assets, *WikiLeaks* has attempted to exist outside the law. The site operated behind a cloak of encryption, seeking to evade the jurisdiction of countries such as the US and distributing sensitive information around the world in encrypted form to trusted collaborators, for release when *WikiLeaks* or its founder were attacked. Unlike mainstream media, therefore, which are subject to licensing restrictions and/or existing ethical codes, and ultimately the law, *WikiLeaks's* own ethical procedures are self-imposed.

It would thus be an oversimplification to claim that *WikiLeaks* was beholden, through its mainstream media contacts, to any one national interest or coalition of interests. In fact, the organization was involved in a tense confrontation about the ethics of publication and the potential for harm to both 'friends' and 'enemies' of the so-called 'War on Terror'. Even during November 2010, Assange was already contacting journalists outside Europe and the US – such as the Brazilian Natalia Viana – about the US Cables. According to Viana, Assange saw this 'as a way of breaking the exclusive contract that tied them to the five most important mediums of communication in the world, and at the same time, increasing the circulation of secret documents about countries that were isolated from the geopolitical center of power'.[4] Phased releases of cables in collaboration with other countries began in April 2011, and *WikiLeaks* chose trusted journalists and publications in countries such as Pakistan (the newspaper *Dawn*) and Jamaica (*The Gleaner*), as well as bloggers such as Viana in countries where Assange chose to avoid the mainstream media. But the fact that this second phase took place some months after the cables were first shared with US/EU media partners made the material less sensitive and should have given the US time to take action to protect security interests, and change diplomatic and military personnel where necessary. Media outside the coalition of US and EU countries had to wait for their access to this valuable material, and wait until after the US and European media had taken their pick of what was most newsworthy, and diplomatic damage limitation had taken place. So whilst *WikiLeaks* leader Julian Assange may or may not be pro-US, the approach to the release of the cables was a negotiated compromise between coalition interests and those outside the US and Europe.

The next section briefly reviews *WikiLeaks*'s basic model, with a focus on the central question of the organization's approach to journal-ism ethics and 'harm minimisation'. We find that in its short history, *WikiLeaks* has experimented with a range of ethical approaches, at times conforming to the more established media ethics of mainstream news providers, and during other periods seeking a more absolute freedom.

WikiLeaks: From wiki to global news organization

WikiLeaks's original idea was a simple one: whereas in mainstream jour-nalism sources are protected by an ethical and legal code, *WikiLeaks* would protect sources by software code. When whistle-blowers post material to the *WikiLeaks* site, they do so through a secure encrypted interface that anonymizes their IP address and records no identifying information. 'Documents can be leaked on a massive scale in a way which combines the protection and anonymity of cutting edge crypto-graphic technologies.' *WikiLeaks* claims to 'keep no records as to where you uploaded from, your time zone, browser or even as to when your submission was made' (Leigh and Harding 2011: 52–53).

WikiLeaks began as a 'wiki' – a site that was open to posting and editing by users. Journalism was at this stage not something done by *WikiLeaks* itself. The idea was that selection and sifting of *WikiLeaks* documents would be 'crowd-sourced' from anyone with an interest in the material. This model was short-lived: not only was there a lack of audience but 'Assange and his colleagues rapidly found that the need to remove dangerous and incriminating information made such a model impractical' (Leigh and Harding 2011: 52). Leigh and Harding observed that 'Assange had now discovered, to his chagrin, that simply posting long lists of raw and random documents on to a website failed to change the world' (Leigh and Harding 2010: 61).

WikiLeaks thus began to take a more hands-on approach to editing during the period 2007–2010 (Dormscheit-Berg 2011: 44–50). Assange formed relationships with mainstream media to gain more impact. Stories would be cherry-picked from leaked material and shared with mainstream media. Assange claims that a 2007 story about corruption in Kenya led to a change of government – after the *Guardian* ran a front-page story on it. According to press reports, the initial Afghanistan War Logs release consisted of around 77,000 documents. When the names of people who might be put in danger had been redacted, another

15,000 or so were published (Benkler 2011: 11). According to Daniel Domscheit-Berg, however, the process was chaotic and *WikiLeaks* lacked the capacity to redact effectively (Domscheit-Berg 2011: 183–184). This was the reason Assange gave media partners access to the material, and over time the arrangements became more formal. Witnesses in a PBS documentary transmitted in May 2011 reported that the *WikiLeaks* 'harm minimisation policy' dates from that time (Keller 2011).[5]

The release of private documents of clients of the Julius Baer Swiss Bank in January 2008 revealed details of their alleged tax evasion and money laundering. Whilst the court order to suppress the *WikiLeaks* release was quickly overturned, the extrajurisdictional status of *WikiLeaks* is confirmed by this episode. *WikiLeaks* remained online despite court orders in a number of jurisdictions outside the US and was accessible globally (Domscheit-Berg 2011: 22).

During 2010, *WikiLeaks* attempted to address mounting concern about an allegedly 'fast and loose' approach to the security consequences of publication of Iraqi and Afghanistan war material. The site formalized a deeper partnership with mainstream media and in particular *Der Spiegel*, the *Guardian, Le Monde*, the *New York Times* and *El Pais*. Alasdair Roberts summarized the nature of this new arrangement for *WikiLeaks*:

> By the end of 2010 it was clear that *WikiLeaks' modus operandi* had fundamentally changed. It started the year with a straightforward conception of its role as a receiver and distributor of leaked information. At year's end, it was performing a different function: still hoping to function as a trusted receiver of leaks, but now working with mainstream media to decide how – or if – leaked information ought to be published.
>
> Roberts (2011)

This shift to a more active editorial position also created new risks. Selecting material for publishing, like actively soliciting specific material, brought to *WikiLeaks* new ethical responsibilities and potential legal liabilities (Benkler 2011). As it developed a harm-minimisation policy there was controversy about the level of professionalism in its approach to redactions. According to Daniel Domscheit-Berg, four days before the US diplomatic cables were to be published, Assange had still not told the *WikiLeaks* staffers preparing the documents for publication to redact names (Domscheit-Berg 2011). The *WikiLeaks* employees did not learn of the issue until editors at German newspaper *Der Spiegel* asked him about progress on redactions. *WikiLeaks* couldn't complete the redactions, so its media partners told it to withhold 14,000 files that contained names. Assange eventually asked the *New York Times* to help to redact but later complained that he had received no help from the paper.

Some of the small number of *WikiLeaks* 'journalists' became increasingly uncomfortable with the procedures and security at the website during 2010. The 'second in command' there, Daniel Dormsheit-Berg, grew uncomfortable with what he saw as the inability of *WikiLeaks* to negotiate the complex ethical balances they faced in relation to national security. He gave an interview to *Der Spiegel* on 29 September 2010 in which he said that

> In recent months we have grown crazily fast and there are technical problems that no one cares about. *WikiLeaks* urgently needs to become more professional in all areas and improve our transparency. But this development is blocked internally. Even for me is not clear how decisions are actually made and who is ultimately responsible. Because of the high pressure with the publication of the American military documents, we have not come to rebuild the organization accordingly. The result is that not all jobs are done correctly.
>
> (Dormsheit-Berg, reported in *Der Spiegel* 2011)

If arrangements within *WikiLeaks* were fraught, relationships with media partners were even stormier, with a long series of disputes and recriminations between *WikiLeaks*, the *Guardian* and the *New York Times*. This led to a formalized procedure, though not a transparent one. By June 2011, Assange was asserting that he would never work with media partners without a written agreement.[6] Part of the difficulty with these relationships, according to him, was that he was constantly challenging the media to be more bold in releasing the cables; and the journalists, citing their own legal and ethical responsibilities, counselled caution. In the following section I examine some of the rules and structures within which conventional news media operate.

Free speech and the media responsibility compact

In order to understand the global ethical terrain on which *WikiLeaks* is operating, it is necessary to understand the national terrain within which journalism ethics has developed. In the jurisprudence of the European Convention on Human Rights (ECHR) and the First

Amendment to the US Constitution, free speech is not an absolute, but balanced with what are considered to be legitimate restrictions of speech. I could face prosecution if I unjustifiably shouted 'fire!' in a crowded theatre since this could endanger people's lives, and there is a range of other restrictions on free speech justified in terms of privacy, reputation, intellectual property, harassment or confidence and other rights.[7] The right to life itself is, of course, most fundamental, and national security considerations such as those engaged in the *WikiLeaks* case can therefore constitute legitimate restrictions on speech.

Media law and policy in liberal democratic countries constitute a set of institutions and practices that structure the speech field and decisions about what should be made public with a presumption in favour of free speech, but in terms of a balance with these other rights. Journalists claiming protection under Article 10 of the ECHR (Freedom of Expression), for example, may be required to demonstrate that they are performing a public interest role and acting responsibly. They do so in terms of a series of free-speech-related privileges – such as the right to protect sources and protection from liability for public interest journalism, which are granted in recognition of the performance of a certain set of functions – chiefly performing responsible journalism in the public interest.[8]

Various authors have debated the historical development of the current settlement in terms of notions of countervailing powers, reflexivity (Eder 2006) and the detailed negotiation and battles that occurred during historical battles over free speech (Pickard 2010). What is clear is that in democracies, the media have had some autonomous power, because of their influence in the electoral market, to repel attempts to control speech.[9] So whilst clear legal limits are defined in relation for example to national security, voluntary self-restraint defines the practice of media responsibility within the nation-state.

Steven Ward has outlined a contract theory of media ethics in which freedoms are granted in return for a commitment to a series of responsibilities (2005). Pickard (2010) has developed the notion that the media exist within a compact of rights and responsibilities. In short, we can understand the institutional position of media, including press freedom and journalistic privilege, as a social compact. The media serve a valuable social function in the facilitation and distribution of public debate, and in return they are granted by society a series of privileges (see Tambini 2012). But the media are not 'free' in an absolute sense. They operate within a tense regulatory settlement. One of the conditions upon which such a compact is based is that the media should work within accepted rules.

The point here is that *WikiLeaks* and similar sites have the potential to operate not only beyond the law, but outside the social compact that governs mass media. Within national free-speech frameworks, media enjoy certain immunities and privileges deriving from freedom of expression but these are granted on condition of good behaviour defined in terms of a nation-state bounded public interest, and national security in particular provides a justification of restriction of free speech. WikiLeaks is free of these constraints, ultimately relying neither on ethical nor legal, but on software code.

It is important to note that this is an institutional rather than a solely normative approach. So-called 'social responsibility' theories of the press and journalism (Siebert et al. 1956) are often merely normative considerations of what journalism 'ought' to be and do. By contrast, my rights and duties approach is a sociolegal, institutional theory of journalism, based on an understanding of the legally constituted practice of reporting and its institutionalized role (see Pickard 2010; Ward 2005, Tambini 2012). A number of theorists are engaged in the urgent task of providing a normative theoretical basis for globalizing media in both a deontological and a neo-Aristotelian[10] framework. The approach of this article owes more to Stephen Ward and Onora O Neill in adopting an institutional, practical approach to ethics.

Parliaments have tended to be restrained in codifying laws on news and journalism, and they defer to self-regulation through codes of ethics. Self-regulation is a collective means of avoiding statutory regulation and a condition of free-speech protection. So long as the media are able to exercise restraint and act responsibly, they can be 'free'. In relation to national security, therefore, whistle-blowers may be subject to prosecution, but news media that publish the material will not be prosecuted, as long as they do so responsibly. Responsibility of the media includes the balancing of national security interests against the public interest in publication.

WikiLeaks's approach to the US cables was thus not in any simple sense pro-US, but it may have been shaped by its relationship to media partners embedded within these national legal frameworks. In order to understand the implication of new communications phenomena such as *WikiLeaks* for current transformations of the public sphere, it is necessary to acknowledge that liberal democratic media including *WikiLeaks*'s partners have operated within a clear institutional-legal context, a social compact of rights and duties. Freedom of expression is not absolute but involves balancing freedom of speech against restrictions that are prescribed by law and necessary in a democratic society. The news media, in particular, enjoy privileges such as qualified journalistic privilege. Those privileges are predicated on a set of responsibilities to observe ethical codes; respect rights of others; and operate in the public interest. *WikiLeaks*, like *The Times* in the Reynolds case (See Clayton and Tomlinson 2009: 1383),[11,12] has argued that in releasing the secret cables it was not doing harm; rather, it was acting ethically, responsibly and in the public interest.

Despite the efforts of Rusbridger and Keller, controversy surrounding the *WikiLeaks* revelations in 2010 centred upon the extent to which publishing the leaked information compromised US national security and particularly the security of the military coalitions occupying Iraq and Afghanistan. Government spokespeople were highly critical of the publication of the US cables, both in the UK and in the US. A spokesperson outlined the UK government position: 'Clearly we condemn the unauthorized release of classified information. The leaks and their publication are damaging to national security in the United States and in Britain, and elsewhere.' It was not claimed that the information would lead to direct threats to life and limb but that 'it's important that governments are able to operate on the basis of confidentiality of information'.[13] In the US the reaction was firmer, and singled out a particular cable, one that was in fact released by *WikiLeaks* and not its media partners: 'On Dec. 5, *WikiLeaks* released a 2009 diplomatic cable from Secretary of State Hillary Clinton detailing key sites worldwide. Among the locations cited were undersea communications lines, mines, antivenin factories and suppliers of food and manufacturing materials... U.S. officials said the leak amounted to giving a hit list to terrorists.'[14] According to Alan Rusbridger writing in January 2011, however, 'barely two thousand of the 250,000 diplomatic cables have been published, and, six months after the first publication of the war logs, no one has been able to demonstrate any damage to life or limb'. Julian Assange has repeatedly made the same claim, though it has been pointed out that US security services would be unlikely to publicly identify cases in which their sources had been endangered, since to do so would itself involve further compromising their sources.[15]

Several celebrated legal cases have sought to balance freedom of expression and national security.[16] These do not offer a clear standard against which *WikiLeaks* may be judged, but there is a consensus that prior restraint cannot reasonably be justified on the basis that politicians or diplomats may be embarrassed: restrictions must protect the public from a grave danger or they are not justified. Whilst the Pentagon Papers case did not agree a test, the Supreme Court's Justice Stewart's dissenting opinion argued that restriction of speech would be justified if publication was sure to 'result in direct, immediate and irreparable damage to our Nation or its people'.[17]

In the Spycatcher case, the European Court of Human Rights rejected the notion that reports could be subject to restrictions in order to protect reputation: the judge argued that restrictions ceased to be justified after the book had become more widely available.

> The purpose of the injunctions had thus become confined to the promotion of the efficiency and reputation of the Security Service, notably by preserving confidence in that service on the part of third parties; making it clear that the unauthorized publication of memoirs by its former members would not be countenanced; and deterring others who might be tempted to follow in Mr Wright's footsteps. The court does not regard these objectives as sufficient to justify the interference complained of.[18]

The court therefore found that restricting the publication of the book was not 'necessary in a democratic society' and that there was a violation of Article 10.

According to the ECHR, restrictions must be 'necessary in a democratic society'. This, according to the Spycatcher judgement, refers to a 'pressing social need' which would be needed to justify restrictions on freedom of expression.[19] The US government alleges that such a pressing social need to prevent publication of at least one of the US cables indeed existed, but *WikiLeaks* and its media partners counter that the apparent lack of fallout from publication may cast doubt on this claim. This lack of apparent consequence is a key aspect of *WikiLeaks's* search for legitimacy. '*WikiLeaks* has a four-year publishing history. During that time we have released documents pertaining to over 100 countries. There is no report, including from the US Government, of any of our releases ever having caused harm to any individual.'[20]

Drawing on international law, a network of NGOs and lawyers developed the Johannesburg Principles[21] on national security and freedom of expression. According to these standards, 'any restriction on expression or information that a government seeks to justify on grounds of national security must have the genuine purpose and demonstrable effect of protecting a legitimate national security interest'. Specifically,

> a restriction sought to be justified on the grounds of national security is not legitimate unless its genuine purpose and demonstrable effect is to protect a country's existence or its territorial integrity against the

use of threat or force, or its capacity to respond to the use or threat of force, whether from an external source, such as a military threat, or an internal source, such as incitement to violent overthrow of the government.

The principles explicitly exclude from justified restrictions those that aim 'to protect a government from embarrassment or exposure of wrongdoing, or to conceal information about the functioning of its public institutions or to entrench a particular ideology or suppress industrial unrest'.[22] So there is a clear line between direct and physical security consequences of publication (which justify restriction) and mere embarrassment (which should not). These legal principles are rarely invoked in court, but they are reflected in daily newsroom practice and voluntary ethical regulation such as the D-A notice system in the UK.

Doing no harm? Responsibility, national security and the US cables

> *WikiLeaks* has developed a harm minimisation procedure to clean documents which might endanger innocent lives...*WikiLeaks* may delay publishing some news stories and their supporting documents until the publication will not cause danger to such people. However in all cases, *WikiLeaks* will only redact the details that are absolutely necessary to this end. Everything else will be published to support the news story exactly as it appeared in the original document.[23]

It is widely asserted that *WikiLeaks* simply 'dumps' large amounts of information into the public domain, and as such acts irresponsibly. Yochai Benkler has measured the extent to which the mainstream exaggerates the number of documents that were published during the US cables release. He found that whereas in fact the initial release was of only 272 documents, 'a substantial majority of newspapers stated as fact that *WikiLeaks* had "released," "published," or "posted on its site," "thousands" or "over 250,000" cables' (Benkler 2011: 19).

WikiLeaks publicly claims that the harm-minimization procedure is always followed:

> When information comes in, our journalists analyse the material, verify it and write a news piece about it describing its significance to society. We then publish both the news story and the original material in order to enable readers to analyse the story in the context of the original source material themselves.[24]

WikiLeaks is also clear that this procedure has developed over time:

> As the media organisation has grown and developed, *WikiLeaks* has been developing and improving a harm minimisation procedure. We do not censor our news, but from time to time we may remove or significantly delay the publication of some identifying details from original documents to protect life and limb of innocent people.[25]

According to Alan Rusbridger of the *Guardian*, 'The final piece of the journalistic heavy lifting was to introduce a redaction process so that nothing we published could imperil any vulnerable sources or compromise active special operations.' (Rusbridger 2011: 5). He claims that the *Guardian* led the redactions on behalf of the other media partners and *WikiLeaks*. 'Once redacted, the documents were shared among the (eventually) five newspapers and sent to *WikiLeaks*, who adopted all our redactions' (Rusbridger 2011: 5). But the road was not a smooth one. According to Assange and the journalists he was working with, the *WikiLeaks* organization was perpetually pressurizing media partners to be more bold and take more risks.

There were disagreements. The *Guardian* and the *New York Times* refused to publish 'Critical Foreign Dependencies (Critical Infrastructure and Key Resources Located Abroad)'.[26] This cable was released by *WikiLeaks* rather than partner organizations.[27]

Assange's own description of the process following the release of the US cables was that

> the cables...have been redacted by the journalists working on the stories, as these people must know the material well in order to write about it. The redactions are then reviewed by at least one other journalist or editor, and we review samples supplied by the other organizations to make sure the process is working.[28]

Whilst the details of the redaction process and the outcome of the process (Did people come to harm as a result of the leaks?) will not be known for some time, if ever, the broad outline of the process is not in dispute. Broadly, *WikiLeaks* can be seen to have outsourced ethical questions regarding publication to its media partners who perform a dual role: on the one hand they select stories on the basis of their public impact and level of public interest, and on the other they redact to minimize potential harm. But harm for whom? Who has moral standing (O'Neil 2000) in this complex of ethical practices and procedures?

Wikileaks' outsourcing of ethics to national mainstream media short-circuits a set of more complex ethical challenges that arise in relation to transnational circulation of media and *Wikileaks* has failed to reflect enough on its own ethical status. The following section unpacks some of the notions of national interest, national security, and the public interest from a cosmopolitan perspective, and outlines some key ethical challenges raised by *Wikileaks*.

Ethics outside the law: A case study

When *WikiLeaks*'s release of diplomatic communications was first reported in Pakistan's *Dawn* newspaper on 1 December 2010, details were removed from one of the cables. The newspaper report, quoting the cable, ran as follows:

> The embassy cables also revealed that small teams of US special forces soldiers were allegedly secretly embedded with Pakistan's military forces in the tribal regions, helping to hunt down Taliban and al Qaeda fighters and co-ordinate drone strikes in the area. 'The Pakistani Army has for just the second time approved deployment of US special operation elements to support Pakistani military operations. The first deployment, with SOC(FWD)-PAK elements embedded with the Frontier Corps in XXXXXXXXXXXX (location blocked), occurred in September (reftel). Previously, the Pakistani military leadership adamantly opposed letting us embed our special operations personnel with their military forces', one of the cables' summary stated.[29]

Given the date, we can surmise that the redaction was the product of the *New York Times/Guardian* redaction process (*Dawn* links to an October 2009 cable published on the Guardian website).[30] Notably, the location of the Frontier Corps that were coordinating the drone attacks has been redacted. From the point of view of the US army, and *the New York Times*, it is clear that such information may be security sensitive, and may even endanger military personnel.

It would be possible to argue that the Pakistani national interest narrowly defined by the Pakistan government at the time – in terms of common cause with the US against the Taliban – was served by redacting the cables. But there was such a controversy in Pakistan about the nature of collusion with the US that Pakistani journalists would have had a strong public interest defence had they published the material, and it is likely that many of them would have been keen to do so.

From the point of view of Pakistani citizens, given the high incidence of civilian deaths caused by drone attacks, the location of special forces and the use of drones was information of paramount public importance. If there is Pakistani army support for the deployment of drone attacks in a given region, Pakistani civilians would have a strong argument that they should know in which regions support was given. The fact that such a deployment was condoned by Pakistan – particularly when the Pakistani government publicly condemned all drone attacks – gives even more weight to the argument to publish this detail from a Pakistani perspective. If *WikiLeaks* adopted a global perspective, or even an international view, the appropriate balance between freedom of expression and national security would shift. Whilst the question of the safety of US special forces will be of paramount importance to the US, and Rusbridger (2011: 5) does not want to 'imperil any vulnerable sources or compromise active special operations', the utilitarian calculus from a Pakistani perspective is more likely to include the safety of Pakistani civilians.

There are other cables that reveal some of the standards applied by editors. One that outlines a request for military assistance from the Pakistani army to the US army reveals information that may be very useful to their enemies, such as how many helicopters are operational, how many are required and the specific number of bridges that are requested.[31] This information could reveal plans of military deployments against militants on the Afghan border. These details were not redacted by the *New York Times/Guardian* redaction process perhaps due the nationally bounded approach to national security and redaction.

As noted above, however, in spring 2011, *WikiLeaks* began to work closely with media partners in a wider range of countries. Media partners in countries including Pakistan were given the opportunity to sort and sift the cables, to select stories relating to cables from their region. The process that the Pakistani daily newspaper *Dawn* went through in assembling the stories based on the cables is described by the paper's journalist Hasan Zaidi.[32] This short account does not indicate that *Dawn* journalists were involved in redacting the cables: indeed, the only redacted cables that were referred to by *Dawn/WikiLeaks* at this point had previously been published (and redacted) by *WikiLeaks*/the *Guardian*.

What seems to be apparent is that redaction rights – and with them, decisions about who has moral standing – were given to US and UK interests, but, in the case of the second phase of cable releases in spring 2011, material selected by *WikiLeaks* and its partners was not redacted by partners in other countries, such as Pakistan. The cables that were published appear to have been published in full. It could, of course, be argued that because of the time elapsed between the original leak (early 2010) and the security services knowing of the leak (mid-2010), and the release by global media partners early in 2011, *WikiLeaks* and partners may simply have assumed that any operational impact would be minimal.

There are thus cases in which the balancing of the public right to know with national security raises fundamental questions for global media. Who are the public? Whose (national) security is under consideration? As Clay Shirky put it,

> Appealing to national traditions of fair play in the conduct of news reporting misunderstands what *WikiLeaks* is about: the release of information without regard for national interest. In media history up to now, the press is free to report on what the powerful wish to keep secret because the laws of a given nation protect it. But *WikiLeaks* is able to report on what the powerful wish to keep secret because the logic of the Internet permits it.
>
> (Shirky 2010)

Those who have sought to generalize a set of universal ethical principles for journalism or the media have tended to focus their efforts on the issue of cultural, linguistic and political diversity, and whether any rules could be sufficiently general to accommodate this difference.[33] Kai Hafez argues that despite cultural particularities – for example, the notion in the Islamic world that 'the idea of responsibility for the community ... in public speech is unique to the Muslim world' – a comparison of codes shows that 'truth, accuracy and objectivity are almost consensual cornerstones of journalism ethics'. (Hafez 2002: 228). Strentz simplifies universal ethical principles into four: use restraint; know thyself; respect others; and be accountable (Strentz 2001). Other commentators extend the list. For Herrscher (2002: 281–282) the ethical principles should be truth; completeness; avoiding conflict of interest; freedom and independence; honesty; respect for privacy and reputation; ethnic and religious tolerance; and importance.

This deontological approach to developing universal codes and ethical approaches indicates that an alternative *WikiLeaks* model could find legitimacy in terms of some global ethical principles, but these principles are so abstract that they would not provide much help with the publication decisions regarding the US cables. Such an approach would not help with the issue of diversity of interest – for example, the fact that national security or national interest differ across boundaries. As we saw with the redaction of Pakistan stories, key justifications for publication based on national security and public interest are often nationally bounded. My analysis thus makes clear that Wikileaks raises more profound ethical challenges than have generally been acknowledged, particularly by Wikileaks itself. The attempt to develop ethical legitimacy for such a site would need to articulate what a genuinely global – or cosmopolitan – public interest would constitute, and its implications for publication ethics.

Conclusion: A global ethical code for WikiLeaks?

David Held defines cosmopolitanism in the following terms: 'In the first instance, cosmopolitanism refers to those basic values which set down standards or boundaries which no agent … should be able to violate.'

> Focused on the claims of each person as an individual, these values encapsulate the idea that human beings are in a fundamental sense equal and that they deserve equal political treatment: that is treatment based on the equal care and consideration of their agency, irrespective of the community in which they were born or brought up.
>
> (Held 2010: 95)

When *WikiLeaks* released all of the remaining unpublished cables in August 2011, this could be described as a cosmopolitan act, or as an irresponsible one. Cosmopolitans would give equal weight to lives in Washington and Waziristan, Birmingham and Beijing. Should *WikiLeaks* have sought somehow to consult both sides of the relationship before publishing? Clearly to do so would be absurd and impractical. After all, the cables originated with the US government, and the US military and the US state department would be the best guide to whether publication itself was likely to lead to harm to US forces or US sources. But the process of redaction, for the reasons explored, resulted in judgements that were made in a nationally bounded and US-centric notion of national security and the public interest.

Despite *WikiLeaks*'s global scope and reach, it seems that its approach in relation to the US cables was asymmetrical: media partners in the

US and Europe, with the *New York Times* and the *Guardian* at the fore-front, were allowed first choice of the initial selection of stories from the cables, and they conducted the redactions within their national and geopolitical context. In terms of the selection they made, it is likely that their concerns were for their national subscriber and purchasing public; and in terms of the calls that were made on the security impli-cations of stories, their focus was on the implications for the national interest of the nations in which they are based, as reflected in their assessments of legal liability. When *WikiLeaks* embarked on a second phase of publications with media partners from a wider group of coun-tries, they were not subject to this national media logic, but by that time the news value of the cables was arguably diminished because of the pas-sage of time, and the security implications were less likely to be direct. There were fewer redactions and these were not made on the basis of protecting the US military.

WikiLeaks's approach was pragmatic. First, it had neither the scale nor the skills to carry out responsible journalism in relation to the origi-nal cables, and may also have sought to spread legal risk with powerful media groups that governments may be reluctant to sue. Second, as long ago as 2007, it had been disappointed by the lack of impact of simply releasing documents. Assange and colleagues found that only by work-ing directly with major outlets, such as national newspapers, could they guarantee that releasing files would generate an impact.

The relationship between *WikiLeaks* and its partner national newspa-pers during 2010 was tense. Unlike its media partners, *WikiLeaks* exists outside the 'social compact' of responsible, public interest journalism. Just as it seeks to use internet architecture to escape the reach of a legal framework in which national security provides established justi-fication of restriction of free speech, the site also struggles with the informal social compact that establishes the ethical practice of responsi-ble journalism. The site, in developing its harm-reduction strategy, has acknowledged a need to maintain its legitimacy, but in the case of the US cables it has done so in a way that raises questions about how to bal-ance nationally bounded and cosmopolitan versions of harm reduction and the public interest.

This chapter has focused on the issue that has led to the most intense scrutiny of *WikiLeaks*: national security. As I discussed in rela-tion to releases of cables relating to Pakistan, the process of publication exhibited an unresolved tension between national and cosmopolitan approaches to the harm principle. The same set of general rules would not generate the same kinds of redaction in the US and in Pakistan.

WikiLeaks has not yet articulated ethical practices for global publication. A selection and redaction process that involved not national but global interests, and gave a Waziristani life the same weight as an American life, would be radical, and would be the appropriate longer-term strategy for *WikiLeaks* to gain support globally. Nationally rooted, nationally regulated media are unlikely to take this step.

WikiLeaks, and other sites that exploit an extra-jurisdictional approach to publication and source anonymity need to clarify their own position as ethical actors, and we need a wider, better informed debate on the transnational challenges for an ethical journalism in which such actors operate. This chapter has hopefully contributed to that new and urgent debate.

Notes

1. 'As part of the review process, we requested the US State Department, which has claimed to have conducted an extensive review of the material of its own over the last few months, to provide the titles of the cables which we should look at with extra care. The State Department refused to provide that information, or negotiate any other arrangement, suggesting that its desire to cover up at all costs eclipses its bona fide desire to minimise potential harm. The State Department gave its side of the correspondence to the *New York Times* and elsewhere at the same time.' *WikiLeaks* FAQ, http://Wikileaks. open-web.fr/static/html/faq.html (last accessed May 2011).
2. The case of the Pentagon Papers is strikingly similar to the *WikiLeaks* case. In 1971 the *New York Times* began to publish historical documents relating to the Vietnam War dating back to 1967. The ensuing prosecution examined whether and under what conditions publishers of leaked secrets should enjoy the protection of freedom of expression guarantees. New York Times Co. v. United States (403 US 713).
3. Such an approach has the additional benefit of avoiding the necessity of taking a position that sides either with the virtue-based neo-Aristotelian camp (Couldry 2010, 2012; Chouliaraki 2008) or with deontological, duties-based approaches.
4. http://www.narconews.com/Issue67/article4417.html.
5. PBS Frontline 30 May 2011.
6. Assange, Julian. Remarks at the Hay Literary Festival, 5 June 2011.
7. See also Castendyck, O, Dommering, E and Scheuer, A (2008), Tambini (2009b) and Harrison and Woods (2007).
8. The theoretical point here is that rights – including those deriving from free expression – are conditional on a notion of responsible behaviour. I develop this point in D. Tambini (forthcoming) 'Conflicts of Interest and Journalism Ethics. A Case Study of Hong Kong', *Journal of Mass Media Ethics*.
9. In the recent history of the development of media laws there are numerous examples of the exercise of press and media power (to frame a policy

or politician, to influence public opinion in order to protect media freedom). Some of these are technical, such as the mobilization of press interests against the application of the Market Abuse Directive (EC Directive 2003/6) in 2002; and some of them are rather populist, such as press attacks on judges (such as Justice Eady in the UK by the *Daily Mail* in 2010) or politicians (such as culture minister, David Mellor, in the 1990s) when they argue for the introduction of new regulations to apply to news and journalism. Such regulatory efforts are often thwarted by media power.

10. See Chouliaraki (2008), Silverstone (2006); and Couldry (2010; 2012) for variants of this approach.
11. *Reynolds v. Times Newspapers Ltd* (2001) (2 A.C. 127). In a defamation case brought by the Irish prime minister, Albert Reynolds, against a UK newspaper, the reporter was protected from liability when it could be demonstrated that she acted responsibly and professionally, even though the report was inaccurate.
12. This test was later criticized for creating 'hurdles' over which journalists had to leap in order to be able to access a public interest defence. Geoffrey Robertson and Andrew Nicol, (2008) *Media Law*, 5th edn. London: Penguin. 3–064–3–065.
13. *Daily Telegraph*, 29 November 2011.
14. Associated Press, 7 December 2010.
15. This point was made repeatedly to Assange by Phillipe Sands QC when he interviewed Assange at the Hay on Wye Literary Festival on 5 June 2011.
16. See for a discussion, for example, of the UK T. Mendel et al. (2000) 'Secrets, Spies and Whistleblowers: Freedom of Expression and National Security in the United Kingdom, Article 19. Notable cases include Spycatcher in the UK and the Pentagon Papers case in the US.
17. Cited by Malcolm Turnbull in a speech to Sydney Law School, 31 March 2011, http://www.malcolmturnbull.com.au/blogs/malcolms-blog/reflections-on-Wikileaks-spycatcher-and-freedom-of-the-press-speech-given-to-sydney-university-law-school/
18. *Sunday Times v the United Kingdom* no. 2. (App no. 13166/87) 26 November 1991. 55. http://cmiskp.echr.coe.int/tkp197/view.asp?action=html&documentId=695585&portal=hbkm&source=externalbydocnumber&table=F69A27FD8FB86142BF01C1166DEA398649.
19. *Sunday Times v the United Kingdom* no. 2. (App no. 13166/87) 26 November 1991. 59c.
20. Wikileaks, US Cables FAQ http://Wikileaks.open-web.fr/static/html/faq.html, last accessed May 2011.
21. The Johannesburg Principles on National Security, Freedom of Expression and Access to Information, the Article 19 International Standards Series, London 1996.
22. The Johannesburg Principles on National Security, Freedom of Expression and Access to Information, the Article 19 International Standards Series, London 1996. Art. 2.a- 2.b, http://www.article19.org/pdfs/standards/joburgprinciples.pdf.
23. *WikiLeaks*: submissions http://*WikiLeaks*.ch/Submissions.html.
24. *WikiLeaks*, http://213.251.145.96/About.html, last accessed 6 April 2011.
25. *WikiLeaks*, http://213.251.145.96/About.html, last accessed 6 April 2011.

26. The 2009 cable listed foreign assets viewed as 'crucial' by the US. Publication was immediately criticized by Sir Malcolm Rifkind (Chair of the Intelligence and Security Committee), who said that the publication was 'bordering on criminal' (MSNBC 6 December 2010), http://www.msnbc.msn.com/id/40526224/.
27. Benkler 2011: 14.
28. Julian Assange in a web chat with readers of the *Guardian* on 3 December 2010, http://www.guardian.co.uk/world/blog/2010/dec/03/julian-assange-Wikileaks.
29. Dawn.com, 1 December 2010, http://www.dawn.com/2010/12/01/pakistani-leadership-'okayed'-drone-attacks-Wikileaks.html, last accessed May 2011.
30. http://www.guardian.co.uk/world/us-embassy-cables-documents/229065.
31. http://www.dawn.com/2011/05/21/details-of-us-military-support-for-pakistan.html.
32. http://www.dawn.com/2011/05/20/putting-together-the-pakistan-papers.html.
33. There have been a great number of attempts to generate universal ethical principles led by journalist associations and UNESCO. See the contributions to the *Journal of Mass Media Ethics* (2002) 17(4). Some contributions highlight the 'do no harm' principle (S. Rao and S. Lee 2005) but most attempts to derive a set of common principles do so by taking a sample of existing codes and examining the overlaps and differences. See also Hafez (2002), Ward (2010).

Bibliography

Alexy, R. (2002) *A Theory of Constitutional Rights*. Oxford: Oxford University Press.

Barendt, E. (2005) *Freedom of Speech*, 2nd edn. Oxford: Oxford University Press.

Beckett, C. and Ball, J. (2012) *WikiLeaks. News in the Networked Era*. Cambridge: Polity Press.

Benkler, Y. (2011) 'A Free Irresponsible Press, Wikileaks and the Battle for the Soul of the Networked Fourth Estate', *Harvard Civil Rights-Civil Liberties Law Review*: 19. Available at: http://www.benkler.org/Benkler_Wikileaks_current.pdf.

Castendyck, O., Dommering, E. and Scheuer, A. (2008) *European Media Law*. Netherland: Kluwer Law International.

Chouliaraki, Lilie (2008) The media as moral education: mediation and action. *Media, culture & society*, 30 (6). pp. 831–852.

Clayton, R. and Tomlinson, H. (2009) *The Law of Human Rights*, 2nd edn. Oxford: Oxford University Press.

Couldry, N. (2010) 'Media Ethics, Media Justice', in Ward, S. and Wasserman, H. (eds) *Media Ethics Beyond Borders. A Global Perspective*. New York: Routledge.

Couldry, N. (2012) Media, Society, World. Social Theory and Digital Media Practice. Polity, Cambridge. Chapter 8.

Deibert, R., Palfrey, J., Rohozinski, R. and Zittrain, J. (2010) *Access Controlled. The Shaping of Power, Rights and Rule in Cyberspace*. Cambridge, MA: MIT Press.

Domscheit-Berg, D. (2011) *Inside Wikileaks. My Time with Julian Assange at the World's Most Dangerous Website*. London: Jonathan Cape.

Eder, K. (2006) 'The Public Sphere', *Theory, Culture and Society* 23(2–3): 607–616.

Eder, K. (2007) 'The Construction of a Transnational Public: Prerequisites for Democratic Governance in a Transnationalising Society', in Sala, V. and Ruzza, C. (eds) *Governance and Civil Society in the European Union, Exploring Policy Issues*, vol 2, 7–30. Manchester: Manchester University Press.

Goldsmith, J. and Wu, T. (2006) *Who Controls the Internet. Illusions of a Borderless World*. Oxford: Oxford University Press.

Habermas, J. (1996). *Between Facts and Norms: Contributions to a Discourse Theory of Law and Democracy*, W. Rehg (trans.). Cambridge, MA: MIT Press.

Hafez, K. (2002) 'Journalism Ethics Revisited: A Comparison of Ethics Codes in Europe, North Africa, the Middle East and Muslim Asia'. *Political Communication* (19): 225–250.

Harrison, J, and Woods, L. (2007) *European Broadcasting Law and Policy. Cambridge Studies in European Law and Policy*. Cambridge: Cambridge University Press.

Held, D. (2010) *Cosmopolitanism. Ideals and Realities*. Cambridge: Polity Press.

Herrscher, R. (2002) 'A Universal Code of Journalism Ethics: Problems, Limitations, and Proposals', *Journal of Mass Media Ethics* 17(4): 277–289.

Keller, B. (2011) *Open Secrets. Wikileaks, War and American Diplomacy*. New York: The New York Times.

Leigh, D. and Harding, L. (2011) *Wikileaks: Inside Julian Assange's War on Secrecy*. London: Guardian Books.

O'Neill, O. (2000) *Bounds of Justice*. Cambridge: Cambridge University Press.

Pickard, V. (2010) 'Reopening the Postwar Settlement for U.S. Media: The Origins and Implications of the Social Contract Between Media, the State and the Polity', *Communication, Culture & Critique* 3(2): 170–189.

Pickard, V. (2011) 'The Battle over the FCC Blue Book: Determining the Role of Broadcast Media in a Democratic Society', *Media, Culture and Society* 33(2): 1945–1948.

Price, M.E. (1994) 'The Market for Loyalties: Electronic Media and the Global Competition for Allegiances', *Yale Law Journal* 104: 667–705.

Rao, S. and Lee, S. (2005) 'Globalizing Media Ethics? An Assessment of Universal Ethics Among International Political Journalists', *Journal of Mass Media Ethics* 20(2&3): 99–120.

Roberts, A. (2011) 'Wikileaks: The Illusion of Transparency', Suffolk University Law School Working Paper. April 2, Suffolk University Law School Research Paper No. 11–19 http://papers.ssrn.com/sol3/papers.cfm?abstract_id=1801343.

Rosen, J. (2012) 'Wikileaks, the World's First Stateless News Organisation', blog post at http://pressthink.org/ 2010/07/the-afghanistan-war-logs-released-by-Wikileaks-the-worlds-first-stateless-news-organization/.

Rusbridger, Alan (2011) 'Introduction', in Leigh, D. and Harding, L. (eds) *Wikileaks: Inside Julian Assange's War on Secrecy*. London: Guardian Books.

Shirky, C. (2010) 'Half Formed Thought on Wikileaks', blog post at http://www.shirky.com/weblog/2010/12/half-formed-thought-on-Wikileaks-global-action/.

Siebert, F., Peterson, T., and Schramm, W. (1956) *Four Theories of the Press: The Authoritarian, Libertarian, Social Responsibility, and Soviet Communist Concepts of What the Press Should Be and Do*. Urbana: University of Illinois.

Silverstone, R. (2006) The Media and Morality: On the Rise of the Mediapolis. Polity.

Strentz, H. (2001) 'Universal Ethical Standards?', *Journal of Mass Media Ethic*, 17(4): 263–276.

Tambini, D. (2009a) 'Transformation of the Public Sphere: Law, Policy and the Boundaries of Publicness', in Harrison, J. and Wessels, B. (eds) *Mediating Europe: New Media, Mass Communications, and the European Public Sphere*. Oxford: Berghahn Books: 47–72.

Tambini, D. (2009b) 'Book review: Oliver Castendyk et al., European Media Law Jackie Harrison and Lorna Woods, European Broadcasting Law and Policy', *Journal of Media Law* 1 (1): 129–133.

Tambini, D. (2012) 'Conflicts of Interest and Journalism Ethics. A Case Study of Hong Kong', *Journal of Mass Media Ethics*.

Ward, S. J. A. (2005) 'Philosophical Foundations for Global Journalism Ethics', *Journal of Mass Media Ethics* 20(1): 3–21.

Ward, S. J. A. (2010) 'A Theory of Patriotism for Global Journalism', in Ward, S. J.A. and Wasserman, H. (eds), *Media Ethics Beyond Borders. A Global Perspective*. New York: Routledge.

Ward, S. J.A. and Wasserman, H., (eds) (2010) *Media Ethics Beyond Borders. A Global Perspective*. New York: Routledge.

15
Journalism, Ethics and the Impact of Competition

Angela Phillips

Journalists, like doctors, straddle ethical extremes. Doctors pledge themselves to saving lives but may also use the same skills to perform ethically dubious plastic surgery on the breasts of anxious teenagers – for profit. Similarly, journalists who learn the skills of investigation, analysis and communication may use them to hold power to account, but also to expose the lives of innocent people and hold them up to public ridicule. In each case the practices that are deployed may be positively harmful when used without ethical boundaries and, in each case, individual practitioners may find themselves tempted by commercial considerations, to push the boundaries of ethical practice, either for their own immediate gain or because market conditions put them under extreme pressure to act unethically. The decision to act ethically is, of course, an individual decision – something that Foucault describes as a 'practice of freedom'. However, as he also explains, the 'practice of freedom' is constrained by power relationships:

> one sometimes encounters what may be called situations or states of domination in which the power relations, instead of being mobile, allowing the various participants to adopt strategies modifying them, remain blocked, frozen... In such a state it is certain that practices of freedom do not exist or exist only unilaterally or are extremely constrained and limited.
>
> (Foucault 1984, cited in Rabinow 1994: 285)

This chapter sets out to examine, through interviews with journalists,[1] the way in which power relationships in the highly competitive environment of the UK press undermine individual ethical practices. It goes on to suggest ways in which ethical practices can be protected and encouraged.

Values ethics and journalism

Peter Preston, former editor of the *Guardian* (arguably one of the UK newspapers most prone to taking ethics rather than audience share as its motive for following a story), wrote in response to calls for curbs on the excesses of UK journalism: 'once you put judgment – individual judgment according to circumstances – at the heart of your job, then rigid codes of ethics don't easily apply...sometimes the story, the necessary story, goes beyond neat boundaries and 20 questions. The only way isn't ethics' (Preston 2011).

It may be true that rule-bound Kantian ethics provide little room for the kind of activities that journalists have to indulge in if they are to worm out information that others want to keep hidden. Operating without the legal back-up provided for the police and lawyers, journalists may resort to half-truths or subterfuge in order to find what they are seeking. Where subterfuge is regarded to be 'in the public interest', it may well be considered legitimate, as David Leigh explained about an investigation into the business connections of Mark Thatcher (son of the then prime minister, Margaret Thatcher):

> One story which I did publish at a time when I was running investigations for the Observer, partially involved subterfuge and a balancing of the public interest against a person's right to keep private business arrangements private...I considered this subterfuge justifiable in the public interest. There was no other way I could have obtained the crucial information.
>
> (Leigh 2011)

However, there are other approaches to ethical behaviour. A more flexible utilitarian approach, favouring the greatest happiness of the greatest number, might suit journalism rather well but usually for all the wrong reasons. Indeed, it is not hard to imagine some journalists arguing that the sacrifice of the human happiness of one philandering footballer is worthwhile if, by publishing the salacious details, the lives of several million other people are brightened. Indeed, Rupert Murdoch comes quite close to that in his defence of his newspapers as a 'public service'. He explains: 'Anybody who provides a service which the public wants, at a price it can afford, is providing a public service' (Murdoch 1989). When his newspapers served up the stories of the famous (and not so famous) by hacking their phones, the argument was made that these stories were interesting to the public and therefore somehow legitimate.

As one of the former journalists of the *News of the World*[2] said at the Leveson Inquiry into the UK Press,[3] 'Circulation defines the public interest. You have to appeal to what the reader wants – this is what the people of Britain want. I was simply serving their need' (Paul McMullan 2011).

Even looked at in a less cynical light, utilitarian ethics has little to offer ethical journalism because of its tendency to ride rough-shod over the needs and rights of minorities. The publication of the Muhammad cartoons in Danish newspaper *Jylands Posten* in 2005 provides a useful opportunity to explore a Benthamite (Sanders 2003: 19) approach to ethics. Clearly, those who decided to publish cartoons ridiculing the Prophet felt that they were upholding the rights of 'ordinary Danes' to freedom of expression, and that the hurt feelings of the minority community should not be considered (Hervik et al. 2008: 31).

The response to the publication could have allowed a retrospective re-examination of this 'ethical' action. Would the editors have made a different decision had they known that the cartoons would trigger riots in the Middle East and a boycott of Danish goods? But one cannot make ethical decisions retrospectively, and they didn't. Indeed, journalists almost universally supported the publication of the cartoons as a blow for press freedom (Phillips 2008: 99). Where doubts were expressed, the editors tended to reach for Mill (Phillips 2007) and there was much debate as to whether the publication was tantamount to shouting 'fire!' in a crowded theatre (Mill 1961 (1859)).[4] Thus it was suggested that the publication had been incautious rather than unethical.

While rule-bound ethics may tie the hands of serious journalists in their attempts to uncover wrong, utilitarian ethics creates a framework that is far too easy for populists to exploit at the expense of minorities. Something different is required if an ethical framework is to cover both ends of the journalistic spectrum. Onora O'Neill, responding to the debate about *Jylands Posten* in the *Guardian*, pointed out the sheer inequity of freedom that does not take power into account. She wrote:

> Once we take account of the power of the media, we are not likely to think that they should enjoy unconditional freedom of expression. We do not think that corporations should have unrestricted rights to invent their balance sheets, or governments to damage or destroy the reputations of individuals or institutions, or to deceive their electorates. Yet contemporary liberal readings of the right to free speech often assume that we can safely accord the same freedom of expression to the powerless and the powerful.
>
> (O'Neill 2006)

O'Neill (see Chapter 2 of this volume) sees the way forward in greater regulation to prevent newspapers from using their power irresponsibly. Regulation does, however, create problems for a free press. Most editors fear that giving the state the power to decide which publications have the right to speak would rob society of a press that is free to 'speak truth to power'. This is not the facile, self-protective argument that it sometimes appears to be. Regulation can be used by the state in order to prevent publication of information uncomfortable for those in power as the very existence of the writer's organization, PEN,[5] attests. Journalists do need legal protections, even in democracies, and laws that protect citizens from harm should not, at the same time, expose journalists to unnecessary pressure.

However, the demand for freedom from statutory control should be balanced by a responsibility for ethical behaviour. The best riposte to the regulatory impulse would be to demonstrate that editors take their ethical duties seriously in an Aristotelian sense of doing what is good in the circumstances and weighing up each judgement at the time. A values-driven approach to ethical decision-making doesn't require rules, nor a simple test of utility, but asks that each action should be judged on the basis of our own lives: 'How should each of us conduct our life so that it is a life any of us should live' (Couldry 2010: 65). It is this ethical sense that is absolutely necessary if editors are to be allowed the freedom to wield media power without restriction.

This is why Peter Preston (2011) is so profoundly wrong when he argues that ethics is not helpful in guiding editorial judgement. Indeed, entirely the opposite is true: without ethical judgement, journalism is little more than a particularly pernicious form of entertainment in which real lives are served up to take the place of characters in a soap opera of the damned.

Hospitality ethics

In a global media environment, where conflicting and many stranded discourses criss-cross both space and sensibilities, ethical decision-making is complex. This is why Roger Silverstone believed that journalists have a very special responsibility. He writes: 'This is not to suggest that journalists should be better than the rest of us as human beings (though why should they not be?), only that they should recognize that what they do...has consequences for the rest of us as human beings' (2007: 184).

Aristotle argued that ethical behaviour and the attainment of a 'good life' is based on living by a number of 'virtues', and, for Silverstone, 'hospitality' is the key 'virtue' of the mediapolis (which is how he defined the state of living in a globalized world). Silverstone took his understanding of 'hospitality' from Derrida. He said: 'Hospitality, an obligation rather than a right, is a primary ethic in a globalised world' (2007: 136–162).

Had the editors of *Jyllands Posten* considered the morality of their position as Silverstone suggested they should have done, they might have considered whether an act of deliberate provocation, via the pages of a mass-market popular newspaper, was the best way to create genuine dialogue about the position of a religious minority in their midst. Had the editor of *Jyllands Posten* asked whether it was 'hospitable' to use the power of a mass-market newspaper to publicly ridicule a minority group, he might have seen the action not as upholding the rights of Danish freedoms but more as a question of bullying Muslims. However, the editor did not view matters from this perspective.

The *Jyllands Posten* case is instructive because the story was sanctioned by editors deliberately to stir up a debate (Hervik et al. 2008). The newspaper involved was a right-of-centre popular daily with a large readership. In this particular instance the editors involved (the arts section editor and the newspaper editor) took the step of commissioning cartoons in the knowledge that they would be provocative because, as they put it, 'we are approaching a slippery slope where no one can tell where self-censorship will end' (Hervik 2008). They may have dressed their decision up as a matter of public interest but the particular public they were concerned with excluded the voice of the Muslim minority and allowed them no balancing right to their own freedom of expression.

Whatever one's view of the ethics in this particular case, there was at least plenty of opportunity for Danish people to hear other views. The liberal, left-leaning newspaper, *Politiken* (with a slightly smaller circulation), defended the right of *Jyllands Posten* to publish the cartoons but denounced the paper's 'demonisation' of Muslims (Hervik and Berg 2007: 25).

Truth-telling

If 'hospitality' can be seen as one of the virtues that should guide ethical journalism in a globalized world, the other 'virtues' must surely relate to what so many journalists themselves see as the key role of a journalist in a democracy: truth-telling. Truth is a slippery concept at the best of times. Even the most conscientious journalists, operating at speed and under pressure, may get things wrong. And it is never easy to know whether what one sees or hears represents what actually happened.

The coverage of the shooting of Brazilian electrician Jean Charles de Menezes by police, on a London tube train, in July 2005, is a stark example of just how difficult it can be for a journalist to arrive at the truth (Phillips 2006). In hindsight it is clear that the witnesses themselves had entirely misinterpreted events so, in interviewing them, journalists were certain to get it wrong. When police added statements that the ensuing enquiry found to be misleading, the job became even harder.

Should these journalists be held to account for failing to thoroughly check their accounts before writing? They had a duty to report the events as they unfolded, using the evidence at their disposal. Were they acting unethically if they failed to expose the 'truth' in the early reports? Here, Bernard Williams provides help. In *Truth and Truthfulness* (2002) he recommends the importance of the two 'virtues of truth': 'accuracy' and 'sincerity'. In other words, what matters is that one records accurately what one sincerely believes to be true. It is the sincerity of the action that inspires trust.

To continue with the de Menezes case, as further evidence emerged, some editors and journalists quickly revised their initial assumptions and assembled a far more accurate version of events. Others stuck by elements of the original story and searched for information that seemed to give credence to the police, even when it became clear that de Menezes was wholly innocent of anything to do with terrorism. Days later the *Daily Telegraph* was engaged in an attempt to unearth information about his immigration status: 'As the body of the Brazilian electrician shot dead by police as a suspected suicide bomber arrived in his home town yesterday, it emerged that his visa had expired more than two years ago' (Steele John, 26 July 2005, 'Puzzle over Shot Brazilian's Visa as his Body is Flown back to Grieving Family', *Telegraph*).

Getting it wrong in the first place was not surprising in the circumstances. The subsequent corrections should have demonstrated to audiences that journalism is a process, not a product, and that those involved in producing the story were sincere in their eagerness to correct earlier inaccuracies. Even the *Telegraph*, which held on to its assumption, against all the evidence, that the police could not have been wrong, did in the end give up on its mission to impugn the character of de Menezes.

Competition and ethics

It is likely that the editors of *Jyllands Posten* and the *Telegraph* would argue that they were acting according to their own consciences. They might have been but too often journalists in the UK report that they are required by their editors to look for the facts that support a particular narrative rather than the facts that might take us closer to the truth of an event. As one news editor on a mid-market UK newspaper explained,

> It isn't [that it's] untrue. It is giving prominence to a minor feature. There has to be some kernel of truth. It may be twisted or biased but there must be some truth. [The paper] works on the presumption that negative news sells – always go for the negative line even if it isn't typical. There is nothing untrue but it isn't a balanced representation. It's been twisted to conform to an idea. If you leave ethics out its good professional journalism and it sells papers.
>
> (interview with reporter,
mid-market popular daily, 2008)[6]

What he is saying, rather baldly, is that in a very competitive market the need to sell papers can override the need to provide the most sincerely accurate account. Given this sort of approach to truth-telling it is perhaps not surprising that trust in journalists is at a very low ebb. A 2010 Ipsos Mori poll for Euro Barometer[7] found that in the UK only 22 per cent of people trusted journalists compared with an average for Europe of 39 per cent.

For journalists this loss of confidence should matter, and not just for personal reasons. Building a trusted brand ought to be a real selling point in the pressured and crowded world of internet news production. There is little evidence, however, that ethical journalism is pushing out the crowd-pleasing excesses. As news organizations fight for market share in an increasingly tightening market (Phillips and Witschge 2011), the fight is on for ever-more lurid stories both online and off. At the Leveson Inquiry into the UK press (2011) it was not the serious newspapers, or the investigative journalists, that came under pressure but the popular press, which appeared to have lost any sense of moral boundaries in the pursuit, by any means possible, of people whose only crime appears to have been that the public had shown an interest in their lives.

News International initially tried to hide behind the idea that the issue of illegal phone hacking was the fault of one journalist who was singled out and jailed for his behaviour. However, persistent probing, mainly by Nick Davis at the *Guardian*, made it clear that the 'rot' went a great deal further and that more journalists at the *News of the World* were involved. As the Leveson Inquiry got under way in September 2011, it became clear that other newspapers were involved, if not in phone hacking then certainly in practices that anyone with even the most tentative hold on a sense of morality would find distasteful. More importantly it became clear that these excesses were not the behaviour of individual mavericks but were the result of policy handed down from editors who are themselves under pressure to increase audience numbers.

As Andrew Marr, former editor of the *Independent*, wrote in a less frantic time,

> The truth is that, except for editors who are highly influential in trusts or companies owning their titles, editors are hirelings. Proprietors regard their editors as talented and interesting servants...The newspaper editor gets status and the apparent respect of the social elite of modern London, but the proprietor gets what he wants.
>
> (Marr 2004: 235)

This brings us back to the point made by Foucault: for an individual to behave ethically, s/he must be free to make moral judgements. In the case of the popular press, that freedom is very much in question. In the UK at least, newspapers are run in a very hierarchical fashion. The editor can be hired and fired on the whim of the proprietor, and s/he has the power to hire and fire his/her staff. Those working in senior positions on the more elite newspapers may have the freedom to set their own agenda in terms of pursuing stories, but for more junior members of staff this is not the case. Many are employed on short-term contracts, or taken on for day shifts as a way of seeing if they will fit in. This reporter had been delighted to pick up shifts on one of the UK's most successful newspapers but he was soon asked to pursue a story that he found ethically repellent:

> I thought the story was appalling. I thought all along that it was a ludicrous exercise with no logic whatsoever and I felt very ashamed about it...I talked to a senior reporter and said that I wasn't very happy about it and he said to keep my head down and say nothing...He said that I would lose my job if I raised it with anybody more senior than him...I set about planning to leave. I'd just arrived so I knew I couldn't leave straight away...I kept my head down, I worked hard, I knew it would be at least a year before I could go. I was in a position the same as everybody who joins the [paper] from a local newspaper in that I was doing shifts on a daily basis. And it was up to them to decide whether to renew my job the next day.

So if I lost my job I wouldn't be able to pay the rent or anything like that which probably isn't an excuse but there was still that thought there.

(Phillips, Couldry and Freedman 2010: 56)

This particular quote could be dismissed as an anomaly, but the pressures described here come up time and again in interviews and research. Richard Peppiatt, who resigned as a journalist for the *Daily Star*, a UK popular newspaper, explained to the Leveson Inquiry how tabloid journalists are expected to operate:

Laid out before you is a canon of ideologically and commercially driven narratives that must be adhered to. The newspaper appoints itself moral arbiter, and it is your job to stamp their worldview on all the journalism you do. If a scientist announces their research has found ecstasy to be safer than alcohol, as a tabloid reporter I know my job is to portray this man as a quack, and his methods flawed. If a judge passes down a community sentence to a controversial offender, I know my job is to make them appear lily-livered and out-of-touch. Positive peer reviews are ignored; sentencing guidelines are buried. The ideological imperative comes before the journalistic one – drugs are always bad, British justice is always soft.

(Peppiatt 2011)

Peppiatt also told the inquiry that another reporter working casual shifts at the *Daily Star* objected to writing anti-Muslim propaganda, and this was how the editors responded: 'She was given every anti-Muslim story to write for about two weeks, so as a result of that she quit. I'm deeply ashamed to this day that I didn't walk out with her. That's the atmosphere: you toe the line or you get punished.'

As Bourdieu observes, 'precarity of employment is a loss of liberty, through which censorship...can be more easily expressed' (Bourdieu 2005: 43). It is a testament to their personal morality that all of these journalists have left their jobs. The former did so quietly and moved on to work at a more serious newspaper where he doesn't come under these sorts of pressure. Peppiatt left with a public letter of resignation and has since been subjected to vilification by his ex-colleagues who have used every method at their disposal to undermine his testimony (Peppiatt 2011).

Some may suggest that unethical practices have always been around and that technology has just provided a boost. However, in a very crowded market, with few jobs to go round, newspapers and news organizations in the UK and elsewhere don't have to look very far for new recruits to take the place of those who take the ethical way out and leave. And in the UK press there has been no legal protection for journalists who object to writing stories that they find morally offensive.

Regulation and the marketplace

As Onora O Neill (2006) points out, in this volume (Chapter 2) and elsewhere, our understanding of press freedom emerged at a time when most publications were small and were themselves struggling, usually on behalf of ordinary people, against the overweening power of the state. That is no longer the case. Operating in the global space, vast news organizations are now attracting ever-larger audiences as the logic of markets and internet search working together gradually squeezes the smaller operations out to the margins (Hindman 2009) and into severe financial stress (Phillips and Witschge 2011). To suggest that, in these circumstances, a news organization should enjoy the same protected rights to freedom of expression as an individual shows a lack of balance in thinking and law.

A completely free and unregulated press can only work if those people at the helm are themselves ethical and expect ethical behaviour from those working for them. For this to happen the 'field' in which they operate must exercise some form of peer pressure that helps to support ethical behaviour. In the US the professionalization of journalism via training, and (until recently) the protection of news organizations from extreme market pressures (Curran 2011), meant that the kind of attacks on individuals and minority communities that are seen in the UK are less common.

In some European countries, professionalization is protected via government subsidy. Research by a number of scholars has demonstrated that 'publicly-subsidized newspapers in Sweden and Norway tend to provide more original, critical, in-depth and multiperspectival coverage than their advertising-dependent counterparts' (Benson and Powers 2010). In both the Netherlands and Norway (Humphreys 1996), government subsidy is tied to editorial freedom. In Norway there is a recognition (by the courts) that journalists require editorial freedom from the pressures of the markets as well as the pressures of the state.

In Denmark, newspapers also receive subsidy, to ensure diversity and a reasonable balance of political views in the national press. *Jyllands Posten* (a right-wing populist newspaper) has the highest circulation but that of *Politiken* (a more serious liberal newspaper) is not significantly smaller and in the Muhammad cartoons affair it took a very different line. There was no 'race to the bottom' with newspapers vying in their crowd-pleasing rhetoric.

In the UK, no newspaper published the Muhammad cartoons. Given the rhetoric produced by all newspapers, in favour of publication, this reticence was widely believed to be commercial rather than principled (Phillips 2007: 65). Nevertheless there were few holds barred when it came to words. Richard Littlejohn, writing in the mass circulation *Daily Mail*, felt able to say: 'The Islamonazis are all as hell-bent on world domination as Hitler' (Littlejohn 7 February 2006).

Even these extreme views would be of less concern if all shades of opinion were represented at a similar volume, as they were in Denmark. In fact, only readers of the *Guardian* (with a readership of 350,000) would have been able to consider a multiplicity of opinions on the issue. The *Daily Mail* (with a readership of 2.3 million) printed 11 editorial articles on the issue. None opposed the publication of the cartoons in principle and not one was written by a Muslim (Phillips 2007).

Andrew Marr observed of the UK newspaper market (Marr 2004) that in the commercial news media the editors are the creatures of proprietors and shareholders, and their first duty is not to uphold democracy and democratic debate but to increase circulation or deliver profit. In any marketplace, where competition is fierce and pressure is applied to increase income, there is the risk that employees will cut corners. Where public safety is not at stake, the workings of the market may be allowed to operate until the smallest organizations, unable to match the cost-cutting of larger rivals, simply go under or are bought up by bigger, more successful predators. There are three key mechanisms by which societies protect the public from this process: via regulation, anti-trust legislation and subsidy. Where public health or safety is at risk, regulation is usually employed to prevent market pressures from eating into safe practices. Hospitals, schools and restaurants in most democracies are regulated and inspected to ensure that standards cannot drop below levels of safety. Schools and hospitals are subsidized for the public good.

Journalism is regulated in much the same way and often for the same reasons – on the one hand to protect it as a public good, and on the other to prevent standards in the marketplace from falling low enough to endanger the well-being of individuals and societies. For example, some form of libel laws are the norm worldwide, as are laws banning hate speech (Hallin and Mancini 2004; Kunelius 2007), and coverage of trials is often regulated to prevent news organizations from undermining basic principles of justice. However, the scope of law varies wildly, as does the vigour of its implementation. In many European countries and in a growing number of other areas of the world, such as Indonesia, voluntary press regulation, combining a level of ethical regulation with freedom from statutory control, is also in operation (Hallin and Mancini 2004). In the Scandinavian countries, press regulation is organized via press councils, but high levels of trade union membership for journalists, who are also well represented on the press councils, provide an additional level of peer pressure towards ethical behaviour as well as solidarity, for journalists who wish to resist unethical practices.

The UK is a particularly important case for the examination of press regulation because it has had a combination of tough laws against libel, week voluntary self-regulation and a hugely competitive national press.[8] During the 1980s, a period of circulation and advertising growth, the power of trade unions, which represented the interests of journalists in the workplace, was gradually whittled away. The self-regulating body, the Press Complaints Commission (PCC), established in 1991 (replacing a more representative body that included the unions), has been run entirely by editors and lay members. Given the extraordinary power of the editors, it was inevitable that the lay members would defer to them so that, in time, the PCC became more concerned with protecting the press than with regulating it. This left news journalism stuck between the power of civil law (which best protects those with the money to employ lawyers) and the market. For low circulation, serious newspapers, the calculation had to be: 'How far can you push the rich and powerful without being bankrupted by a libel case?' For high-circulation newspapers, legal action became a business expense, to be weighed in the balance sheets against the benefits of increased circulation.

Where commercial profit is the sole motivation for running stories then, to rewrite Peter Preston (2011), it is clearly not reasonable 'to put judgment – individual judgment according to circumstances – at the heart of your job'. In a hugely competitive marketplace, too often the only reasonable judgement is whether or not the information has entertainment value – not the possible damage to the person who is attacked or ridiculed. 'In such a state it is certain that practices of freedom do not exist or exist only unilaterally or are extremely constrained and limited' (Foucault 1984), and therefore the ability to act ethically is severely limited.

The freedom to act ethically requires a framework in which there is a balance created between freedom of speech for journalists and for ordinary people. These rights can be rebalanced without at the same time introducing draconian regulations that hobble legitimate enquiry. One way is to provide ordinary people with a legally binding right of reply (Media Reform 2012). For people who have been attacked in the media, the sense of injustice burns deeply. They speak of feeling 'violated'. For them, the right to speak back and correct misrepresentations may be the most powerful means of righting wrongs. It is hard to attack such a simple means of rebalancing the power invested in the right to freedom of expression. The editors should not flinch from changes that improve democratic accountability and offer to ordinary people just a small fraction of the power that news organizations assume for themselves. The right of reply is already provided in a number of countries, including Brazil. It has the great value of being simple and cheap to implement and it does not discriminate between rich and poor people or publications. The Council of Europe provides guidance on the drafting of such legislation and it is already embedded in law in a number of European countries.

Good journalism requires tough-minded people who will investigate in places where many would rather they didn't go. For this they need to know that they will not be prosecuted for work that is carried out in the public interest. A public interest defence needs to be embedded in law. By protecting serious journalism it should then be easier to make use of existing legal powers to ensure that frivolous invasions of privacy and mischievous inaccuracies can more easily be dealt with via tribunals or courts. However, the best safeguard against the misuse of investigative power is to ensure that journalists have the freedom to be truly ethical actors with the backing of statutory employment protection and the right to join a trade union. It should not be possible to discriminate against employees who decline to produce material that they consider to be unethical.

Finally, if society believes that news media has a dual role, and should also support and facilitate democratic debate, then it has to provide the same safeguards as it does to ensure that the education system functions for the good of society and not merely for profit. News-gathering and dissemination is not a profit-making business unless it is combined with entertainment and celebrity news, and heavily supported by advertising. In order to underpin the democratic functions of news and free it from over-reliance on gossip and scandal, in a fiercely competitive online environment, news organizations may also need a degree of subsidy. The fiercely competitive UK news market provides a warning for other democracies as to what can happen to ethical decision-making as competition increases online. If ethical news is necessary to the functioning of democracy, it needs to be protected.

Notes

1. Quotes used are taken from in-depth interviews with national newspaper journalists in 2001/2 and 2007/8. The interviews were part of two qualitative research projects looking at the work of ethnic-minority journalists in mainstream newsrooms (2001/2) and journalists' use of sources (2007/8).
2. The *News of the World*, Britain's largest circulation, Sunday newspaper, owned by News International, was closed in the summer of 2011 in the wake of a scandal about phone hacking.
3. The Leveson Inquiry into the culture, practice and ethics of the UK press was established on 13 July 2011, by the UK prime minister, to examine the role of the press and police in the phone-hacking scandal.
4. In *On Liberty* (1859) John Stuart Mill writes that all speech should be allowed unless it is capable of causing physical harm. The example most often quoted of a 'speech act' that cannot be allowed is that of crying 'fire!' in a crowded theatre and causing a stampede.
5. PEN is an international organization that campaigns for freedom of expression and defends writers whose freedoms have been infringed.
6. Interview carried out by the author for the Leverhulme Spaces of the news research 2008.
7. www.ipsos-mori.com/.../ben-page-a-crisis-in-trust-september-2010.
8. As we go to press the UK Parliament is debating changes to regulations, and laws on defamation, that may, if adopted, create a more balanced regulatory regime.

Bibliography

Benson and Powers (2010) *A Crisis of Imagination: International Models for Funding and Protecting Independent Journalism and Public Media* (A Survey of 14 Leading Democracies). Washington, DC: Free Press.

Bourdieu, Pierre (2005) 'The Political Field, the Social Science Field and the Journalistic Field', in Rodney Benson and Eric Neveu (eds) *Bourdieu and the Journalistic Field*. Cambridge: Polity.

Couldry, Nick (2010) 'Media Ethics: Towards a Framework for Media Producers and Media Consumers', in Stephan J.A. Ward (ed) *Media Ethics Beyond Borders: A Global Perspective*. Routledge.

Curran, James (2011) *Media and Democracy*. Abingdon, Oxon: Routledge.

Foucault, M. (1984) in Rabinow, P. ed (1994) *Ethics: The Essential Works of Michel Foucault*, Vol. 1. Harmondsworth: Penguin.

Hallin, Daniel C. and Paolo Mancini (2004) *Comparing Media Systems*. New York: Cambridge University Press.

Hervik, Peter (2008) 'The Original Spin and its Side Effects: Freedom Speech as Danish News Management', in Eide Elizabeth, Risto Kunelius and Angela

Phillips (eds) *Transnational Media Events: The Mohammed Cartoons and the Imagined Clash of Civilizations*, 59–80. Nordicom: Gothenburg.

Hervik, Peter and Clarissa Berg (2007) 'Denmark: A Political Struggle in Danish Journalism', in Kunelius Risto, Elisabeth Eide, Oliver Hahn and Roland Schröder (eds) *Reading the Mohammed Cartoons Controversy: An International Analysis of Press Discourses on Free Speech and Political Spin* Arbeitshefte Internationaler Journalismus. Dortmund: ProjektVerlag.

Hervik, Peter, Elizabeth Eide and Risto Kunelius (2008) 'A Long and Messy Event', in Eide Elizabeth, Risto Kunelius and Angela Phillips (eds) *Transnational Media Events: The Mohammed Cartoons and the Imagined Clash of Civilizations*. Stockholm: Nordicom.

Hindman, Matthew (2009) *The Myth of Digital Democracy*. Princeton University Press: Princeton.

Humphreys, Peter J. (1996) *Mass Media and Media Policy in Western Europe*. Manchester: Manchester University Press.

Kunelius Risto, Elisabeth Eide, Oliver Hahn and Roland Schröder (eds) (2007) *Reading the Mohammed Cartoons Controversy: An International Analysis of Press Discourses on Free Speech and Political Spin*, Arbeitshefte Internationaler Journalismus. Dortmund: ProjektVerlag.

Leigh, David (2011) *Evidence to the Leveson Inquiry*, www.levesoninquiry.org.uk/.../Witness-Statement-of-David-Leigh.pdf.

Littlejohn, Richard (2006) in Angela Phillips (2007) 'The UK: A very British Response', in Kunelius Risto, Elisabeth Eide, Oliver Hahn and Roland Schröder (eds) *Reading the Mohammed Cartoons Controversy, An International Analysis of Press Discourses on Free Speech and Political Spin* Arbeitshefte Internationaler Journalismus, 76. Dortmund: Projekt Verlag. Marr, Andrew (2004) *My Trade: A Short History of British Journalism*. London: MacMillan.

McMullan, Paul (2011) *Evidence to the Leveson Inquiry*, http://www.levesoninquiry.org.uk/wp-content/uploads/2011/11/Transcript-of-Afternoon-Hearing-29-November-2011.txt.

Media Reform (2012) *Ethics Briefing Paper*, http://www.mediareform.org.uk/policy-research/ethics/briefing-paper-on-ethics.

Mill, J. S. (1961) [o.p. 1859] 'On Liberty', in M. Cohen (ed) *The Philosophy of John Stuart Mill*, 185–319. New York: Modern Library.Murdoch, Rupert (1989) 'The James MacTaggart Lecture, Freedom in Broadcasting', in Franklin, Bob (ed.), *Television Policy, The MacTaggart Lectures*, 133. Edinburgh: Edinburgh University Press.

O'Neill Onora (2006) 'A Right to Offend', *Guardian*, 13 February 2006, Guardian Media Pages.

Peppiatt, Richard (2011) *Seminar 1: The Competitive Pressures on the Press and the Impact on Journalism*, 6 October 2011, www.levesoninquiry.org.uk/.../Presentation-by-Richard-Peppiatt.doc.

Phillips, Angela (2006) *Good Writing for Journalists: Narrative and Style*. London: Sage.

Phillips, Angela (2007) The UK: A Very British Response, in Eide Kuenlius and Shroeder Hann (eds), *Reading the Mohammed Cartoons Controversy, An International Analysis of Press Discourses on Free Speech and Political Spin*, Arbeitshefte Internationaler Journalismus, Dortmund: Projekt Verlag.

Phillips, Angela (2008) 'Who Spoke and Who was Heard in the Cartoons Debate?', in Eide Elizabeth, Risto Kunelius and Angela Phillips (eds) *Transnational Media Events: The Mohammed Cartoons and the Imagined Clash of Civilizations*. Stockholm: Nordicom.

Phillips, Angela, Nick Couldry and Des Freedman (2010) 'An Ethical Deficit? Accountability, Norms, and the Material Conditions of Contemporary Journalism', in Natalie Fenton (ed.) *New Media, Old News*. London: Sage.

Phillips, Angela and Tamara Witschge (2011) 'The Changing Business of News: Sustainability of News Journalism', in Peter Lee Wright, Angela Phillips and Tamara Witschge (eds) *Changing Journalism*. Routledge.

Preston, Peter (2011) 'Ethics Aren't the Whole Story', *Guardian*, http://www.guardian.co.uk/media/2011/sep/11/ethics-arent-the-whole-story-when-the-news-is-really-big.

Sanders, Karen (2003) *Ethics and Journalism*. London: Sage.

Silverstone, Roger (2007) *Media and Morality: On the Rise of the Mediapolis*. Cambridge: Polity.

Williams, Bernard (2002) *Truth and Truthfulness: An Essay in Genealogy*. Princeton: Princeton University Press.

World Values Survey (2006) 'Confidence in the Press', http://www.wvsevsdb.com/wvs/WVSAnalizeQuestion.jsp.

16
When Practice Is Undercut by Ethics

Barbie Zelizer

We live in an age where, as an issue, ethics seems to be up for grabs, debated as fervently by those outside the community as by those inside. But what is the community that needs to decide on ethical standards? Where do its boundaries lie? And how does one determine what matters, who falls in line, what emerges and by which agenda? The recent scandal surrounding the *News of the World* is a case in point, where a panoply of unethical practices by members of the news media, the police and the political establishment fermented intense public discourse regarding which ethical course to take in recovery from the damage wrought by the scandal. Though most held the news media – and, in a more narrow form, tabloid journalism – primarily responsible, the calls for heads off splashed across the wide spread of institutional settings and ranged across a long list of ethical violations. As this volume goes to print, it remains unclear whether the extensive navel-gazing fomented by the scandal will result in anything more than a high moment of rhetorical hand-wringing.[1]

I argue in this essay that the response to the *News of the World* scandal is but one example underscoring what is particularly problematic about establishing principles of ethical usefulness with regard to journalism. Specifically, I will argue that journalistic practice – as it takes shape in news gathering, news presentation and news distribution – defies the establishment of meaningful ethical standards. In querying their usefulness, this chapter also raises the possibility that ethical standards, as they are realized by ethics codes, cut short the potential for ethical practice on the ground.

The problem with ethics

Journalism ethics are regularly touted as offering important standards of action to which journalists can and should aspire in practice. Ranging across a panoply of subjunctive earmarks for action – truthfulness, accuracy, fairness, integrity, service to the public good, impartiality and accountability – ethical standards, following what Aristotle labelled 'phronesis,' or practical wisdom, provide what is thought to be an instrumental high ground of journalistic practice. But such standards are aired far more regularly and supported far more stridently by academics than by journalists themselves, who tend to eschew and deride their presence, exhibiting what one columnist recently called an 'instinctive journalistic aversion to official codes of conduct'.[2]

Ethics, by and large realized in journalism by ethics codes, have always presented a multidimensional quandary for journalists. As conceptual projects, ethics and journalism are built upon a different directional understanding of the relationship between thought and action. Drawing from philosophy, ethics tend to work from the top down to establish stable codes of action that negotiate universal and particular means and ends; earlier invocations tended towards universal standards and more recent ones towards situated particularity. By contrast, journalism tends to work from the bottom up, its practitioners needing to negotiate and renegotiate constantly shifting sources of contingency in practice. That difference has driven to no small degree the negativity amongst most journalists towards ethics codes. They see dominant approaches to ethics as simplifying, restricting or ignoring the various materialities by which the news is crafted. In the eyes of the editor of the *Australian Journalism Review*, it is possible in many places around the globe to 'practice as a journalist for years and never so much as look at an ethics code'.[3] Or, as the associate director of a UK non-profit devoted to journalism ethics recently observed, 'the proscriptions on journalistic behavior are many and obvious, but they all have one thing in common: they are not worth the paper they are written on'.[4]

The problem with ethics derives in large part from the multiple vagaries of action with which journalists must wrestle as part of doing work, and the difficulty that ensues in establishing standards for shifting practice. Beyond offering a generalized edict to 'do the right thing', ethics codes tend to prescribe levels of specificity that have little bearing on the ever-changing grounds of journalistic practice. The first ethics codes in journalism came into being in the late 19th and early 20th centuries, aligned with the ascent of a model of professionalism and a particular notion of modernity. Richly implicated in the quest for truth, that mindset saw rationality, objectivity, impartiality and reason as the modes of engagement which journalists could offer those needing information about the world,[5] and the ethics codes that resulted reflected its values.

Ethics codes thus mirrored a transformation in journalists' affiliations from reigning work models of partisanship to those of objectivity, and justified those hoping to promote journalism as more of a profession than an occupation. In so doing they set in place a prism for evaluating journalistic practice that was aligned with particular expectations of professionalism in a particular kind of modern context. In the US the first use of the word 'ethics' in a journalistic context surfaced in an 1889 essay on press criticism, written after the *Philadelphia Public Ledger* attempted during the 1860s to set new rules of fairness and accuracy for covering the American Civil War.[6] Sensationalist coverage of the Spanish American War helped to prompt the adoption of the first code of ethical behaviour, established in 1922 by the American Society of Newspaper Editors and embraced four years later by the Society of Professional Journalists (SPJ). Repairing to a broadly scoped notion of serving the larger good that grounded the authority of professional-minded journalists in a modern age, the notions of ethical conduct it forwarded were seen as offering journalists protection from growing rates of corporatism in the surrounding culture, intensifying political attacks and public disillusionment with the press. Codes remained more or less stable until after the Second World War, when the famed Hutchins Commission offered a more socially scientific rationale for journalistic responsibility.[7]

Since then, many news organizations have tried to buttress ethics codes by implementing self-regulating news councils, such as the UK Press Complaints Commission, or by setting up in-house public editors or ombudsmen. They have also experimented with different kinds of situated ethics that are more primed to accommodate change and that are presumed to shift with new technologies, new journalistic practices, and changing economic and political conditions. Perhaps the most eloquent defence of ethics has come from Theodore Glasser and James Ettema, where they sidestep many of the pitfalls in rigid ethics codes by defining 'being ethical' as the process of 'being accountable'.[8] By and large, however, journalistic ethics codes still continue to fall short of reflecting the range of circumstances undergirding journalism.

Such is the case across the array of practices that constitute newsmaking. For instance, news-gathering takes shape in situations largely beyond the control of journalists, where rapidly unfolding news stories, high stakes, a marked degree of risk and inherent unpredictability are all part of the ground that journalists must navigate on their way to making news. News presentation, complicated perhaps more than ever before by corporatism, privatization, sensationalism and convergence, is often decided without the input of the journalist who gathered the news. And news distribution in today's online environment has multiple shapes, platforms and audiences, making one form of a news story a thing of the past. Instead, multimodal journalists are regularly expected to rework news angles for multiple objectives alongside non-journalists who are doing the same. These contradictory forces on the ground not only undermine the project of ethics in journalism – of inspiring shared rules of conduct that distinguish right from wrong, good from bad – but raise the question of ethics' relevance at a time when journalistic practice itself eludes standardization.

Journalism is thus more porous, more unstable, more variegated and less authoritative than might be assumed. Though it may be relatively easy to delineate one's ethical aspirations as a journalist, it is far more difficult to translate those aspirations into practice across the range of situations with which journalists regularly engage. Its variable standards of action patched together largely on a case-by-case basis and often via improvisory responses to unpredictable and emergency-like situations, journalism's capacity to repair to an aspired to but largely abstract ethics code remains a sideshow, supporting a more general journalistic disregard for abstractions that is exacerbated by 'a busy newsroom... impatient of any form of reflection which doesn't contribute to a result or which may slow things down'.[9]

The value of ethics codes in journalism is further complicated by the temporal, geographic, institutional and technological parameters of newswork, each of which presents additional challenges to the idea of a shared ethics. They are worth considering in turn.

Temporality and ethics

Temporally, journalism exhibits a remarkable affinity with what came before, and journalists tend to repeat behaviour across time. For that reason and despite repeated declarations of their egregious status, the same ethical violations tend to be committed again and again across the landscape of journalism's past and present.

Why is this so? Journalists do what they can to secure coverage of the news. An elastic affinity between news practice and abstract codes of action reveals how marginal ethics codes have been in changing this aspect of newswork. In fact, many of the unethical practices now being critiqued in the *News of the World* scandal – using deception and impersonation to secure information, cozying up to officials, disregarding the privacy of others, a rush to sensationalize – were exhibited as early as the penny press and yellow press during the 1800s. Though details differ, the violations have been remarkably persistent across both the high and the low grounds of journalism.

For instance, one such practice – journalists paying sources for information, also called chequebook journalism – has generated a long and illustrious history. As ABC anchor Chris Cuomo noted recently, 'the commercial exigencies of the business reach into every aspect of reporting... It's the state of play right now.'[10] Though paying for information tends to be discredited primarily as a tabloid practice, where it is thought to 'taint' the value of the information being secured, it has in fact surfaced across much of journalism and at times has been instrumental in generating important information relay. In 1963, *Life* magazine paid $150,000 to dressmaker Abraham Zapruder for his filmed sequence of the assassination of US President John F. Kennedy. Seven years later, *Esquire* magazine paid $20,000 to US Lt. William Calley for his version of the story of the My Lai massacre. More recently, CNN paid $10,000 for an interview with a Dutch citizen who had overpowered the so-called Christmas Day bomber midair in a transatlantic flight. Given the questionable ethical nature of the means used to obtain information, should any of these news stories not have come to light? Without a clear rank-ordering of ethical violations – by which ethics codes might establish that serving the public good trumps other wrongs in journalism – the unethical nature of news-gathering in each case might have denied the US public fuller information critical to its functioning as a body politic. Furthermore, ethics codes offer a sliding scale of evaluation: If paying for information was acceptable in these cases, who is to say where its appropriateness ends?

And yet, despite evidence of its instrumentality and its intensification over time, paying for information has been vilified by nearly every existing ethics code in journalism. The SPJ, for example, maintains that journalists should never pay for information, under any circumstances. No wonder that US presidential candidate Herman Cain recently pulled out the SPJ's code of ethics in defence of his being charged with sexual harassment, suggesting that the code may have become more useful for those looking to scapegoat the media than for those needing behavioural guidance.

Temporally speaking, then, codes of ethics in journalism have not done much to eradicate unethical behaviour. They have done an even less impressive job of clarifying what to do when decidedly unethical practices produce an ethical public engagement with the news.

Geography and ethics

Geographically, the capacity to make a case for ethical standards is no easier. Despite journalism's global spread, the range of circumstances in which journalism is practised around the globe is testament to the inability to prescribe either one standard for all or any standard for some.

Ethics codes in journalism are largely an invention of the industrialized democracies of the West and global North, where the usually voluntary issuance of guidelines has been common across major news organizations. Most news organizations today boast their own codes of ethics. Offering a set of best practices without an accompanying official or legal mechanism for enforcement, these codes tend to be pre-emptive in open societies 'to ward off any potential government interference with the freedom of the press'.[11]

The geographic bias of these attributes, part of a mindset that positions certain kinds of journalism and a certain kind of modernity as the backdrop to the accomplishment of ethical behaviour, is problematic when considering how little of the mindset is replicated across journalism's many platforms around the world. Certain privileged forms of journalism – the notion of a free and independent press; the idea of a fourth estate or the public's right to know; the embrace of neutrality, facticity and objectivity – are central in ethics codes, often uncritically positioned at their core. But they have never been the practice in much of the world.

In countries where soft authoritarianism, transitional governance, government-owned media, odd mixes of colonialism and post-colonialism, blends of secular and religious authorities, self-censorship and government interference are prevalent, ethics codes bear a particularly tenuous relationship with journalistic practice. Driven by a different kind of modernity – one connected as much with repression, social order and authority as with hopes of free expression – in such countries, aspired to standards of action shrink in relevance for most practising journalists.

Examples abound: How does one determine 'conflict of interest' when journalists are so badly paid that they need to take more than one job? What does 'truth' look like when it is overshadowed by the threat of punitive action or persecution? What does 'public interest' or 'civil society' mean in a region whose public institutions are driven by corruption? Can 'impartiality' exist in locations with no tradition of civil society? In such places, the very term 'codes of ethics' may be a problematic by-product of governmental attempts to control the dissemination of information. New journalistic practices have emerged to accommodate these complicated circumstances, such as the anonymous *Blog Del Narco* in Mexico and the citizen-run *Weibo* in China, both of which attempt to sidestep institutional self-censorship yet whose actions might be considered unethical by some.

Even the practice of paying for information has spawned additional action of a presumably unethical nature in response to rampant institutional corruption. So-called 'brown envelope journalism' references a complex undertaking of interchanges between officials and journalists in the African media, by which the former pay for information to be relayed and the journalists and/or news organizations readily accept the payment.[12] Similar practices exist in both China (*hongbao* or 'red envelope journalism') and Russia (*zakazukha*).[13] Without this kind of interchange, information does not readily flow, making its implementation critical for journalism's existence, despite its decidedly unethical nature. And given the global flow of news, the transportation of information from these problematic interchanges means that ethical violations undergird journalism in even the open societies of the West and the global North, if only from afar.

No surprise, then, that when considered geographically, ethical standards take on many faces. As has been widely argued, 'promoting ethical standards in journalism cannot be separated from the advancement of human rights and welfare in general'.[14] Though ethics may abstractly be seen as having value, their positioning in local contexts can render them redundant, troublesome and even the source of institutional adaptation or political danger.

Institutional culture and ethics

Institutionally, the challenges have been no less strident. Journalism today exists as part of a large institutional culture, where politics, economics, social welfare, education, security and other institutional settings regularly impede on what might be thought of as autonomous news-making. The intricate web by which multiple institutions exist in a complicated symbiosis with the news media reveals entrenched attributes of institutional culture, which shed doubt on the workability of any ethics that target only some of those responsible for its shaping.

The characteristics of contemporary institutional culture, particularly as it has evolved in open societies of the West and the global North, are all too familiar. Among them are widespread institutional corruption, a concentration of media ownership, a culture of promotionalism, extensive kowtowing to power, interinstitutional dependency, corporatism, a gravitation towards impunity and cover-up, a resistance to change, opposition to transparency, an entrenched sharing of power, commercial profit above all and a revolving door of personnel. Relevant to ethics because the parameters necessitated by other institutional settings can easily intrude on what might be thought to be ethically correct for journalists, they raise the question of how viable ethics can be when much of news is driven by a culture that includes journalism as only one of many settings.

Such was certainly the backdrop to the *News of the World* scandal, where much of the unethical behaviour at the heart of the affair involved a complicated interweaving of three supposedly separate institutions – journalism, politics and the police service. As one observer for the Poynter Organization noted, with all of the interinstitutional collusion that surfaced, 'this should've been the fifth season of *The Wire*'.[15] Though observers have been keen to pinpoint which narrow part of the larger institutional context is most culpable, generally assigning blame to UK tabloid journalism, it is not at all clear whether the disconnect between journalism, writ large, and its non-journalistic institutional neighbours is deserved. In fact, the intimacy across institutions might merit as close attention as that being paid to the interiors of the *News of the World*.[16]

Codes that single out unethical action in certain quarters, while keeping the broader agents of responsibility afloat, are all too plentiful, raising fundamental questions about which ethics matter and to whom. In fact, given the widespread scope of institutional intimacy, it is probable that action of multiple kinds will violate some notion of ethics somewhere. A journalist's most routine questions might require sources to betray confidence. Commercial imperatives – keeping ratings high or subscriptions up, pleasing sponsors – often displace the ethical limitations of privacy. Educational cues – a desire to keep children shielded from negativity or brutality – can censor the ethical insistence on the public's right to know.

Institutional considerations give a different status to the practice of paying for information. First, a larger ethos of competition becomes strident in an era of shaky economics. When other news organizations, high and low, regularly pay for information, doing so can easily be reconstituted as a necessary condition for journalists to remain in the game. Second, other institutions pay for information – lawyers pay expert witnesses, police services pay snitches – relativizing its unethical nature as a practice. Third, much of this blurring across different institutional domains is not controllable by either reporters or editors, making the supplanting of ethical behaviour beyond the purview of individual journalists themselves.

Journalism's publics also intervene at will so that the body responsible for producing the coverage that should reflect ethical principles is not necessarily the same one that makes ethical decisions about the news. Intervention comes from multiple quarters of the public. Politicians, lobbyists, human-rights workers and involved citizens all make the call about what topics news should address and in which ways – in journalism's name but not always with journalism's sanction. But whose ethics need to remain at the core of a debate between bereaved parents, who do not want details of their dead child aired, and politicians, who feel that covering the death has instructive civic value?

Institutionally, then, ethics codes in journalism reflect a simplified understanding of the complicated context in which journalists work. They tend to apportion blame to only some of those committing ethical violations, while leaving the broader institutional culture, and its offending institutions, largely intact.

Technology and ethics

Today's online information environment poses additional challenges to the viability of ethics codes in journalism, particularly around the persistent questions of who is a journalist and what journalism is. An intricate blending of so-called professionals, amateurs, quasi-professionals and part-time bloggers continues to push the question of how to set in place an ethics that can apply to the varied practitioners in journalism's landscape and the extensive range of practices in which they engage.

Simply put, journalism is no longer operated only by journalists. Not only are news-gathering operations more visible than ever before, but the importation of practices of crowd-sourcing, tweets and online postings by employed journalists on digital and social media and the ever-increasing role played by citizen journalists all undermine the establishment of shared or standardized behaviour of any kind.

Furthermore, the range of the online environment enhances the issue of global responsibility for journalists. With journalism now operating on global platforms with the hope of global impact, the question of what it might mean to be globally responsible as a journalist depends in no small part on an understanding of ethical behaviour that reflects practice on the ground.

Multiple questions thus arise about the viability of ethics codes and technology, which, given the rapid rate of technological diffusion, promise to be out of date almost as soon as they surface.[17] For instance, most existing ethics codes in journalism mention the accountability and/or transparency of those doing the reporting. And yet the anonymity associated with many online postings, particularly visual ones, renders those objectives unattainable. Left unclear are the ways in which news organizations must balance the public good against their inability to display accountability and/or transparency.

Such was certainly the case in 2009, when an anonymous cell-phone video was uploaded to *YouTube* of an Iranian demonstrator being shot to death in Tehran. Though the mainstream news media had no detail about who had produced the video, after extensive discussion they ran it across the board.[18] Ethical questions went beyond the anonymity of the cell-phone owner: What does visual privacy mean in an age of cell-phone cameras? Can retweeting be seen as ethical? How should journalists manage the cannibalization of material, when the lack of technical or temporal barriers facilitates lifting information from one site for use elsewhere?[19] In each case, the viability of upholding different standards of accountability and/or transparency on different journalistic platforms remained at issue.

Technology further complicates considerations of the ethics of paying for information too. Not only does the online environment intensify competition but it does so in ways that make unmanageable the kinds of checking aspired to in less frenetic circumstances – corroborating information, piecing together fragments of a larger story, contextualizing incongruent information. Again, paying for information can take place at one point in the global flow of news and then be used to justify what appears to be ethical news-gathering down the line. For instance, when the celebrity news site *TMZ* broke the news of Michael Jackson's death in 2009 within minutes of his dying, journalists were initially reluctant to report the story and delayed its circulation, driven by TMZ's willingness to pay its sources for information and unwillingness to admit when it had done so. Yet, within the hour, nearly all of the US mainstream media had swallowed their discomfort and reported the news, with little discussion of the unethical behaviour that potentially produced it in the first place.

In short, journalistic ethics codes cannot operate today as if they are separate from the ethics practised by those beyond journalism. Ethics discussions continue to repair to outdated notions – such as an insistence on clear boundaries around privacy – which do not sufficiently take heed of how difficult it is to establish and police such conditions given today's technological landscape. Some news organizations have begun to offer guidelines to their employees on mining the internet – the BBC, National Public Radio and the *Washington Post*, for example – but most still act as if journalists exist in a professional ghetto, where the newer presence of digital and social media is not necessarily part of the picture and where ethical standards for journalists are far from reflecting what unfolds on the ground. What hope, then, can journalism ethics codes have of changing the landscape of unethical practice if many of journalism's non-journalistic collaborators and competitors and their practices reside there too?

A technological view of journalism's codes of ethics thus underscores the gaps in practice currently not addressed by ethics codes. Not only are such gaps instrumental in understanding journalism in today's online environment but they obscure the unfolding of unethical action that finds its way back into mainstream news.

Conclusion

This chapter argues that collective ethical standards are all but impossible to achieve in journalism and that even codes of situated ethics do not come close to reflecting all that journalism constitutes. It also argues that ethics codes may fall short in what they can offer journalists, whose collectivity is regularly undermined by the temporal, geographic, institutional and technological settings that they must navigate. Without such collectivity, the possibility of realizing shared standards of ethical action remains in peril.

The point here is that it is doubtful that ethics codes can be imagined in journalism in any viable fashion. This is not to say that journalists should not aspire to be ethical insofar as that means 'doing the right thing'. But in their present encapsulation as collective codes of action, ethics tend to be the least worried over, debated and enacted by those whose behaviour remains the most targeted by the magnifying glass of others. In fact, ethics in journalism tend to draw the most attention when an ethical code is egregiously broken, as in the *News of the World* scandal, and such attention comes from outside journalism far more fervently than from inside. These circumstances are hardly a propitious way of determining ethical standards for journalists.

The difficulties with establishing ethics codes in journalism have been shown to be multiple and repetitive. Such codes presume a collective that may not exist; draw from a clarity of purpose and authority of decision-making that are more aspired than real; pay little heed to the intrusion of others in deciding what counts; and fail to raise the question of whose ethics are at stake and for what purpose. Ethics, as conceptualized since the days of Aristotle, may be more improbable in journalism than we think.

This is not new. Nearly 30 years ago, Jay Black and Ralph Barney laid out the principles that made media codes of ethics unviable in their eyes. Among other things, they argued that ethics codes helped the regulators more than those who were being regulated, regulated the neophytes more than the established practitioners, and satisfied those lured by the promise of ethical behaviour more than those tracking its implementation.[20] In other words, 'codes arise in response to public demand but they are framed to cause the least commotion.'[21]

Why, then, do we continue to insist that some kind of ethics code must be applicable to journalism? Part of the reason may rest in an ambivalence about all of the circumstances that allow journalism seemingly untouchable authority: its reliance on practices that unfold largely behind closed doors; its insistence on power without commensurate degrees of accountability; its ballooning public stature when things go right; and its easy access to tools and platforms of self-enhancement. Part, too, may derive from an ambivalence about the certain kind of modernity with which journalism aligns. As we ponder its historical myopism, mechanically shifting centres, overt confidence about the future and blinding belief in rational reasoning, journalism's status as one of its high achievements comes to the fore. Ethics, at some primal level, offer a step back into simpler times. In conjuring up a premodern moment, one replete with value and aspiration and good, we cling to them perhaps because they lessen our own existential ambivalence. But they do not solve the problems we face living in today's world.

For the danger of adopting codes of ethics in journalism may be more serious than implied thus far. It may in fact be that calls to journalism ethics prevent an ethical engagement with the news. News images in so-called open societies offer a litmus test in this regard. Repeatedly positioned as the target of various appeals to 'decency', 'privacy', 'taste', 'appropriateness', 'sensitivity' and the so-called cereal test of journalistic depiction, images are by no means certain candidates for display in journalism. The question of which images surface in the news airs so regularly and so uncritically that we have backed ourselves into the improbable position of seeing less and imagining more. How often are pictures of vital public events –war, terrorism, corruption – pushed from public display? What this does to the ethics of our shared global space and the health of our body politic is worrisome. For in admitting that we are willing to see less in the name of a so-called 'ethical' display of images, are we not at the same time enabling a less ethical address to the issues, events and problems that those images are used to depict? Furthermore, in playing to a so-called 'ethical' treatment of news events, mainstream journalism has lost its sway as the 'go-to' place when violent events occur. This has facilitated the intrusion of citizen journalism and citizen-run new media, which in the best of cases provide much-needed coverage. In the worst of cases, however, their involvement allows for the news agenda to be run by those who understand the power of information relay but may use it for more nefarious purposes. The coverage of beheadings of captive individuals in Iraq from 2006 onwards, whose photos were taken and circulated by the militias who committed the killings as they were in process, remains a vivid example. We are, then, in the midst of a sea-change about what journalism ethics could and should mean. A far greater relevance of praxis should by now be clear. But even that does not resolve the question of what ethics are for if they facilitate less coverage of the news than we might otherwise provide and receive.

Journalism regularly addresses the space between what we read, see and hear versus what we know and understand. A call for collective ethical standards, as embodied in ethics codes, may thus undo what should be most ethical about journalism: it undermines the principles of full and complete journalistic relay; it reifies ethics even when ethical standards may be at cross-purposes with critical news coverage; it justifies the universal at the expense of understanding the particular; and it allows for the intrusion of others to make the call about which news to address. Why, then, are we concerned with a workable journalism ethics without first considering more fully what we want from journalism?

Notes

1. Barbie Zelizer (2012) 'How to Give Meaning to the Hand-Wringing After Scandal', *Media, Culture and Society* 34(5): 625–630.

2. Ruth Marcus, 'Herman Cain Harassment Story Was Good Journalism,' *Washington Post*, 7 November 2011.
3. Ian Richards (2009) 'Uneasy Bedfellows: Ethics Committees and Journalism Research', *Australian Journalism Review* 31(2): 35–46.
4. Bill Norris (2000) 'Media Ethics at the Sharp End', in David Berry (ed), *Ethics and Media Culture: Practices and Representations*, mediawise.org, see http://www.mediawise.org.uk/www.mediawise.org.uk/display_pageac86.html?id=574.
5. Barbie Zelizer (2011) 'Journalism in the Service of Communication', *Journal of Communication* 61(1): 1–21.
6. W.S. Lilly (1889) 'The Ethics of Journalism', *The Forum*, 503–512.
7. The evolution of journalism ethics is traced in Clifford Christians, John P. Ferre, and Mark Fackler's (2003) *Good News: Social Ethics and the Press* (New York: Oxford University Press); Hazel Dicken-Garcia's (1989) *Journalistic Standards in Nineteenth Century America* (Madison: University of Wisconsin Press); Ronald Rodgers's (2007) "Journalism Is a Loose-Jointed Thing": A Content Analysis of Editor and Publisher's Discussion of Journalistic Conduct Prior to the Canons of Journalism, 1901–1922', *Journal of Mass Media Ethics*, 22 (10): 66–82; and Lee Wilkins and Bonnie Brennen (2004) 'Conflicted Interests, Contested Terrain: Journalism Ethics Codes Then and Now', *Journalism Studies* 5(3): 297–309.
8. Theodore L. Glasser and James S. Ettema (2008) 'Ethics and Eloquence in Journalism: An Approach to Press Accountability', *Journalism Studies* 9(4): 512–534.
9. George Brock (2010) 'Road to Regaining the High Ground,' *British Journalism Review* 21(4): 19.
10. Chris Cuomo, quoted on 'CNN: Reliable Sources', CNN, aired 12 June 2011, http://transcripts.cnn.com/TRANSCRIPTS/1106/12/rs.01.html.
11. Eugene L. Meyer (2011) *Media Codes of Ethics: The Difficulty of Defining Standards*, 4.Washington, DC: Center for International Media Assistance and National Endowment for Democracy.
12. Terje Skjerdal (2010) 'Research on Brown Envelope Journalism in the African Media', *African Communication Research* 3(3): 357–406.
13. Yuezhi Zhao (1998) *Media, Market and Democracy in China*. Champaign-Urbana: University of Illinois Press; Katerina Tsetsura and Dean Kruckeberg, *Transparency, Public Relations and the Mass Media: Combating Media Bribery Worldwide*. New York: Routledge.
14. Eugene L. Meyer (2011) *Media Codes of Ethics: The Difficulty of Defining Standards*, 5. Washington, DC: Center for International Media Assistance and National Endowment for Democracy.
15. Steve Myers (2011) 'Phone Hacking Scandal a Corruption Story, Like Enron and Countless Others', Poynter.org, 20 July 2011, see http://www.poynter.org/latest-news/top-stories/139853/phone-hacking-scandal-a-corruption-story-like-enron-and-countless-others.
16. For more on this, see Barbie Zelizer (2012) 'How to Give Meaning to the Hand-Wringing after Scandal', *Media, Culture and Society* 34(5): 625–630.
17. S. Buttry (2011) '21st Century Journalism Requires 21st Century Code', *Quill* 99(2):16–19.

18. This is discussed in detail in Barbie Zelizer (2010) *About To Die: How News Images Move the Public*. New York: Oxford University Press.
19. *Cameras Everywhere* (2011) New York: WITNESS, 9 November 2011. See http://www.witness.org/cameras-everywhere/report-2011/full-report. See also Angela Phillips (2010) 'Transparency and the New Ethics of Journalism', *Journalism Practice* 4(3), 373–382.
20. Jay Black and Ralph D. Barney (1985) 'The Case Against Mass Media Codes of Ethics', *Journal of Mass Media Ethics* 1(1) (Fall/Winter): 27–36.
21. Jay Black and F.C. Whitney (1983), *Introduction to Mass Communications*, 432. Dubuque: Wm. C. Brown.

Index

Printed and bound in Great Britain by
CPI Antony Rowe, Chippenham and Eastbourne